The High Victorian Movement in Architecture 1850-1870

W. Burges, competition design for Crimean Memorial Church,
Constantinople, 1856/7 (from the *Builder*, 1857, 151; cf. Plate 85).

The High Victorian Movement in Architecture 1850–1870

Stefan Muthesius

School of Fine Arts and Music
University of East Anglia, Norwich

Routledge & Kegan Paul   London and Boston

In memoriam Carola Pevsner

First published in 1972
by Routledge and Kegan Paul Ltd
Broadway House,
68–74 Carter Lane,
London, EC4V 5EL
and 9 Park Street,
Boston, Mass. 02108, U.S.A.
Photoset and printed in Great Britain by
BAS Printers Limited, Wallop, Hampshire
Set in 12 pt Apollo, 1 pt leaded

ISBN 0 7100 7071 3

Contents

Contents

vi

Illustrations

Acknowledgments

First of all I have to thank my parents for their patient support over many years and my teachers, Professor Sir Nikolaus Pevsner and the late Professor K. H. Usener at Marburg, for help and encouragement. I am deeply indebted to Paul Thompson, Nicholas Taylor and Priscilla Metcalf, who went through the manuscript and greatly improved it.

I am extremely aware of how much this book depends on the help of and discussion with my fellow researchers who generously shared their information with me. I have to thank S. Beattie, J. Brandon-Jones, S. Bury, D. Buttress, R. Chafee, P. Clark, N. Cooper, R. Dixon, S. Dürr, D. Evinson, J. Fawcett, P. Fontaney, J. Franklin, J. Gage, M. Girouard, R. Gradidge, T. A. Greeves, A. Grieve, C. Handley-Read, D. Hansen, J. Harris, J. House, P. Howell, E. Hubbard, P. Joyce, B. Kearney, A. King, G. Kokkelink, R. Lewcock, D. Linstrum, D. Lloyd, S. Lyle, G. McHardy, R. Macleod, M. Martin, R. Middleton, S. Millikin, C. W. Mullen, M. G. Murray, J. Newman, J. Paul, D. Richardson, M. Richardson, H. Rosenau, J. Schuchard, G. Stamp, P. Stanton, Sir John Summerson, W. Vaughan and many other members of the Victorian Society and students at UEA.

Furthermore, this book could never have been written without the help and liberality of the Library of the Royal Institute of British Architects. My thanks also go to other institutions and libraries: the Church of England, the National Monuments Record, the Victoria & Albert Museum, the British Museum Library, Westminster Public Library, the Libraries at Manchester, Liverpool, Dublin, Newcastle and Leeds.

Finally my thanks go to all those who made it possible for me to travel extensively, to my typists, photographic technicians and Gordon Barnes for allowing me to use his excellent photographs.

Introduction

This book is concerned with a particular movement in English mid-nineteenth-century architecture, as a development of and departure from the Gothic Revival. It is not a detailed survey of mid-Victorian buildings, nor a sequel to Henry-Russell Hitchcock's book on Early Victorian architecture. It concerns something much more cohesive, a trend that grew from modest beginnings around 1850 to affect buildings throughout the country by the end of the next decade. The intention is to investigate the early development of this trend in more detail than the later stages of the next decade.

This movement was an important phase in the career of many architects, for most of whom it stimulated their first work and early successes, although their careers as a whole and their personal backgrounds can only be touched on very briefly. For some years, especially in the early fifties, these architects kept in close touch with one another as members of the Ecclesiological (former Cambridge Camden) Society. The propagation of their ideas was one of the chief aims of the Society's publications. Nevertheless, this movement of the fifties cannot be called the result solely of the activities of the Ecclesiological Society, as High Church architecture in the forties could be called a product of the Cambridge Camdenians in its unique blend of liturgical reform and architectural principles. In the fifties, the Society served only as one forum among several.

The Ecclesiologists' position in the emerging professional world of that time is not easy to define. On the whole these architects tended not to design commercial buildings. Liberals and townsmen were a minority among their clients, at least before the sixties; most were landed gentry, new and old, partisan to the narrower Church and church-building doctrines. When, in the sixties, more secular work was given to more of the Ecclesiologist architects, and their principles were influencing 'commercial' architects, a new group branched off, advocating 'art' architecture rather than 'surveyor' architecture.

Most of the buildings described in this book are churches, still the outcome of the continuing effort of the Established Church after the 'Million-pound' Act of 1818. But after 1850 few architects devoted themselves solely to church design, as some did before 1850. So this book is not concerned with any one type of building as such, since most of the changes in planning during the fifties and sixties depended on factors other than liturgical or practical function. Thus the Ecclesiologists were concerned with traditional kinds of buildings and traditional materials and only occasionally did they face the challenge of new functional and technical problems. Their interest lay with formal and theoretical architectural problems in a narrower sense.

The main formal traits of buildings of the High Victorian Movement are easily described. St Peter's, Vauxhall, and Congleton Town Hall, to cite two of the better known buildings from the early 1860s [Plates 106–7 and 91], are relatively simple in plan and outline and the overall treatment is equally simple except for some concentrated ornament. Details such as the corners of windows and doorways tend to be clear geometrical forms. Wall surfaces are kept flat, varied only by that undisputably High Victorian element, the polychromy of different materials, dimmed though this is by a century of grime. Little of this particular kind of polychromy appeared before 1850 and no such strict principles of surface treatment were observed in later Victorian architecture; nor can they be found in the other mid-Victorian work that did not follow the movement's principles.

This purely formal description seems more relevant than the investigation of the meaning of these forms, historical or otherwise symbolical. But recent iconological research in art and architectural history, as well as sociological methods, have to a large extent replaced the methods of purely formal description, because they are thought to provide a greater degree of objectivity. On the other hand, the view that art is pure form seems to have been particularly relevant to many nineteenth- and twentieth-century artists as well as being used as an art-historical method. What seems to follow for the student of Victorian architecture is that, in addition to the formal description of buildings, one ought to trace the origin of this very notion of pure form; how did it develop out of the symbolical connotations of architectural forms and how did it relate to the social, functional and moral considerations in architecture?

It is not difficult to find out what Victorian architects thought about architecture. The majority of the better known architects, in the humanist tradition of the thinking artist, wrote many books and articles in the specialized periodicals. Most of these writings were concerned with historical architecture, but the predilections, the reasons for the selection of particular historical buildings and the way they were described and sketched resulted from the architects' views about architecture in general and coincided with what they thought their own buildings should look like. It is a well known fact that in the nineteenth century – as in previous centuries – architecture and architectural history developed and progressed side by side. What is usually stressed is the imitative nature of nineteenth-century architecture, but what should be equally stressed is the creative aspect of architectural history, when hitherto unnoticed historical buildings are described with the help of new general architectural ideas.

The formal notions with which we will be largely concerned seem to have stemmed from the aesthetic of the 'picturesque' and 'sublime', dating from the eighteenth and early nineteenth centuries. They were closely interrelated with symbolical considerations, especially about nature, and also with rational-moral considerations: in what way form follows function or in what way form follows construction. The different answers to these questions seemed more and more to be influenced by aesthetic choice: 'truth' in planning in the forties meant complex aggregations of irregular forms, descendants of the picturesque; in the fifties truth meant simple massive forms, the offspring of the concept of the sublime. The emphasis on colour in architecture can also be called a purely formal element. On the other hand, there was not yet an open demand for 'form' as such; this can only be found later in the century with the Aesthetic Movement and in *art nouveau*, as well as in the writings of Fiedler and Wölfflin in Germany. But by no means did this mean the end of moralistic considerations in architecture, and critics and architects of the present day are still troubled by the same problems.

An explanatory remark may be called for on two terms which I have used very little. I have avoided using the word 'style' because it is not precise: in the nineteenth century it meant the symbolical value of architectural motifs, their historical and geographical significance, and it was used for the general historical classification of buildings. In the art historical jargon of the twentieth century it means abstract formal analysis, used whether as a tool for classification or for its own sake. Thus the word 'style' can cover the two aspects I am trying to disentangle. The same applies to the term 'Gothic': in a sense I am describing High Victorian Gothic buildings, but the main emphasis is intended to be on elements which derive from other sources and which can be applied to other nineteenth-century revivals such as the neo-Romanesque or even neo-Renaissance. This does not, of course, mean that terms such as Gothic or classical should be abandoned for this period; as general classifications they remain indispensable.

Pugin and the Ecclesiologists in the 1840s

Of English architecture at the death of George IV it could be said that never in the centuries since Henry VIII had it been 'so feeble, so deficient in genius, so poor in promise'.[1] Yet it was possible to describe the end of the early Victorian phase, twenty-five years later, with 'a rising instead of a falling cadence'.[2] The first buildings of the phase we call High Victorian were under way. To understand the development of the High Victorian phase that concerns us in this book, we must examine its origins, that is, the evolution of the Gothic Revival in the 1840s.[3] At the beginning of Victoria's reign the prime movers were Augustus Welby Northmore Pugin[4] and the group of writers and architects associated with the Cambridge Camden Society, originally founded in 1836 and renamed the Ecclesiological Society in 1846.[5]

Both Pugin and the Ecclesiologists were initially impelled by an antiquarian interest in medieval architecture, but they were also influenced by the need for liturgical reform, on pre-Reformation models, then being advocated in the wake of the Oxford Movement. Pugin's activities can be summed up briefly. He combined a variety of architectural, religious and social beliefs: a romantic religious zeal and love for the symbols of the Middle Ages, mainly deriving from German and French Romanticism; a belief in the superiority of the social system of the Middle Ages; a demand for 'truth' of construction, inherited from the French Rationalist tradition of the eighteenth century; a strong sensitivity to materials and colours, inherited from the English Picturesque mainly through his father, a topographical and architectural draughtsman. Pugin welded all these concepts in his books by means of an extremely concise language, often couched in the satirical style of the day, accompanied by numerous illustrations closely related to his text and polemics. His work as an architect, although by no means small, was limited by his conversion to the Roman Church, and the Ecclesiologists, largely by following his ideas, assumed the leading role from about the mid-forties onwards. Only a few aspects of Pugin's work will be mentioned in the course of this chapter. He died at forty in 1852 but perhaps, judging from what little he contributed after about 1846, his early death may not have to be called an architecturally premature one. The Ecclesiological Society was dissolved in 1868, at a time when new movements were under way.

The Ecclesiologists did not confine themselves to antiquarianism as did other societies for the study of medieval architecture which sprang up during these years.[6] They provided regulations for the building of new churches which from the beginning were closely adhered to by their architect-members and soon by the whole of the 'High Church'. These architects – mostly very young – maintained close contacts with each other. With their insistence on a set of architectural-liturgical principles they recall artist-societies like the Lukasbund (Nazarenes) of some young German painters at the beginning of the century, or the Pre-Raphaelites of 1848, with all the enthusiasm and impermanence of such situations. In 1850, George Edmund Street, one of the youngest architects of the society, advocated a group of 'devout church architects'; yet it was Street himself who later criticized the Society for being exclusively concerned with church building.[7]

Most of the principles of the Society were enunciated from 1841 onwards in numerous editions of *A Few Words to Church Builders*,[8] and also in 1841 the periodical the *Ecclesiologist*, appearing five times a year, was started. With its aim 'to furnish information, which they [the members] have a right to expect but cannot easily obtain', and with (as was said some years later) 'its character strictly practical',[9] the *Ecclesiologist* should be considered one of the first practical architectural journals, with – if one forgets its ecclesiastical limitations – a certain priority over the *Builder* (which began in 1842–3).[10] Especially important was the systematic criticism of projected or newly erected buildings according to aesthetic and other architectural principles, as well as for their fulfilment of liturgical requirements, which usually meant harsh criticism of buildings not erected under the auspices of the Society.

Historicism

Many trends in the architectural theories of the forties go back to 1800 and beyond; that is to say, the exploration and classification of historical architecture; the application of historical motifs and forms in new buildings, and controversies involved on this point; the aesthetic of the 'picturesque' and 'sublime', and the discussions about fitness, construction and materials.[11]

To begin with the first of these elements, 'style', we realize that knowledge of architectural history had increased enormously during the first decades of the nineteenth century. Discrimination of English medieval styles was further pursued, mainly through the researches of Rickman, and exploration of medieval architecture on the continent had also begun. The post-medieval architecture of Britain, from the Tudor to the later seventeenth-century, began to be of interest. Furthermore, classical architecture had been enriched by the study of the Renaissance in Italy and elsewhere. By the beginning of the forties motifs from all these sources were being used. Many architects practised several different styles at the same time; for example, P. C. Hardwick built churches in a fourteenth-century Gothic style, country houses in Elizabethan and Tudor styles, hotel and office buildings with classical façades.[12]

The position of Pugin and the early Ecclesiologists in this context is well known. They undertook to discriminate between the phases of English medieval architecture even more meticulously than Rickman. One recalls Eastlake's words 'the late days of early Middle Pointed'.[13] At the same time they wanted to limit the choice of style for new buildings. Only 'Middle Pointed', and in some cases 'Early English' were permitted.

'Imitation' of past styles remains a matter of controversy today. In general, nineteenth-century architecture in this respect is still dealt with polemically,[14] especially in the case of Pugin, of whom estimation ranges from criticism of the assumed contradiction between his 'advanced' theories and his demand to imitate a past style of architecture, to belittling of the elements of imitation in his work.[15] Yet these polemics seem of little use, if one tries to trace more closely the history of the various reasons for the imitation of historic styles. Initially one should not assume the same knowledge of architectural history then as exists now, but rather enquire how much was known and how that knowledge developed. Although one may point to a mere quantitative increase in the knowledge of details, one has to look at the general situation of architectural opinions in order to explain new findings in architectural historiography. Thus rationalist theory played an important part in research into Gothic in the 1830s and 40s: the various phases were described as developments of more 'constructive' or more 'decorative' treatment. In the following decades it was mainly the aesthetic of the 'picturesque' and 'sublime' which provided the instrument of discovering new phases of historic architecture. Consequently it is not advisable to compare nineteenth-century buildings to older ones in the light of today's art-historical standards, which have developed so much further. Historic buildings have to be viewed in the way they were seen in the nineteenth century. We must try to reconstruct the Victorian vision of the past from pictures and descriptions, and then see the Victorians' own buildings and their choice of historical motifs, in the light of that reconstruction. This is, of course, not to deny that many individual features can only be explained by identifying them with some particular historic precedent, but within this short survey there will be little room for such identifications, and, in any case, these individual features must also be seen in a larger context. In the architecture of the 1850s in England windows may be found which can only be explained by direct comparison with fourteenth-century Venice, yet it is questionable whether these windows would have become so well known, if the aesthetic of

*Pugin and the
Ecclesiologists
in the 1840s*

the 'picturesque' and 'sublime', especially as summoned up by Ruskin, had not drawn attention to the medieval architecture of Italy in these particular years.

Other reasons for the choice of historical motifs were symbolic, the historic or geographic significance of motifs. Here important changes took place in the late thirties. The Ecclesiologists and Pugin insisted strongly on differentiating between the 'Christian' and the 'pagan' significance of motifs. Moreover, architecture came to be seen as an exponent of the social conditions of its inhabitants, and the choice of motifs was therefore linked with the wish to encourage particular states of society. Only when this relationship between architecture and society had been observed, could the criticism arise that one should not imitate former periods, because one could not expect the social background to be the same. This criticism was linked with demands that architects should not copy, but be 'original'. Pugin and the Ecclesiologists derided the practice of imitating several 'styles' in the same design; yet the general debates on 'copyism' were sharpened by their insistence upon one particular 'style'.

Furthermore, conflicts arose between the various reasons for following a historic style. When there were changes *within* the fields of particular reasons, different styles were proposed. This led to clashes among the fields of reason. For instance, a change in the field of aesthetics in the forties led to the recommendation of Italian motifs in contrast to English motifs, and this clashed with the supporters of a national approach. As a consequence, the importance of symbolic reasons, including national ones, was greatly reduced, at least in the Ecclesiological Society. Since most 'style' discussions of that period were concerned with symbolic reasons, the Ecclesiologists rarely took part, and consequently such discussions will be gone into only marginally here.[16]

For the Ecclesiologists, from the late forties onwards, the choice of historical motifs was not so much determined by consideration of symbols as by considerations of form and construction. 'Gothic,' said Street in 1852, 'is emphatically the style of the pointed arch and not of this nation, or of this or that age' (see below, Chapter 3).

Picturesque utility in Ecclesiological architecture

The development of the aesthetic of the 'beautiful', 'sublime' and 'picturesque' in eighteenth- and early nineteenth-century philosophy and psychology cannot be gone into here. The decades after 1800 saw the spread of these ideas into most types of architecture, whereas previously they had only been applied to painting, landscape gardening and garden buildings. Briefly, the new aesthetic was concerned with a development of modes of representation that had been discussed long before: in the case of 'the picturesque' a certain mode of landscape painting, in the case of 'the sublime' a kind of rhetoric. Emphasis was on the subjective element, the reaction of the beholder. Forms and arrangements of forms were intended to provoke strong reactions: the irregularity of the 'picturesque' was to cause surprise and nourish curiosity; the monotony and vastness of the 'sublime' were to elicit terror and to overwhelm the beholder. The importance of such aesthetic categories grew during the eighteenth century, they were discussed by Burke, and reached their peak in the writings of R. Payne Knight and Uvedale Price around 1800, where their purely formal significance gained importance over their psychological and associational significance.

Price had published his *Essay on Architecture and Building* in 1798. In the following decades such ideas were popularized through a large number of books on gardening and country houses, villas and cottages, where, in conjunction with antiquarian research, the various 'styles' were presented to illustrate the different principles. In the thirties J. C. Loudon was the chief propagator and in 1842 a Scotsman, Sir T. D. Lauder, even re-edited Price's writings on the picturesque. By then these principles had begun to influence the architecture of churches and at least one very important public building, the Houses of Parliament, designed in the mid-thirties. In the forties their influence combined with other trends in architectural thinking.[17]

The prevailing principle in the forties was the picturesque. Pugin combined it with an anti-classical theory of proportion: in his *True Principles of Pointed or Christian Architecture* (1841) he wrote, 'the different details of the edifice are multiplied with the increased scale of the building; in classic architecture they are only magnified.'[18] The 'preconceived uniform shell' of a building, as the *Ecclesiologist* put it,[19] should be replaced with what has been called 'agglutinative planning'.[20] This disintegration of proportion is equally applicable to the minor parts of a building. When Pugin said the elevation should follow the plan he did not mean to determine all the exterior subdivisions or storey heights and the position and size of the windows; they could be as haphazard as the arrangement of the ground plan itself. As a typical example Pugin's own church at Ramsgate, built in 1846,[21] may be taken [Plate 1]. The nave and the chancel are of different heights with a square crossing tower between. There is a south transept and a south aisle to both nave and chancel. The roofs differ in height, both in respect of the eaves and of the rooflines. Hardly any relationship can be seen between the openings of the different walls, and the interior spaces are separated by heavy arches.

However, for Pugin and the Ecclesiologists the aesthetic of the picturesque was not an end in itself but was combined 'with the demand for *bienséance* and *convenance* of Classic French architectural theory . . .', and 'to consider utility now became not a matter of common sense but

5

1 A. W. N. Pugin, St Augustine's church, schools, 1846 etc. and 'The Grange' (left), Pugin's own house, 1841 (from the *Builder*, 1853, 376). 'Picturesque utility', aesthetics and ethics combined, is the principle of this layout. It must be a very faithful realization of the architect's ideals, since he paid for most of the buildings himself. Each part of the building is treated as a separate unit, different in size and covered by a separate roof.

of truthfulness'.[22] A building was to show its various purposes, not in the cheap and elementary solutions of the earlier French theorist Durand, but in the greatest possible complexity of arrangement.[23] Pugin, like Durand, subjected proportion to 'utility': '. . . the scale and proportions of buildings we have to consider . . . under the head of architectural propriety,' he wrote,[24] but, of course, he had nothing uniform and symmetrical in mind. It has been said that the 'functionalism' of the Ecclesiologists was 'more symbolic than practical',[25] but on the contrary, it seems that the new adherence to fitness was more 'real' and 'practical' than it had been before, especially if compared with the symbolical method of applying various historical motifs to buildings of various uses. Architects now tried to emphasize differing functions by irregular and individualized plans.

The writings of the Ecclesiologists were not in the old tradition of

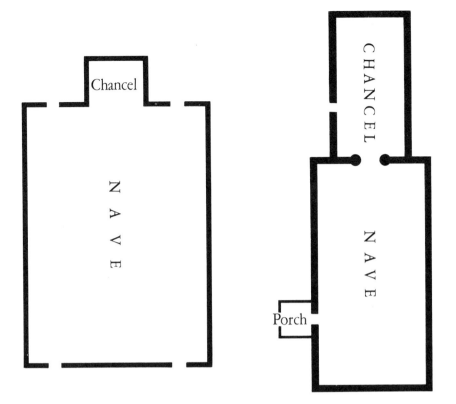

2 Contrasted plans of churches (from *A Few Words to Church Builders*, published by the Cambridge Camden, later Ecclesiological, Society in 1841). A church should not be a 'preaching box', but preference should be given to the ritual on the altar. Even the smallest church should have a spacious chancel, clearly distinct from the nave, and a porch on the side of the nave.

architectural treatises as to a certain extent those of Pugin still were. They were only concerned with special types of buildings and with the particular use of those buildings as the mainspring of form: they thought all commentary on church buildings should be based on religious, not general architectural principles.[26] Yet the *Ecclesiologist* was not concerned with 'religious controversy, we believe what the Church believes . . . but its material expression is our province.'[27]

A church, it was argued, should have at least two units – nave and chancel – which should be clearly distinguishable both from the out-side and from the inside. A porch, not on the west front, but on the southern side of the nave, not too far from the west, was to be added. In *A Few Words to Church Builders*, a good and bad example are compared [Plate 2]: the 'bad' example is, of course, a typical preaching box. 'Undoubtedly the greatest problem in re-introducing chancels was the rather basic one of finding a use for them.'[28] By 1850, however, opposition had waned, and chancels were used mostly by the choir, which also had been reformed according to Gregorian models. Within the chancel further divisions were made; towards the east the sanctuary was accentuated by the fittings as well as by different kinds of windows and sometimes a different roof.

There were no compelling ritual reasons for the other parts of a church, so that these could be added according to individual requirements. One aisle could suffice; it is much better 'to build one aisle as it ought to be, than to run up two cheaply'.[29] The tower – for smaller churches a bellcote is sufficient – should not be placed symmetrically.

The impression of a great variety of shapes was also required of the interior of churches. The classical type of arrangement of the eighteenth and early nineteenth centuries, which usually included versions with Gothic motifs, had a unified plan and all the fittings were arranged in an orderly manner and decorated with the same motifs as the architecture. The *Ecclesiologist* in contrast wanted an asymmetrical arrangement of fittings of various materials such as stone altars, sedilia and wooden movable and immovable furniture.[30] Besides this, for the impression of interior space as a whole, the aesthetic of the 'picturesque' and 'sublime' called for darkness, 'the sombre and subdued light, which was characteristic of all Early English Churches'.[31]

Equally important were the trends in building types not immediately connected with liturgy. Perhaps the most surprising features are those which form part of the churches but which serve only practical purposes: the chimneys which stand out prominently from sacristies and even from churches are the most striking examples of this.[32]

In the building of parsonages the *Ecclesiologist* again advised that 'the exterior ought to be adapted to the internal requirements.'[33] The general arrangement followed that of the type of a small country house which had developed shortly before.[34] Its main characteristics were the loose relationship of servants' quarters with the main building and the external expression of the great hall and staircase by means of a great window breaking through the divisions of the storeys.

An even more typical example of the new attitude to 'fitness' was provided by schools and especially village schools. The precepts were laid down in the article 'Schools' in 1847.[35] There were to be a certain number of rooms of various sizes and shapes, with smaller and bigger classrooms, cloakrooms, toilets and porches. All these were to have separate roofs and gables and one-storey buildings were preferred. The dwelling house of the teacher was to be treated as another separate unit, and situated at right-angles to the school. As with churches, fittings were also described in great detail.

All the same, the material aspects of 'fitness' did not reign exclusively. As 'form' and usage had to be interrelated as much as possible, it was logical to proclaim that where there were no ritual uses there should be no 'church-like' features; yet with smaller classrooms, which were attached to bigger ones, it was difficult to prevent their 'looking like little chancels'.[36] In the programmes of Pugin, as in those of the Ecclesiologists, all buildings had some relation to the church, a certain level in the church-hierarchy. The ideal building-type for a school was the monastic college[37] – 'a quadrangle is the proper form of a school'[38] – where the many stages within the hierarchy could be shown most clearly, from the church or chapel to the humble outbuildings. Many examples of this type can be found from the late forties onwards. This special hierarchy of 'decorum' must largely be seen as a reflection of the general traditional hierarchy of all buildings. George Gilbert Scott speaks of two kinds of 'utilitarian architecture' i.e. 'buildings which answer their purpose', meaning fitness, and the building which has 'just that amount and that kind of good looks which suit its class and its uses; and that these good looks are derived from a natural and rational manner of decorating the forms which its uses suggest'.[39] Thus the simplicity of the smaller buildings of the Ecclesiologists must always be seen as a result of the observance of ecclesiastical propriety, as well as of rational and aesthetic tendencies.

The other limitation came from the landscape background of the 'picturesque'. Buildings could not be thought of as separated from 'unspoiled', 'natural' surroundings. It is perhaps characteristic that a continuation of the article 'On Ecclesiastical Grouping' in 1845,[40] which was to have dealt with the 'juxtaposition of a church with buildings', never appeared. By far the most usual setting for Ecclesiologists in the early years (owing also to the more aristocratic clientele) was the rurally grouped church, the parsonage, the school and occasionally a small group of cottages in the manner of the 'model-villages', where the church took the place of the country house in dominating the hierarchy.[41] Numerous publications in the forties dealt with village churches in various parts of England. For architects like William Butterfield and Street, the publication of lectures and illustrations of such medieval buildings served as one of the starting points of their careers.[42] Street's detailed descriptions of simple features of those buildings are among the most remarkable art-historical writings of the time, especially his lecture 'on the Probability of some churches in Kent and Surrey being by the same Architect . . .' of 1850.[43]

Already in the late forties tendencies were beginning to change. The Ecclesiologists tried to restrict the number of parts in a church and they were no longer as certain of the motifs and symbols. Soon they tried to restrict the 'rough country look' as well. All this, however,

*Pugin and the
Ecclesiologists
in the 1840s*

did not result so much out of considerations of fitness or from social considerations, but from a change within the aesthetic of the 'picturesque' and 'sublime'. Considerations of fitness will not, therefore, be considered systematically, although the trends in various types of buildings will be summarized in Chapter 7.[44]

Masonry construction

Discussion of elevations and external aspects such as masonry – that is, broadly, the subject of 'construction' – would appear to be a more complex matter than that of planning. But in general, the Ecclesiologists went about it in a similar way. The concern was again with ethics as well as aesthetics, with the demand for 'truthfulness' in construction and the external treatment of materials, and with the respect for the visual qualities of the various materials used.

The catchword again was 'real' or 'truthful'. 'The essential elements are strength, utility and reality, which alone constitute true beauty,' declared the *Ecclesiologist* in an article of 1843 entitled 'On Simplicity of Composition, especially in Churches of the Early English Style'.[45] In spite of the traditional hierarchy of 'decorum' the richer kinds of decorative treatment of buildings through mouldings, tracery and so on were strongly criticized: 'nothing is left to itself . . . nothing is plain,' was the complaint about contemporary church-building; 'plain' was another catchword of the period. The demand for sincerity in the use of materials went so far that *A Few Words* was able to reach the conclusion, 'let every material be real . . . , let mean materials appear mean.'[46] Whitewash was a crime ('How to remove Whitewash', 1847).[47] Here the ethical demands, as in the case of fitness, were heightened by religious zeal, just as the Lukasbrüder or the early Pre-Raphaelites linked realist submission to detail with religious enthusiasm. An important result of the insistence on 'truthfulness' in construction was the belief that different materials ought to be represented by different shapes and motifs. It followed that those parts of a building, or of its decorations or fittings, which were not of stone, ought to be represented by forms differing from those for stone, which was one of the starting points for a whole field of design termed the 'applied arts'.[48] Architecture, in turn, became very much the affair of construction in various kinds of stone.

As in the case of 'picturesque utility', where the aspect of fitness itself was nothing new, naturally there had previously been many investigations into materials and problems of construction. In fact the Ecclesiologists' writings, from a purely technical point of view, were not nearly as elaborate as the building treatises of the day. On the other hand, these building manuals never claimed to include a whole point of view toward architecture.[49]

In his own church architecture, Pugin initially continued the tradition of 'gothic rationalism'. This was the idea of Gothic as framework construction where a great amount of space and especially of height could be obtained with a minimum of material, and with a maximum of ingenuity of construction. These concepts, which originated in France, found some followers in England in the twenties and thirties,[50] but in subsequent decades here were not adhered to much further, whereas in France they reached their apogee during the next decade.

In England it was the element of the continuous wall which gained importance. The antagonism between framework construction and flat wall surface could already be found in the eighteenth century – it is only necessary to compare Laugier's theories with Boullée's designs.[51] For the English it was not so much the surface of a whole wall, but the treatment of the masonry itself, which was important.

Here the elements of the aesthetic of the 'picturesque' and 'sublime' were stronger. For Pugin as for many architects and theorists, as well as for architectural watercolourists and draughtsmen ever since Piranesi, rough masonry formed an important element in architecture. 'The rubble wall of antiquity . . . [impresses] the mind with feelings of reverend awe,' Pugin wrote.[52] But aesthetics and ethics are again fused in another consideration of Pugin's: the kind of proportioning of the shapes of the building material on the wall surface. He argues against the use of regularly cut, big stones for masonry: 'not only are the stones which are used in the ancient buildings exceedingly small, but they are very irregular in size . . . '; and he also demands 'that the jointing might not appear a regular feature and by its lines interfere with those of the building'.[53] The proportioning of the building stones should be completely random so that it contrasts as much as possible with the more regular and bigger jointing at corners and openings. In his illustration [Plate 3] Pugin shows parts of buildings which are identical as regards motifs and measurements, and only differ as to the arrangement of the masonry: one shows regular big stones, whose proportions are related to those of the subdivisions of the buildings, while in the other no calculated relationship exists between the wall surface and the divisions. Pugin's later buildings, especially those with flint and stone dressings, continue this device [cf. Plate 1].[54] The surface of the wall is considered as a continuous neutral area, which is to be subdivided according to the requirements of the interior. This appears a logical step from the principles of free planning mentioned above: an irregular arrangement of the whole would have conflicted with a regular subdivision of the wall-surface – a step which may be described as the final dissolution of the Classical principle of symmetry in architecture. As a further consequence, also in line with the demands in planning: no irregularity for its own sake. In an article entitled 'On Masonry' in 1846 architects are warned not to use stones which vary too much in their size. Builders began to

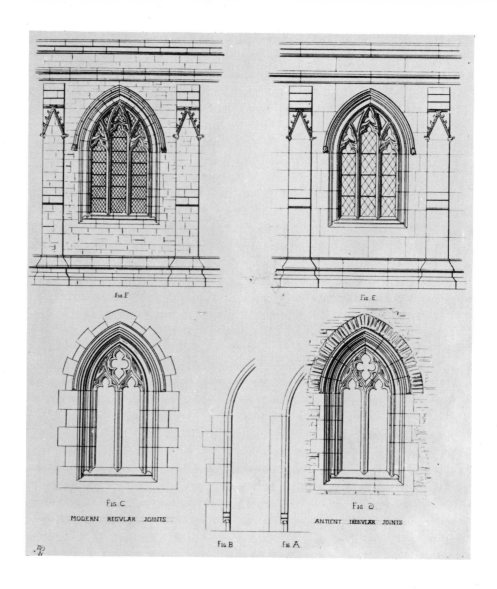

3 A. W. N. Pugin, contrasted masonry (from *The True Principles of Pointed or Christian Architecture,* 1841). In his verbal and visual polemics Pugin contrasts good, ancient examples with bad modern practice. The detailing of masonry elevation was subject to laws similar to 'picturesque utility' in planning: stones should be small and irregular in size. According to Pugin the ancient walls of this kind were much stronger than the modern ones. He clearly inherited the old liking for rough walls, but he imbued it with a moral sense of constructional 'truth'. Therefore a rough wall, showing its random masonry is no longer just a limited picturesque alternative to normal classically proportioned elevations, but a universal principle for every kind of masonry in all types of buildings. Pugin stands at the beginning of the overriding concern for masonry and wall surface, in its moral and its visual aspects, which is an eminent characteristic of the High Victorian movement and later English architecture.

try irregular jointing, and one soon saw the prodigies of 'irregularity'. It is best if 'you are neither induced to examine and commend the ingenuity with which the difficulties of a bad building stone are overcome, nor are you called on to join the vulgar admiration of "such big blocks".'[55]

Massiveness

The other related development of the forties was a demand for simple and heavy masses. The increased emphasis on massiveness aesthetically undermined the belief in a rationalist framework conception; instead of a minimum mass, a maximum of mass was now desired. 'Massiveness' was an attribute stressed in countless old and new buildings. The element of the 'sublime', which comes in here very strongly, had been mentioned much less than the 'picturesque' during the preceding decades, but it had always been less clearly defined, and the 'picturesque' had included many elements of the 'sublime'. Now much in the descriptions recalls Burke's earlier analysis, or Boullée's buildings, although the term 'sublime' itself was very rarely used.[56]

Among a few architects mainly concerned with country houses, there was also a tendency to turn from picturesque elaboration to the simplicity and massiveness of the 'sublime', and this was most noticeable in some of the work of Anthony Salvin (1799–1881). In his 'castles' at Peckforton (Cheshire), begun in 1846, and Alnwick, built from 1854 onwards, he used plain masses, vast surfaces only interrupted by small simple chamfered windows. Yet Salvin stands apart from the tendencies dealt with in this book in so far as for him this plainness seems to have only been one style among others, signifying thirteenth-century Gothic; he also built Louis XIV country houses and classical office buildings. Some time before, James Wild tried to combine 'Doric' and 'Egyptian' severity with *Rundbogenstil* motifs in what appears to be an isolated example in England: his Christ Church in Streatham shows plain yellow-brick walls pierced by small openings (1840).[57]

However, for the Ecclesiologists 'sublime' is not only an aesthetic or stylistic alternative but also a general moral principle. 'Low and massive' walls were found in many remote rural churches, as the *Ecclesiologist* noted in 'Simplicity of Composition' in 1843. The *Ecclesiologist* dwelt at length on the contrast between 'simple massiveness' and 'plainness' on the one hand and a highly decorated 'meagreness' on the other [cf. Plate 12]. It is possible that here the Ecclesiologists were also directly influenced by Uvedale Price's writings which, as we have mentioned, were reissued the year before. Price also opposed 'plain simple Gothic' to 'meagreness', for example in towers with corner pinnacles.[58]

'Rustic' churches of the forties

These tendencies were immediately exhibited in some new churches. Pugin already shows some 'rustic' trends in his churches at the beginning of the forties, for example St Oswald's, Old Swan, near Liverpool, begun in 1840 (replaced in recent years by a bigger church except for the tower),[59] had buttresses which projected very far out and also a very large roof, giving the whole a low, pyramidal appearance. At St Barnabas, Nottingham, 1842,[60] it is the continuity of surface which is noteworthy, and the reduced treatment of the windows with little exterior recession. Pugin chose the 'lancet style', a common alternative to traceried windows at that time, but he reduced the mullions to simple chamfers.

In many churches of the next years these characteristics can be noticed again and again: a tendency toward low and broad proportions, a diminishing importance of buttresses in relation to the body of the church, a flattening of tracery in relation to wall surfaces, and a simplifying of rooflines. The broad base and the low, sloping section of the church affect the proportions of the whole building. The effect on the buttresses is that they now become fewer and fewer, instead of projecting regularly from walls and corners as they did when the idea of Gothic as 'framework' was still maintained. At Pugin's St Barnabas, they are missing at some corners, and at other corners they form a continuation of the wall surface, as on the porches. In his later churches, such as Ramsgate, Pugin dispensed with buttresses altogether.

Similarly, tracery was more and more integrated into the wall, to lie flush with the wall surface. In the article of 1844 on 'Early English Lancet', some odd examples of this kind were noticed: 'windows of this kind are seldom recessed; their mullions usually stand flush with the outer wall, as in fact forming part of it.'[61]

It was suggested that mouldings should be treated as simply as possible also. In a book devoted entirely to mouldings, F. A. Paley's *A Manual of Gothic Mouldings* of 1845, the following remark can be found: 'and yet mouldings are merely the ornamental adjuncts, not the essentials, of architecture. Some buildings of the best periods were quite devoid of mouldings; whence it is evident that they are not necessary even to a perfect design.'[62] An early example of flush tracery is in the aisle windows of Pugin's church at Brewood (Staffs.) of 1844;[63] but in general this form spread only in the fifties, at a time when plate tracery, coming from other sources, also gained importance.

The demand for a simplification of the roofline can be found in 'On Simplicity of Composition', and in some of his later churches Pugin let his eaves project over the wall. Later, roofs edged by parapets were given up and replaced by projecting bargeboards, one of the most striking examples of 'cottage-design' applied to churches.[64]

*Pugin and the
Ecclesiologists
in the 1840s*

Little has to be said about the interior of churches for which the essential element, the new attitude to planning, has already been described. Again the proportions become lower and the impression of massiveness prevails, especially through the broad splay of those windows which lie closely behind the exterior wall surface. The arcades are mostly reduced to the barest essentials, and since there are no vaults there are no superimposed pillars or other such complications. Only a short piece of blank wall remains above the arcades, for in most smaller churches the clerestory is eliminated. A kind of low 'hall church' is the result.

The most important feature of the interior was the wooden roof. The history of the renaissance of medieval roofs since the early forties was based on the familiar reasons: ceilings had to be 'medieval', 'picturesque' and 'truthful' and consequently the traditional flat Georgian plaster ceilings were condemned. In the later forties there was a tendency towards simplification, in contrast to the hammer-beam roofs at first imitated.[65]

Two very characteristic examples of the 'rustic' kind of design were by George Gilbert Scott.[66] At the beginning of the forties Scott had already used the 'lancet style', but in two churches of 1846–7 he put aside the whole complicated system of small, slender pillars and arches usually associated with this manner.[67] He left the outside of Christ Church, Ramsgate [Plate 4], and St Anne, Alderney,[68] of 1846 and 1847 as bare as Pugin had left St Barnabas, Nottingham, and on the whole the character of Scott's churches is even broader. These buildings by Scott pose a special problem, for he does not seem to continue this particular mode of design. He goes on with his more elaborate former manner of 'lancet' as well as with traceried churches;[69] only in the mid-fifties does his work regain interest in this context. It might well have been that the young Street, who was his assistant from 1845 to 1849, was influential here: some features in other works of Scott of these years have already been ascribed to Street.[70] Street's own first documented larger work [Plates 5, 6] begun in early 1847, the church at Par (Biscovey, Cornwall),[71] bears a strong resemblance to these two churches by Scott, especially Ramsgate. Tracery and mouldings are reduced and overall height in proportion to width is low, particularly in the case of the tower.[72] The tendency to integrate the tracery into the wall can also be seen very strongly in one of the aisle windows, where two lancets and a circular opening are pierced through the wall with no framing members. The interior shows many purposely 'rough' features, such as the very irregular quoining and the primitively shaped beams of the roof; on the other hand some features of the chancel are treated very elaborately, such as the arcadings in the eastern wall, as well as the coping of the outside of the east wall. Other architects continued these tendencies in the early fifties; a few more examples will be discussed in Chapters 3 and 4.

Pugin and the
Ecclesiologists
in the 1840s

4 (below left) G. G. Scott, Ramsgate, Christ Church, 1846. Begun at the same time as Pugin's church nearby (Plate 1), the approach is different: for smaller churches, the influence of the picturesque was even stronger, features from the 'cottage orné' were taken over, such as rough masonry and a great emphasis on the roof, no parapets and coping, but projecting eaves. What is influential for later developments is the relative importance of materials in the visual impression of the whole and the simplicity of treatment of contour and detail, cf. especially the windows.

5 (below right) G. E. Street, Par (Biscovey), Cornwall, church, begun 1847 (Courtesy National Monuments Record). Street's first building was designed when he was still in G. G. Scott's office. He continued the manner of Scott's church at Ramsgate, where he might have had a share in the design. Street also very clearly adhered to the principle of keeping the different parts of the church distinct, nave, chancel, one aisle ('better one aisle than to run up two cheaply') and the tower, placed on the side of the nave.

J. L. Petit

*Pugin and the
Ecclesiologists
in the 1840s*

John Louis Petit (1801–68)[73] was chiefly concerned with another aspect of architecture, which has not been dealt with so far: the rendering of architecture in drawing and watercolouring. The function of architecture in landscape painting was very similar to that of a 'picturesquely' designed architecture in its landscaped surroundings.[74] Architecture was subservient to landscape; it took part in different moods. But gradually the representation of architecture became a distinct genre, just as 'picturesque' principles themselves were applied to buildings not in parks. It became a subsidiary branch of landscape drawing, nurtured by the spread of the watercolour technique. At about the same period, roughly around 1800, architects began to provide 'picturesque' perspectives of their projects,[75] and in turn watercolourists and illustrators began to design architectural details and furniture, like Pugin's father, Augustus Charles Pugin. At first the range of motifs, moods and means of rendering architectural effects remained very limited: the mood of 'ruinousness' was the most

6 G. E. Street, Par, Cornwall, church interior, begun 1847 (Courtesy National Monuments Record). The interior of Par is as simple as the exterior, apart from the fittings in the east end.

Pugin and the
Ecclesiologists
in the 1840s

popular. But gradually with the increase of travel and the greater demand for topographical and scholarly accuracy that mood lost importance.

Petit's drawings are actually less faithful to detail than those of many other contemporaries, for example Samuel Prout.[76] Petit's main intention – he always used the same technique, short pen-strokes of even breadth – was to render the changing effects of light and shade on crumbling surfaces of masonry. But in some places – and this tendency increases with the years – parts of the wall are left free and contours get sharper and more continuous. The buildings are more and more interpreted as simple-shaped masses. Petit seems to have been the first draughtsman to accompany his drawings with theoretical, that is to say mostly aesthetic, comments. His two books of the forties must be mentioned here: *Remarks on Church Architecture*, 1841 and a later edition in 1846,[77] and *Remarks on Architectural Character*, 1846. He seems to be the first author of the forties to stress the importance of 'horizontal lines',[78] which became another important concept in the early fifties. Other aspects need not be gone into here, his 'character' stands for almost everything: massiveness, plainness, 'individuality' in the choice of motifs and, of course, the unity of the building and a landscape background. In the fifties Petit continued publishing and as there are no essential changes these works can be mentioned here. He had very little interest in colour. His biggest work, *Architectural Studies in France,* appeared in 1854 [Plate 7]. Here he dealt with interiors as well, where the tendency for sharp and regular corners also prevails. Again and again drawings show simple pillars and pilasters, arches and barrel-vaults and in his text he stressed the importance of 'unbroken surfaces' and 'squareness of moulding'.[79] Petit, who had seen much of European architecture, chose in this volume groups of Romanesque churches in the south-west of France to make his points. He recommends these 'styles' for imitation, because they were less 'developed' than the more complicated kinds of northern Gothic. But on the whole it did not matter from what historical period this aesthetic of simplicity chose its examples. In his lecture 'A Few Remarks on Italian Architecture'[80] he looked at Roman architecture where he again found 'unbroken surfaces, rectangular edges, plain square orders' and so on and his paramount example in the *Studies* was not St Front at Périgueux[81] but the simplified interior of the model of St Paul's Cathedral of 1673.[82]

Polychromy

The article on Masonry in the *Ecclesiologist* of 1846 was mainly concerned with 'Kentish rag', that is a manner of 'rustic' surface resulting in a wide use of this form of limestone for town and country churches alike. In the following years, however, attention turned more to the

*Pugin and the
Ecclesiologists
in the 1840s*

inherent qualities of the materials themselves. A regard merely for varieties of surface treatment came to be considered a literally superficial and 'untruthful' attitude toward materials. Kentish rag was increasingly discarded in advanced circles, for the most important quality of materials now seemed to be something else: colour.

A new kind of architectural polychromy was one of the consequences of theory and practice of the forties and early fifties. Interest in architectural polychromy had started a little earlier, as a result of discoveries and researches in the field of classical archaeology. In the 1820s T. L. Donaldson and I. Hittorf had for the first time attached some significance to the colour of which they found traces in classical ruins. Controversies arose over the reconstruction of these traces, whose aesthetic implications still remain to be investigated.[83] In the forties the interest in architectural polychromy became very strong. Owen Jones started to publish his descriptions and theories on the use of colour in architecture, beginning with his views of the Alhambra and examples of Cosmati mosaics in 1842.[84] At the same time, processes of printing, especially chromolithography, provided

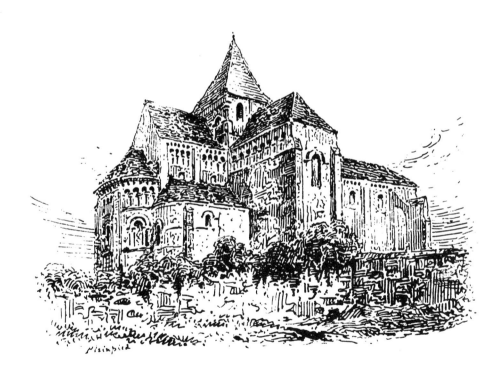

7 Church at 'Plainpied' (Plaimpied-Giraudins, Cher) drawn by J. L. Petit (from his *Architectural Studies in France*, 1854). England as well as the continent was searched for precedents for the small 'rustic' church. Petit preferred those of the south-west of France which in his vigorous style of drawing are invariably reduced to simple masses.

19

the means for wide dissemination of strongly coloured pictures. Colour began to be freed from the complicated contours of form and from the domination of tone. In contrast to controversial adaptations to classical motifs, emphasis was put on the more lavish use of colour on flat surfaces. Pugin was also concerned with questions of coloured decoration as early as 1841; his main point was that the laws of flat surfaces ruled out the use of illusionistic motifs as for example 'the ancient paving tiles . . . being merely ornamented with pattern, not produced by any apparent relief, but only by contrast of colour'.[85]

Pugin's investigations into coloured decorations with Gothic motifs were soon continued by John Whichcord and others.[86] The *Ecclesiologist* took up the question in an article on Decorative Colour in 1845.[87] 'We would have every inch glowing' – again aesthetic demands were proclaimed with religious enthusiasm – ' . . . Puritans would have every inch colourless.' Like many other artists in England at this time, the Ecclesiologists were also influenced by the coloured decorations and fresco paintings of the contemporary Munich school.[88]

As it is not difficult to guess from the foregoing, a conflict arose: the painting of the walls contradicted the call to leave masonry as it was. At this point the *Ecclesiologist* introduced an argument which Ruskin and his followers were shortly to take up: all that matters is that there should be no deceit as to the material of which the decoration is made.[89] Pugin continued to object. He refused to paint the interior of his later churches and he wrote in 1850 that Lord Shrewsbury and not he himself had been responsible for the interior of his early church at Cheadle[90] which he began in 1841 and where the walls and pillars are encrusted with coloured plaster. In his own church at Ramsgate there was nothing but 'solid stone walls and moulded work'. That he was not castigating all colour when he wrote this was shown by his further remarks: ' . . . do not let anyone imagine that I am deprecating the legitimate use of colour in church decoration, but it should be defined within proper limits . . . roofs, altars. . . .'

But arguments had already developed further. Pugin's opinions were commented on by the *Ecclesiologist* which agreed with him about Cheadle, but maintained that something was missing from Pugin's remarks, namely: 'one of the problems, which revived pointed architecture of the nineteenth century, enterprising and scientific as it is, will have chiefly to work out . . . is constructional polychromy'.[91]

'To make colour with the body', which had already been mentioned as a possibility in the article 'On Decorative Colour', was to be one of the main concerns in architectural writing and building activity in the next decade. For this reason all other kinds of coloured decoration, and especially fresco-painting, played a remarkably small part in the architectural discussions.[92]

*Pugin and the
Ecclesiologists
in the 1840s*

In 1844 and 1845 the secretary of the Ecclesiological Society, Benjamin Webb, travelled extensively in northern Italy where he found many more examples of the approved elements. His thoughts and observations were first laid down in a lecture 'On Pointed Architecture as adapted to tropical climates' in 1845.[93] Time and again he speaks of 'massiveness', 'unusual thickness of the walls', 'great breadth', 'great simplicity' and 'plainness', especially with regard to the medieval architecture of Tuscany. On the other hand he is not sure what forms to recommend in detail: 'probably [one] ought to study simplicity of mouldings.' He is undecided about continuous wall surface, which was unpicturesque: 'the architect . . . will gladly avail himself . . . of every opportunity of breaking the external surfaces by different planes of elaborate panelling.' But some lines above he says: 'the architect must carry up his walls boldly even though they present an uniform blank surface. Buttresses he will probably avoid.' Similarly he is uncertain about other elements, especially verticality: 'I do not profess to understand, however, how so vertical an effect is obtained in Giotto's tower – which is a square building in horizontal storeys, so far from tapering that the top is of the same area as the base and to which the spire was never added – except it arises from the unequal height of the stages themselves.' The notions of simplicity are also extended to planning and interior space. Besides 'interior gloom', Webb specially noticed the extensiveness of the interiors: 'immense area, . . . great space', 'hieratic plan', a notion which was soon to conflict with those of complicated picturesque planning.

As a reason for all these devices, Webb emphasized an argument which had already been used before by Pugin and others: the local climate.[94] The hot weather of those countries required interiors which had to be shut off from the outside as much as possible. But this argument was less important in itself (Webb also wrote that the same kind of thick walls may serve against the cold in the north) than as serving to exclude the symbolic meaning of forms and motifs; there was not much need to pay attention to their national significance. As Webb wrote: 'At last, if the result be unlike an English church, what will that matter, provided we have a building correct in plan and details [i.e. ritually] and accurately suited to the particular climate?' Webb also criticized the contemporary church at Colabah, India, by J. M. Derick,[95] which he said 'reads the problem thus: Given, an English church to fit it for the tropics. Instead of, Given, the tropics, and such *principles* of architecture, to build by the latter a church to suit the former'. It was now possible for a good church to be built without English medieval motifs and within a few years the climatic justifications were forgotten and the aesthetic considerations openly prevailed. The term 'tropical' had a special ring architecturally during the next years, but in the fifties it became confined to buildings which were erected in actual tropical zones.[96]

Webb's notes appeared in their entirety as *Sketches of Continental Ecclesiology* in 1848. Although on the whole the account is more concerned with liturgy, many of his descriptions of buildings anticipate Ruskin and Street. In San Zeno at Verona he points to the interior where 'nothing occupies the surface of the wall under the clerestory windows'.[97] In Sant'Anastasia in the same town he admires the tracery which consists of 'a plane of stone which is cut into two lights . . .'.[98]

Brick

It was the search for coloured material as well as the new feeling for massiveness which led to a new evaluation of brick. In 1841 *A Few Words* had still said that 'brick ought on no account to be used'.[99] The cheap yellow brick of the flat Georgian wall surfaces became unpopular. But now Webb again and again mentioned the material of his Italian churches. Probably the first publication entirely devoted to this subject was Thomas James's pamphlet 'On the Use of Brick in Ecclesiastical Architecture – on Ecclesiastical Brickwork in Italy' of 1847.[100] The colour of the brick, contrasted with other colours, was described in many examples. The best type of building for brickwork seemed to be the tower. The campanile at Venice shows 'no decoration . . . common brick yet beautiful in form and colour'. Many other observations point forward to later descriptions by Ruskin and Street: the campanile at Vicenza 'is carried up the whole height of the same size'.

The other element, 'massiveness', can also be found in a long account of Albi Cathedral of 1847, with its ' . . . side chapels excavated out of the immense thickness of the walls . . .'; 'we have no doubt that the material has influenced the form of the buttresses . . . broad and shallow segments of circles . . . altogether conceived in a gigantic spirit,'[101] and R. C. Carpenter's project of Colombo Cathedral of the same year was criticized: 'the detail might be made more suitable to brick, e.g. columns . . . not clustered compositions.'[102] Italy was, of course, especially rich in examples of brick and 'constructional polychromy'. James pointed to the 'bold richness of colour . . . [in the] alternate stripes of brick and stone' in many examples.

Apart from Italy, medieval brick buildings in many other parts of Europe caught the attention of British architectural travellers. According to Charles Fowler in 1850 the 'prevailing character' in German medieval brick buildings was 'simplicity' and 'massiveness'. The same was found in buildings in Spain.[103]

English medieval connoisseurs had, of course, been travelling in Italy for many years. But Thomas Hope's and Robert Willis's books, which appeared in the mid-thirties, were largely concerned with classifications by way of rational analyses of the problems of construction and decoration. In the early forties a number of books containing coloured illustrations appeared. But generally only the coloured decorations of the interiors were taken into account; Street later criticized the lack of colour in Gally Knight's illustrations of north Italian churches in the forties.[104]

The fact that this appreciation is a result of the particular aesthetic and theoretical disposition of the Ecclesiologists is shown by some comments of a member of the Schinkel-Schule, Ludwig Runge, who during the same time found that there is very little decoration with coloured materials in Italian medieval architecture, a fact of which he approved. 'Variously coloured materials only rarely occur in the brickwork of architecture in Italy, and only in small patterns and as a special adornment. Those very finely treated and differently shaped forms which are already there would very easily get disturbed if the colours were given more space.' His illustrations, the most surprising thing about his book, show many monuments familiar from the descriptions of Benjamin Webb or Ruskin, but the manner of rendering the architecture is very different.[105]

The use of coloured brick in buildings in England before the mid-forties does not seem to have amounted to much. Thomas James and later Ruskin in *The Stones of Venice* pointed to an early contemporary example, Wild's Christ Church, Streatham, of 1840. Yet the exterior use of coloured brick is very slight, and the building seems more remarkable as an early example of brick-massiveness than of constructional polychromy. Apart from that, it had one of the first sumptuously coloured decorations in the interior by Owen Jones. Other examples of coloured brick are the diaper works on buildings with perpendicular or Tudor motifs, such as Hardwick's Lincoln's Inn Library of 1843.[106]

At this point, the account should proceed with Street's and Butterfield's work immediately following the years 1848–9. In 1849 and 1850 Butterfield started to build the Model Church of the Ecclesiological Society, All Saints, Margaret Street, which from its beginning was supposed to incorporate the new principles. Street was more active in lectures and articles. In his article 'On Town Churches' of 1850 he appears to be influenced by Webb, Ruskin and Butterfield. Yet before dealing with all these we have to concern ourselves with a writer, John Ruskin, who developed ideas similar to those reported so far, but with infinitely more detail. Street's activities in the early fifties will be dealt with in Chapter 3, Butterfield's, including All Saints, in Chapter 4.

Developments abroad

The next chapters will be concerned with the successful development and application of these principles and their powerful influence in England in the next two decades. This might be the moment to look across the Channel to see whether there are any similar developments. At first sight quite a few similar things might be found in the forties. In Germany some architects, especially Gaertner in Munich, had tried to combine Greek simplicity and medieval motifs by imitating Byzantine or south Italian forms. In the forties their influence spread widely. In Hanover A. D. Andreae, a little known architect who died young in 1846, built a remarkable addition to the old Rathaus (1845), combining a relatively free, asymmetrical spacing of the openings with astounding massiveness and continuity of surface. Very remarkable, also deriving from the same background, is the Dane Bindesbøll's polychrome project for a zoological museum of 1844, again combining Doric severity and Italian Romanesque flat-pattern decoration.

However, this path does not seem to have been pursued much further. When German architects spoke of the combination of various periods they were mostly thinking in terms of motifs, not of abstract forms, and the general formal tendency from the late forties onwards

8 C. Naissant, Paris, Notre Dame de la Gare, Ivry, 1855. Although not Gothic, the churches by Naissant, an architect who deserves more attention than he has been given so far, were intensely admired by the *Ecclesiologist*: 'the severity and plainness of detail is most extraordinary'.

was towards the 'picturesque' and away from the remnants of the neo-classical 'sublime'. It was not until the later sixties that tendencies moved a little in the direction they had taken in England. Also the early Puginian Ecclesiologists' phase of insisting on Gothic motifs for symbolic reasons developed in Germany from the later forties onwards, so that Gothic architects insisted for a long time on northern thirteenth- to fifteenth-century motifs. So the curious situation arose that while the German Gothic Revivalists of the fifties, especially A. Reichensperger of Cologne, were well informed about the developments in England, there was hardly any English influence. The Ecclesiologists, in turn, thought very little of their German counterparts.

In France the situation was, on the whole, more different from that in England. A strong movement towards simplicity and the adoption of Byzantine or 'primitive Romanesque' forms occurred in the late forties. Claude Naissant, probably one of the first to follow these tendencies, was in fact strongly praised by the *Ecclesiologist* in 1855: 'the severity and plainness of detail is most extraordinary,'[107] referring to Saint-Lambert, Vaugirard, begun in 1848. Even more powerful is the slightly later church, Notre Dame de la Gare at Ivry (1855) [Plate 8]. On the whole these buildings look almost as if they derived from Petit's descriptions and illustrations. Yet although this tendency became quite a powerful one in church building – one only needs to think of Sacré Coeur in Paris, begun in the seventies – it was, if not directed against the Gothicists, at least a tendency distinct from neo-Gothic, and the Gothicists did not take part in it. However, Viollet-le-Duc seems to have been influenced by this tendency towards massiveness, as is shown in some of his later works, such as Saint-Denys-de-l'Estrée at Saint Denis, begun in 1864. Again contacts between England and France seem to have been quite frequent (see Chapter 6), but very little influence can be detected in either direction.

two

John Ruskin

Ruskin's writings on architecture are as voluminous as his writings on the other arts. We shall discuss only those elements that relate to the architectural concepts of the Ecclesiologists. In other words, only Ruskin's contribution to High Victorian architectural ideas in a narrow sense will be outlined here, precisely because this problem has received little attention so far.[1]

Ruskin's starting point for his interest in architecture was broadly similar to Petit's: the study of buildings and their settings by means of sketches and watercolours; the concern with the aesthetics of the 'picturesque' and 'sublime' together with ethical considerations; and the ignorance of, or even contempt for, practical considerations in architecture. But it was in his intensity of seeing and describing that he surpassed his contemporaries. Although Ruskin had written about architecture before, a deepening of his interest took place in 1845, about which he wrote much later in *Praeterita*:

> Hitherto all architecture, except fairy-finished Milan, had depended with me for its delight on being partly in decay. I revered the sentiment of its age, and I was accustomed to look for the signs of age in the mouldering of its traceries, and in the interstices deepening between the stones of its masonry. This looking for cranny and joints was mixed with the love of rough stones themselves, and of country churches built like Westmoreland cottages.[2] Here in Lucca I found myself suddenly in the presence of twelfth century buildings, originally set in such balance of masonry that they could all stand without mortar; and in material so incorruptible, that after six hundred years of sunshine and rain a lancet could not now be put between their joints.
> Absolutely for the first time I now saw, what medieval buildings were, and what they meant. I took the simplest of all facades for analysis, that of Santa Maria Foris-Portam (Lucca), and thereon literally began the study of architecture.[3]

> The inlaying of San Michele (Lucca), as opposed to Gothic pierced lace work . . . the pure and severe arcading of finely proportioned columns of San Frediano (Lucca) doing stern duty under vertical walls, as opposed to Gothic shafts with no end and buttresses with no bearing . . .[4]

The change in his attitude may first be observed in the field of drawing [c.f. above p. 17; Plates 9, 10]. In 1846 Ruskin added to the second edition of the first volume of *Modern Painters* a number of paragraphs on the drawing of architecture.[5] He condemned linear elevations as 'unintelligible and meaningless abstracts of beautiful designs'. On the other hand, he was opposed to 'the habit of executing every-thing under one kind of effect or in one manner'. The draughtsman should not follow 'the love of mere ruinousness' and he should not 'substitute rude fractures and blotting stains for all its [i.e. the building's] fine chiseling and colour'.[6]

In 1845, Ruskin discovered that he preferred the simpler Italian medieval style to the more complicated northern Gothic style. He had already travelled and sketched in Italy, and his changed views are shown in two drawings by him of Santa Maria della Spina at Pisa, one made in 1840 [Plate 9] and one in 1845 [Plate 10]. The earlier drawing shows an abundant use of small linear patterns, the later one patches of light and shade which expose form and surface. A dense and complicated network of lines covers the surface of the building, whereas in the later drawing surfaces remain unbroken; much stronger contrasts of light and shade bring out the contours and edges of the buildings, not linearly, but with a more three-dimensional character. The anatomy of the masonry is clearly shown. A detail of the façade of San Michele at Lucca of 1845 shows this even more strongly: the decorative figures are shown to be part of the stonework, defined and surrounded by an inlaid mosaic ground, some of which has dropped off.[7] Ruskin used a different manner in his drawings to Pugin or Petit, a development which should be investigated in a much larger context of architectural and landscape drawing. His drawings remained sketchy in their general handling, but became much more accurate in the rendering of construction and materials especially as he tended to limit himself to views of small details.

Engravings of a number of his sketches form an essential part of his books on architecture. In 1851 he published a separate collection of plates under the ponderous title *Examples of the Architecture of Venice, Selected and Drawn on Measurement from the Edifices*.[8] This of course contained nothing like conventional elevations and per-spectives, but a completely haphazard mixture of architectural and sculptural details.

Very often these drawings recall photographs. It was in these years that photography became available to those interested in historic architecture and it was soon hailed as the best way to 'render' such objects. In fact, the later Pisa drawing is said to have been done after a photograph. Although Ruskin had known about photography before, he had not appreciated its value: ' . . . wholly careless at that time of finished detail, I saw nothing in the Daguerrotype to help, or alarm me; until now at Venice I found a French artist producing exquisitely bright small plates . . . as if a magician had reduced the reality to be carried away into an enchanted land. . . .' And in a letter of 1845 he wrote: 'every chip of stone is here . . . it is a blessed invention.' From this time onwards architectural photography was increasingly used. In 1857 an Architectural Photographic Association (later Society) was founded to promote 'the sharpness and precision . . . of the delineation of buildings' by photography.[9]

After finishing the second volume of *Modern Painters* in 1846, which contained some substantial passages on architecture, Ruskin concentrated more on the subject, in 1846 in northern Italy and in 1848 in Normandy. In 1847 he laid down many of his views in a long review of Lord Lindsay's *Sketches of the History of Christian Art*.[10] Early in 1849 he completed *The Seven Lamps of Architecture*.[11]

The Seven Lamps of Architecture

Much of *The Seven Lamps,* or principles (Sacrifice, Truth, Power, Beauty, Life, Memory, Obedience) continues his *Modern Painters,* thus remaining within the tradition of the English aesthetic treatise.[12] This was unusual in a book entirely devoted to architecture, although Burke and Uvedale Price had included some architecture in their treatises. Yet, as with them, *The Seven Lamps* contains almost no practical details on the subject.

In the chapter on 'Truth', Ruskin begins with moral demands, but

9 J. Ruskin, Santa Maria della Spina at Pisa, drawing, 1840 (Courtesy London, Courtauld Institute of Art, Witt Collection).

10 J. Ruskin, Santa Maria della Spina, Pisa, pen and wash, 1845 (Courtesy
Ruskin Museum, Sheffield). When Ruskin drew the building in 1840 he
emphasized the picturesque, spiky outline, the richness of small-scale
decoration and the general impression of decay. By 1845 his notions of
what architecture should be had completely changed. We seem to look at
a different building: the emphasis is on surfaces and shade is used to
produce clear outlines. The intense light reveals what seems to be the
most important quality of the masonry: colour (as can be proved from
other contemporary sketches by Ruskin; previously he had rarely used
colour for architecture). Italy, i.e. the medieval buildings of northern Italy,
offered by far the best examples of this kind of masonry. Ruskin was not
the only one who realized this in these years; the Secretary of the
Ecclesiological Society, Benjamin Webb, had reported about the same
buildings in the same year, 1845.

soon modifies their importance. Like Pugin he warns of 'structural deceits', but that does not mean that all the parts of the building have to be 'constructional', for 'it is just as lawful to build a pinnacle for its beauty as a tower'; what is important is to show a clear distinction between 'decorative' and 'constructive' parts. More important is the discussion of 'surface deceits'.[13] Ruskin elaborates on what the Ecclesiologists had already said in their article 'On Decorative Colour' before, he condemns only 'false representation of material', as in the case of false jewels. The various means of coating a rough wall are not condemned, for example, 'whitewash . . . though often (by no means always) to be regretted as a concealment, is not to be blamed as a falsity. It shows itself for what it is, and asserts nothing of what is beneath it.' The same applies to slabs of marble: if it is clear that 'a marble facing does not . . . imply a marble wall, there is no harm in it .'

For Ruskin, form is always determined by the material of which it consists and the way in which it is constructed; on the other hand the choice of a material and a method of construction means an aesthetic choice among possible forms. Referring to the use of iron, which was a much debated question in these years, he has to admit that 'we can hardly allege anything against them [cast-iron ornaments] since they are always distinguishable, at a glance, from wrought and hammered work, and stand only for what they are,'[14] and on the prospects of an iron architecture he writes: 'Abstractedly there appears no reason why iron should not be used as well as wood; and the time is probably near when a new system of architectural laws will be developed, adapted entirely to metallic construction.' But Ruskin prefers 'the surface of the earth, that is to say, clay, wood or stone' and the modes of construction proper to those materials. It follows from this choice – which at one point Ruskin calls a 'prejudice' that is based on a long tradition – that iron buildings are 'not architecture at all'.[15] Ruskin was less tolerant later, when he despised iron architecture mainly because it was not hand-made. The 'iron-problem' in the fifties comes up in a later chapter. What matters here is that 'architecture' is defined by describing the physical properties of stone. It is a formal choice: for Ruskin, ethical choices in architecture crystallize around something else, namely architectural painting and sculpture, to which we come later.

Form and material become to a very great extent identical. Moreover, architectural form consists not only of the forms in which the designer shapes the material, but also of the traces of external physical influences: wear and weathering are an integral part of it [Plate 11]. Ruskin demands that there should be no restoration, that is, no replacing of old material by new material of the same shape, 'and as for direct and simple copying, it is palpably impossible. What copying can there be of surfaces that have been worn half an inch down?'[16]

Here again, drawings might illustrate the shift of emphasis; in almost any contemporary archaeological drawing one can still find a differentiation between those lines or shaded parts which characterize the state of the material, and those lines which, as it were, more abstractly delineate the contours of the parts of the building: in Ruskin's drawings this difference has disappeared. Although Ruskin's views on restoration did not seem to have an immediate influence on restorations at the time, they were some of his most influential and revolutionary ideas in the end. It was only after a general spread of the 'Arts and Crafts' view of architecture that in 1877 William Morris founded the Society for the Protection of Ancient Buildings to urge that buildings ought to be repaired rather than 'restored'.

For Ruskin at that time the most important qualities of materials

11 J. Ruskin, 'Wall-Veil Decoration, Renaissance and Romanesque'
(from *The Stones of Venice*, Vol. I, 1851, XIII).
A 'contrast' that reminds one very strongly of Pugin (cf. Plate 3). The
Renaissance treatment is totally formal, mechanical and concerned with
the surface only; in the Middle Ages the ornament of the surface was part
of the body of masonry. More than Pugin, Ruskin emphasized the element
of decay of the materials as a sign of the 'life' of a building as a physical
being. Consequently Ruskin argues that it is impossible to 'restore' a
building; one can only repair, but not replace, the materials of the
building, a view which became more influential in the 1870s and 80s
with the Anti-Restoration and Arts and Crafts Movements.

were their inherent colours. He preferred strongly-coloured stones:

> The transparent alabasters of San Miniato, and the mosaics of St. Mark's are more warmly filled and more brightly touched by every return of morning and evening rays; while the hues of our cathedrals have died like the iris out of the cloud; and the temples whose azure and purple once flamed above the Grecian promontories, stand in their faded whiteness, like snow, which the sunset has left cold.[17]

Further discussions of the use of coloured materials elaborate portions of the second volume of *Modern Painters* and his review of Lord Lindsay's book: colour and form have little to do with each other, strongly-coloured areas should not bear a complicated outline. Ruskin very often writes of 'spaces of colour' instead of forms of colour, and there are also 'simple masses of colour'. Suitable shapes are circles and squares.[18]

Ruskin also prefers the substance and surface of hard stones, 'polished surface and iron heart, not rough looks and incoherent surface',[19] as he says in *The Stones of Venice*. Consequently the surface of walls should be left uninterrupted. Ruskin speaks of 'smooth', 'broad', 'lineless', 'unbroken surface', of 'flatness' and 'breadth of surface',[20] a definite change from the forties when the general opinion in the picturesque tradition was, as Pugin expressed it, 'play of light and shade consequent on bold relief and deep sinkings are so essential to produce a good effect.'[21]

In looking at buildings in their entirety, these considerations are supplemented by the more familiar demands of the 'sublime': 'vast flat surfaces' which should be 'gathered up into a mighty square'. Also the buildings must be 'bounded as much as possible by continuous lines . . . one visible bounding line from top to bottom, and from end to end' [Plate 12]. The same applies to circular forms. Other elements of the sublime are 'mere size' and the continuous repetition of arcadings – all described in the first paragraphs of the 'Lamp of Power'.[22] These concepts go back to Burke in the middle of the eighteenth century and Ruskin's words remind us momentarily of the unbuilt designs of Boullée, with their vast cubes and unbroken surfaces. But, when Boullée wrote of 'surface continue', or 'muraille absolument nue',[23] these walls were for him primarily the enclosing planes of his three-dimensional 'corps', whereas Ruskin hardly ever took the whole of a building into consideration. There is a characteristic difference in the concept of the cornice: whereas Boullée (and, even more, Ledoux) had reduced the cornice to a small projecting slab so as not to interfere with his basic forms, Ruskin strongly advocated projecting cornices, made up of several parts and especially like the machicolations of Italian medieval palaces.

For Ruskin the term 'mass' was not restricted to matter but could be applied equally to matter and areas of shade – although Ruskin proposes at one point to 'restrict the term "mass" to the portions to which proper form belongs, and to call the field on which such forms are traced, interval'. But the relevance of shade is diminished by his emphasis on flat surfaces; in his next book, *The Stones of Venice*, light and shade are hardly mentioned. In *The Seven Lamps,* Ruskin tends to restrict the element of shade to the consideration of features added to the simple wall surfaces of buildings and he thinks 'a noble surface of stone . . . a fairer thing . . . than most architectural features it is caused to assume. But however this might be . . . the wall . . . is supposed to be given and it is our craft to divide it.' Shadows must have a homogeneous darkness, 'broad sunshine, starless shade':[24] their

12 J. Ruskin, 'Towers, Medieval and Modern' (from *The Stones of Venice*, Vol. I, 1851, VI).

The Ecclesiologists had already been opposing the 'simple massiveness' of their rustic churches to the 'ornate meagreness' of many contemporary buildings. Ruskin now puts the Campanile at Venice side by side with one of the towers of Free Church College in Edinburgh, built in 1846. He admits that the latter has been rendered a little too much on the meagre side, and he also stripped the Loggia off the Campanile to increase its grandeur. A tower – and most other buildings as well – should be 'one bold square mass of brickwork' outlines must be sharp, and he shows examples where he finds the recesses 'cut as sharply through them as if they had been struck out by a stamp'. Ruskin looks at the development of window tracery in these terms: 'At first there was a state, where there were only penetrations in the shield of stone.' Those penetrations became larger and the solid parts 'caught the eye of the architect'. Then, tracery was more and more subdivided, and Ruskin deplores 'the substitution of line for mass', as in his simplified comparison of two styles of Gothic detail, 'linear and surface Gothic', in *The Stones of Venice*.[25] As we shall see later, plate tracery with simple geometrical openings, very often lying flush with the wall, became a favourite form of window in the fifties and sixties.

Ruskin's attitude towards architectural decoration clarifies the new attitude towards architecture as 'building': 'sculpture is the representation of an idea, while architecture is itself a real thing . . . reality ought to have reality in all its attributes.'[26] Architecture has lost its symbolic significance; it is something which can only 'express' what it materially consists of. Ruskin describes a complicated range of different kinds of decoration from the more naturalistic to the more abstract; but in general he recommends that decoration be set in 'bold' opposition[27] to architecture; it is seen in its quality of telling a story as 'painting' or 'sculpture'. It then matters little what relation it has with the building: the most important consideration is that it should be 'readable'. Ruskin is concerned with the subjects of such sculpture in long parts of the 'Lamp of Beauty' and 'Lamp of Memory' (see below).

The Stones of Venice, I

Soon after the appearance of *The Seven Lamps, The Stones of Venice* was announced. The first volume appeared early in 1851, volumes II and III in 1853; it is the first volume that is most important in our context and is easily separable from the other two.[28]

Ruskin divided his subject into two broad categories, 'Construction' and 'Decoration'. Of course his maxims on construction were no builders' manual.[29] He ignored any structural complication, such as vaulting,[30] describing only the simplest aspects of masonry walls, arcadings and their basic elements, but that in enormous detail. He wrote many pages on the simplest elements of masonry construction, for example its horizontal layers. He compared the 'stratification of the wall'[31] to the stratification in mountains; in describing Mont Cervin (the Matterhorn) he stresses the importance of underlying courses of hard rock, 'the masonry of the mountain itself', that hold it together in spite of mingled and overlying courses of loose shale: an example of stability 'attained with materials of imperfect and variable character' from which he concludes 'that it is better and easier to strengthen a wall . . . as of brick, by introducing carefully laid courses of stone, than by adding to its thickness'.[32] The fact that a wall is a series of layers should be shown as distinctly as possible on the surface, and the two-dimensional elevational character of that surface is less important than the indication of those layers. Ruskin writes of 'epochs in the wall's existence',[33] of 'expression of growth or age of the wall', and the cornice is 'the accomplishment of the wall's work'.[34] This layering can also show off various natural colours of stone or brick with layers of marble, again a crucial feature in the architecture of the later fifties. Yet generally, he thought, stratification should be reserved for thick walls; with thinner walls it is better 'to throw the colours into chequered patterns'. Ruskin also applies his concept of clarity and simplicity of outline to the thickness of walls, a 'condition of structure being that it is of equal thickness everywhere'.[35]

Some pronouncements of *The Seven Lamps* about 'weight of earth' or 'the mere weight of a great wall'[36] are given a more literal sense in *The Stones of Venice*. What Pugin had done for the surface of the wall, to consider it as something neutral in shape and proportion, and what Ruskin continued in the field of coloured decoration in *The Seven Lamps*, was now laid down for the whole mass, the thickness, of the wall.[37] Here again, as so often in nineteenth-century art, theory, by describing factors in a work of art in terms of nature in the physical sense, widened the field of purely formal considerations.

In many other ways *The Stones* continued *The Seven Lamps*; 'blank surface' should not be disturbed by buttresses: the same applies to 'bold rounded and polygonal surface'. Where one has to build buttresses,[38] they should be shown as part of the walls: 'through the buttress and the wall alike, the courses of its varied masonry are seen in their successive order.'[39] Openings should have rectangular edges, which should be kept free of decoration. The outer surface of the wall and the surfaces of the splay, the archivolts, are not to be treated as two different parts of a wall and decorated in a different manner: they ought to be shown as two facets of the same body of masonry. 'A rude border [is] all [that is] needed',[40] 'plain openings in the walls, studiously simple and unmoulded at the sides'.[41]

In Ruskin's long and detailed chapters about columns and capitals and so on, he felt it important to distinguish clearly between the different parts of an arcade. Shafts should be isolated and preferably monolithic: that is, either what Ruskin called 'detached block shafts' or clusters of these, never fused into 'nebulous' piers. Arcades should be isolated from the surrounding wall.[42] The continuity of horizontals is more important than the continuity of verticals: one may even disturb the vertical continuity of superimposed arcades by 'changing their [the columns'] places in the upper stories'.[43]

It is not difficult to guess what shape should be given to a tower:

already in *The Seven Lamps* Ruskin had praised campaniles that run up undisturbedly, as preferable to towers linked with the rest of the building [Plate 12]. A tower should not diminish its breadth in its upper parts and a horizontal termination is better than an acutely pointed one. The impression of massiveness is paramount, as in the campanile at Venice, 'one bold square mass of brickwork'. 'A tower may, indeed, have a kind of buttress, a projection, or subordinate tower at each of its angles; but these are to its main body like the satellites to a shaft, joined with its strength, and associated with its uprightness, part of the tower itself.'[44]

Here the difference of Ruskin's kind of 'sublime' from earlier phases of that aesthetic comes out most clearly; 'mass' does not apply to regular geometrical shapes, but to something which can be moulded freely within simple and grand outlines, even something – and this would be a premonition of the dynamism which later decades saw in architecture – that generates itself, as the term 'uprightness' might suggest.

There is very little specifically on interiors of buildings. Nearly everything which has been related so far applies to both exterior and interior as well. Ruskin briefly deals with roofs, but not feeling competent to treat vaulting, he confines himself to wooden roofs, which really have little to do with stone architecture. Smaller roofs, he writes, are often 'put together on the ground . . . and put on the walls like a hat'.[45] Yet their inner surfaces should be smooth – 'curved surfaces . . . sweeping vaults'.[46]

Ruskin and architectural theory

Ruskin was not familiar with the practical problems of architecture, but neither can he be called an architectural theorist in the traditional sense. But by bypassing theory he undermined it. Ruskin does not undertake to deal with specific types of buildings or groups of types at any length – here he differs from Pugin and the Ecclesiologists of the forties. He himself sees no reason for doing so. Again, for him a building is basically 'construction', what he writes about is 'form' conditioned by the nature of the materials used. The shapes given to individual buildings by their various uses are of no principal importance, because they are always different:

> The various modes in which these parts i.e. the elements
> discussed so far are capable of combination, and the merits
> of buildings of different form and expression, are evidently
> not reducible into lists, nor to be estimated by general
> laws . . . nay, there were never probably two edifices erected
> in which some accidental difference of condition did not
> require some difference of plan or of structure.[47]

Of course, there is no room left for abstract laws of proportion. In *The Seven Lamps,* they were mainly thought to derive from the inspirations of the individual artist,[48] but now they are considered as the results of the various functions of the individual buildings, in the way Pugin had discussed the problem. In the case of columns, proportions were to be determined by their size and the weight of the wall above, again not by the traditional laws of proportions for these members; for example, there could be very short, thick, shafts.[49]

In the question of 'style' Ruskin proceeds in the direction outlined in the writings of the Ecclesiologists in previous years. He denies symbolic value e.g. of roof shapes; there are only climatic differences.[50] But, like the Ecclesiologists, he cannot allow imitation of a completely free range of historical motifs. He recommends various phases of north Italian medieval architecture,[51] a range of motifs from which one may select freely, but the point is that the forms and motifs he recommended contain, in their simplicity, hardly any specific geographical or historical significance.

By selecting from Ruskin's writings the concepts which correspond to those of the Ecclesiologists, it seems possible to clarify his influence on High Victorian architecture. Recent research has found Ruskin's influence on architecture a most controversial matter.[52] Even Hitchcock gives no clear answer.[53] It seems that a sharper distinction ought to be made between Ruskin's influence on the High Victorian movement in a narrow sense, and his influence on painting, sculpture and the applied arts, which of course includes those arts also when they were closely connected with architecture. This second influence, best expounded in the famous chapter 'The Nature of Gothic' in the second volume of *The Stones,* is much better known than the first,[54] although it affected architecture in hardly more than a negative way. His influence on the Arts and Crafts view of architecture as 'honest building' can only be mentioned in passing, as it belongs to the 1880s and 1890s.

Elements of the second influence in their application to architecture replaced the emphasis on the constructional and formal aspects dealt with here. Those concepts are already to be found in the two books of 1849 and 1851, sometimes in blatant contrast to the theories selected here. Ruskin distinguishes strongly between 'architecture' and 'building': 'no-one would call the laws architectural which determine the height of a breastwork or the position of a bastion. But if to the stone facing of that bastion be added an unnecessary feature, as a cable moulding, that is architecture.'[55] Or, 'The delight which you take in ornament [has] no connection with that which you take in construction or usefulness.'[56]

In the following two volumes of *The Stones of Venice* (1853), Ruskin completely left the field of common types of building, so beginning what has been termed his 'defection';[57] 'Architecture is dependent . . .

on the delicacy of design . . . the perfection of colour, the preciousness of material, the legendary interest [of the sculptures].'[58] He knew
it was not possible to make ethical demands on construction, since
all construction always 'shows what it is', and can only be judged in
its forms and colours. Ruskin's ethical demands in architecture were
concerned with the effort every individual puts into purely decorative
features, into painting and sculpture. Soon Ruskin moved further in
that direction to enquire into the social conditions which would or
would not allow the craftsman to enjoy working on these features.

At first, this might seem a simple return to pre-rationalist demands
for more decoration in architecture. But there are more differences
than there are similarities. There is no demand for an orderly distribu-
tion of decoration within a tight system of classical 'disegno', which
always comprised buildings as a whole and meant that everything was
devised by an authority which could be a long way from the execution. Ruskin wanted plainness and massiveness for the building itself
in contrast to concentrated efforts of sculpture and painting. Probably
the most important corollary to his theories was that rules of social
hierarchy no longer applied or were at least bypassed. For Scott, an
architect with a fair amount of rationalism in his outlook, this hierarchy still existed; as he wrote; important buildings have to be
decorated, unimportant ones have to be left plain. The only effort
that mattered for Ruskin was that which the individual artist took
with the decoration, regardless of its degree of perfection and regardless of the purpose or standing of the building. Ruskin in *The Seven
Lamps* refused to accept a hierarchy from ecclesiastical down to
secular, which the Ecclesiologists were so fervently trying to reaffirm
in the forties, but which gradually slackened in later decades; 'thus
we have church-building, house-building, ship-building' – as against
'architecture'.[59] He secularized the religious enthusiasm which he took
over from the German Romantics. In *The Stones* he argues against the
religious symbolism of some 'German Critics'.[60]

The influence of his emphasis on painting was hardly felt before
1858 (see Chapter 7), whereas his views about architectural sculpture
were influential from about 1853. Otherwise his contacts with contemporary architectural circles were not very intense. He knew some
of the architects personally, but very little about their works, and his
comments hardly stood out from the mass of architectural criticism of
the day. Ruskin did not become a critic of contemporary architecture
in the way he had become a critic of painting.[61]

Theory and building in the early fifties: Street, White and others

Before describing the first building to incorporate the new principles on a large scale, All Saints, Margaret Street, in Chapter 4, we must introduce some architects whose work and writing showed a more gradual acceptance of the new ideas and who continued the tendencies of the late forties into the early fifties.

Writings by Street and others

George Edmund Street (1825–81), at the time of his first church at Par briefly described in Chapter 1, stood at the beginning of one of the most successful careers of the Gothic Revival. At first, as often happens, he was more prolific with theories than with buildings, with a kind of architectural journalism, opinions on current problems, contributed as lectures to architectural societies and as letters to journals: between 1850 and 1860 more than twenty papers and smaller communications appeared in the *Ecclesiologist* alone.

Although Street's architecture of the fifties has been fully described and discussed by Hitchcock[1] more needs to be said both about Street's writings and about his smaller buildings of this period. His letter of 1850 on 'Town Churches'[2] was an important amendment to the principles of the Ecclesiologist, and was not unrelated (Hitchcock to the contrary) either to what Ruskin was writing or to what Butterfield was building at the time. Many of Street's principles may be found in Benjamin Webb's article of 1845 and Petit's books of 1841 to 1854. Street's phrase, 'prominence of horizontal lines' reminds one of Petit, and his 'harmonious combination of horizontal and vertical' was hinted at by Webb, in opposition both to Pugin's emphasis on verticals and to the followers of the trend toward low rustic buildings. The sublime 'repose', 'grandeur' and 'regularity of parts' seem to derive from Ruskin. Street also argued for what Butterfield was doing at just that time: 'I would . . . use . . . brick . . . simply on account of its superior smoothness and evenness of surface.' He also praised Butterfield's unbroken rooflines on St Augustine's, Canterbury. Street rejected 'rusticity' and 'Kentish rag',[3] less for functional reasons than as a result of the aesthetic of the sublime (although some aspects of that aesthetic had earlier on contributed to the more 'rustic' trends of architecture such as 'horizontality'). In general, less distinction seems to have been made between town and country churches in the fifties than in the forties, when, at least in principle, a clear hierarchy of ecclesiastical buildings was observed. Only in the later fifties was a new aesthetic of the sublime linked with practical considerations of building types specifically suited to towns.

Street continued these ideas in a long lecture on 'The True Principles of Architecture and the Possibilities of Development' in 1852.[4] At the beginning he joined in the general chorus of these years complaining against copyism – 'reviving what is defunct, simply on antiquarian grounds' – and proposed a radical rationalist solution to the problem. For him, as for many other theorists, in 'all architecture . . . the first principle was most eminently constructional . . .', and in this context, the Gothic arch was a most important feature. For Street, and here he went beyond Pugin, the Gothic arch should be regarded exclusively as the 'pointed arch': 'Gothic . . . is emphatically the style of the pointed arch and not of this or that nation, or of this or that age (. . . I so much prefer the word pointed, in describing our form of architecture, to any other that has been proposed . . .).' Street also refused other symbolical connotations of the pointed style besides national ones: 'The steep pitched element [of the roof] is not an element of the pointed style; on the contrary, steep and flat roofs are accidents depending entirely and solely on the variations of the climate . . .'

> And let me protest warmly against the too common method
> of argument . . . , that the question between the two styles
> is one merely of taste, or of fitness, or dependent on sym-
> bolism, when in reality there are grounds on which differ-
> ence of opinion may always fairly exist; whereas as to the
> relative merit of the styles, in the matter of construction,
> no one, I suppose, would ever think of arguing.

It was appropriate to select motifs and forms from the whole range of historic architecture: 'We have to go to all these lands to discover in what that development varied from our own, in what it was superior, and in what inferior.' In his letter on Town Churches, he had already written: 'My own feeling is that a diligent study of many of the examples which the large continental churches furnish, would, if accompanied by a thorough knowledge and respect of those Anglicanisms . . . do very much for us.' He cites French churches, Saint-Germain l'Auxerrois in Paris and Saint-Pierre at Chartres which he had seen in the summer of 1850.

In his article on Kent and Surrey churches[5] Street had already recommended the use of features from the 'best' periods of a style, and from those regions where it had fully developed, instead of imitating the medieval forms of the particular region in which the new building happened to be erected. Such a regional frame of reference, or 'antiquarianism', was suitable only for restorations.

But again, Street did not follow the direction of the Gothic Rationalists in France. He was not interested in framework, but in coherent masonry: 'is it well to forget that all construction is horizontal?' he asked. Again, he spoke of 'repose' and 'grandeur'. He even recommended the classical cornice; not, of course, for it forms in detail, but only for 'that which is its real beauty, the horizontal line'. He also made some comments on colour, especially about 'various stones or marble, laid in horizontal courses throughout the buildings'. He contrasted this kind of decoration with that of Late Gothic work, especially the flint and stone churches of East Anglia: 'in all these the stone work is all arranged in view to effect and not at all to construction.' Details such as profiles of mouldings he regarded in Ruskin's way, as vehicles of light and shade.

In one important aspect Street followed Benjamin Webb rather than Ruskin: in the way in which he deals with interior space. Again 'grandeur' was important, but of a space within range of the eye, i.e. of similar dimensions in each direction, height, length and width:

> The rise from west to east should always be most gradual;
> the spaces between each step considerable, and gradually
> diminishing as they approach the east. By this the eye
> obtains a concave line of ascent, rather than a convex;
> and an idea of ease in the approach is formed, which
> contrasts delightfully with the apparent difficulty of the
> convex line. In arrangements of steps leading up to a higher
> level, and on extending a portion of its width, they should
> always be sunk into it, and not put against it. Then they
> give the idea of being cut out of the mass, which is to be
> ascended, instead of being like step-ladders put on against it.

It was this 'hollowness' of three-dimensional space which Street seemed to grasp much more clearly than Ruskin or any other writer or architect of these years. Another consideration concerned the interior as well as the exterior. So far, Street wrote, most interiors had been made either very light or very dark, but he preferred 'those lovely alternations of light and shade . . . when nature gives them to us in brilliant sunshine'. Thus, in analogy to the concepts of strong contrasts of light and shade on wall surfaces, he advised the architect 'to concentrate the admission of light on particular points'. As a consequence, it was better that in many places 'a considerable piece of wall' should remain unbroken, which should then contrast strongly with the openings. Finally, he recommended the 'wonderful beauty of the apsidal east end'.[6]

In his next lecture 'On the Revival of the Ancient Style in Domestic Architecture',[7] Street combined his aesthetic recommendations with other arguments. At first he complained that 'the domestic development lags behind the ecclesiastical', a point that William White had already made two years before at a meeting of the Ecclesiological Society (see below p. 42). Pugin also had already tried to apply the new principles to secular work. Street now argued that Gothic meant neither something specifically churchlike nor something antiquarian: 'however much the symbolic principle may have had to do with particular arrangements and forms, still the main features of the Pointed styles were clearly constructional.' He then pointed out that one could depart from those precedents according to the requirements of 'modern comfort', and described in this connection practical details of window-constructions. In the case of furniture, historical motifs should be almost entirely excluded, as in Pugin's later furniture: 'they were not Gothic, certainly, in the ordinary cabinet maker's sense: . . . no pointed arches, . . . crockets, finials, . . . but really simple, with no more material consumed in their construction than was necessary for their solidity, and no sham or incongruous ornaments.'

Again he propounded the aesthetic of the sublime: 'horizontality', 'mass', regularity, 'grandeur'; 'simple features' should prevail, 'repeated one after another in a long and unbroken succession'. He then tried to justify this aesthetic point of view with functional reasons, just as Pugin had used practical considerations to justify the aesthetic of the picturesque: 'I think the medieval builders always strove as much as they could to simplify their plans. . . . The consequence is, that in old designs one sees long lines of roofing and no attempt at a display of gables, except where they are positively necessary.'

But after all that, Street admitted that 'our style' had so far found very limited application to street architecture – an admission that amounted to severe criticism of the movement from one of its members. For the purpose of a specific town architecture, this 'style' had to be altered and enriched with forms from other periods, which was one aspect of his call 'to accommodate our architecture to every want of this nineteenth and most exigent of centuries'. But except for some vague mention of streets in Germany, Würzburg and Bamberg (probably the eighteenth-century houses there), Street could only cite James Wild's Northern Schools (St Martin's Schools) of 1849–50, with its storeys of continuous arcading, a building of considerable historical importance and directly influenced by *The Seven Lamps* [Plate 145].[8] Street himself did not go further into the subject of 'street architecture', a recurrent topic in architectural writing soon to be taken up by Gilbert Scott (see below, Chapter 7).

Similar opinions were expressed by William White[9] during the early fifties. White became a friend of Street when they were both working in Scott's office in the late forties.[10] At the beginning of his career, White was as well known as Street but in later decades his work was much less important. In a lecture in 1851 'On some of the principles of design in Churches',[11] White recommended 'strength', 'massiveness' and 'repose'; 'it seems to me that *breadth* is the first quality to be obtained in every building, for this may, and often does, exist almost alone.' He also recommended an equilibrium between horizontals and verticals, for the interior as well as the exterior: 'that it is not the great *length* of the vertical lines . . . which gives to Gothic architecture its character . . . if our churches are not broad as well as long, the east not visible from all parts of the church . . .'. He agreed with 'my friend Street' when he mentioned 'horizontality' in a lecture on 'Some Points and Causes of Failure in Modern Design'[12] for which his sketchy illustrations were also published [Plate 13]. White repeated the well known progressive demands of the time, but he mainly applied them to schools and vicarages, a field of design which was lying, as he said, 'tardy behind' that of church building.

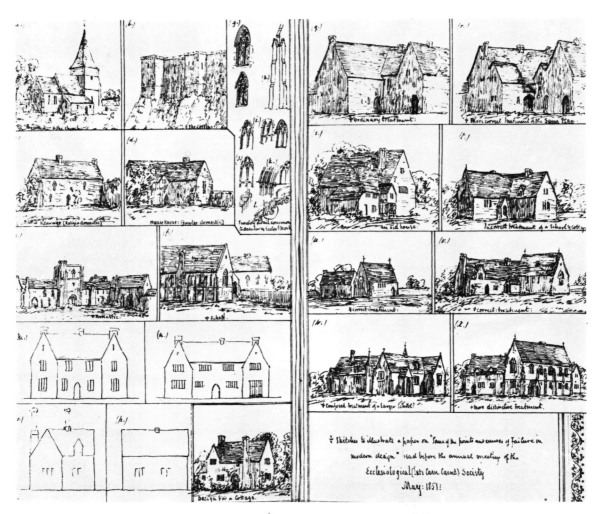

13 W. White, illustrative sketches for a lecture on 'Modern Design' (from the *Ecclesiologist,* 1851).
White's proposals are directed towards 'picturesque utility' as well as indicating the hierarchy from more ecclesiastical parts of the building down to more domestic ones; one can also observe a general swing away from the picturesque towards simple massiveness.

White confirmed what the Ecclesiologists had already hinted at in the forties: 'ritualism and symbolism are in churches, what the suitableness of a building to its application and uses is in other cases of design,' but he added characteristically that this suitability was 'in the case of churches not so easy to find out'. In many other ways he anticipated Street's lecture of 1853. In his illustrations he contrasted: 'confused treatment of a school' and 'more distinctive treatment'. 'Massiveness' is again based on both considerations, utility and aesthetics: 'thick walls comfort both in appearance and in reality.' He shows broad, low houses, very similar to the cottage-schools Street was building in those years.[13]

Another book belongs to the same group, *Designs for Country Churches* of 1850. The author, George Truefitt, was active in the Ecclesiological Society as well as in the Architectural Association, but on the whole he built and wrote very little. He demanded, like Street and White, 'repose' and 'breadth' in his short comments on his designs, which are very similar to village churches by Street, like Colton or Filkins, low, heavy, with massive corner buttresses[14] [Plate 14].

Buildings by Street

The arrangement of early *Ecclesiologist*-approved churches has been described in the first chapter. As regards 'style' and treatment of details, two versions prevailed in 1850: the larger 'Middle Pointed' church with two aisles, elaborately traceried windows and high towers (a few representatives of this type will be described among the early churches of Butterfield in Chapter 4), and the small rural church on a reduced plan, with simplified tracery. The latter type mattered most, in practice, for the architects under discussion here: young men usually had to be content with small jobs at the beginning of their careers; we shall see only a gradual influx of new elements into this type.

We saw how Street's work began with his very 'rustic' church at Par (Cornwall) [Plates 5, 6] of 1847. But he did not continue this rough treatment. In his church at Treverbyn (Cornwall)[15] of two or three years later, he used traceried windows of the familiar kind ('Decorated' motifs). On the other hand, very ornate features such as the eastern window arches of Par do not occur here. The mouldings of the interior of the eastern window at Treverbyn are very simple, all windows except the one in the east lie flush with the walls. Here the first effects of the new opinions seem to come in. The *Ecclesiologist* noted both the elaborate and the 'rough' aspects at Par without commenting on the contrast: 'the eastern triplet is elegantly hooded and shafted . . . the rudeness and simplicity of an old church, . . .

the allowable clumsiness of the medieval churches of the poor and distant districts.' One may assume that the elegant parts were demanded by the hierarchy of church symbolism. Street, as we have seen, condemned roughness in his Town Church article; as to the relation of elaborateness to roughness, he said something which could be read as a criticism of Par: 'rough masonry must necessarily preclude the use of elaborate enrichments . . . it will be found as a rule in old work, that the masonry was first improved, and then the detail, enrichment in fact commenced with the whole surface of the wall.'[16]

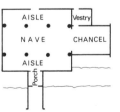

14 G. Truefitt, *Designs for Country Churches,* 1850.
By 1850 the massive appearance, the large roof and a simplified system of buttresses had become the accepted mode for country churches.

Street was not able to carry out a large church in the next few years. Hitchcock has discussed his project for Hobart, Tasmania, (1851)[17] especially in relation to Butterfield's St Matthias, Stoke Newington, with its high clerestory and its oblong tower placed over the chancel.

Smaller traits of the new principles occur in country churches of the next years: the carefully treated stone-surfaces and the simplified interior roof at Colton (Staffs.), 1850;[18] the simplified interior (the chancel arch projects from the wall and has no special support, as at Hobart Town) and the aisle without buttresses at Eastbury (Berks.), 1851;[19] the polygonal apse at Filkins (Oxon.) of c. 1853.[20] The church at Milton under Wychwood (Oxon.), 1853–4 [Plate 15],[21] is characterized in its western parts by an emphasis on the vertical: the nave projects further west than the aisles, and whereas the western corners of the aisles are emphasized by diagonal buttresses, the nave has only one central buttress which leads right up into the bell-turret. The tall windows of the west front are not centred between corner and buttress, but are pushed against the buttress, which partly cuts off their hood-moulds.

15 G. E. Street, Milton under Wychwood, Oxon., church, 1853.
Street now rejected the 'rustic' for churches as he had practised it in his earliest works (see Plates 5–6). His methods became more sophisticated: the smooth masonry is contrasted with carefully executed decorative details, there is a tendency to concentrate openings in order to obtain larger areas of blank surface.

This tension between blank wall and opening is tested in many subsequent buildings. At the church at Tilehurst (Berks.) about 1854,[22] only one window is set in the middle of the south wall and the contrast between the elaborate stringcourses and the blank flint on the chancel wall is also characteristic of Street's way of designing. The larger church at Boyne Hill (Maidenhead), 1854–60,[23] [Plates 16, 17] Street's most important executed work so far, developed this contrast further, and its interior gained in height and clarity.[24]

As for Street's domestic architecture of this period, in its general arrangement, the play of regular and irregular features was also characteristic. Both in plan and in roofline these buildings appear rather regular, but within that quiet outline the design is full of movement, as for example at the vicarage at Wantage, c.1850,[25] the Sisterhood there, c.1854,[26] and the College at Cuddesdon (Oxon.).[27]

The range, that is the degrees of importance accorded to domestic and collegiate buildings, is very marked. This difference may be found even within one building, as at Cuddesdon College, between the domestic wing and the chapel wing. For smaller country buildings,

16 G. E. Street, All Saints, Boyne Hill, Maidenhead, begun 1854 (from the *Builder*, 1860, 769).
A typical group of church (its western parts were not executed as shown here), vicarage, school-rooms, school-master's cottage, with the hierarchy of decoration clearly shown.

17 G. E. Street, Boyne Hill, church interior (Courtesy National Monuments Record).
The interior of Boyne Hill owes a great deal to All Saints, Margaret Street, by Butterfield, with its 'constructional polychromy' and its general feeling of spaciousness (cf. Plate 32).

18 G. E. Street, school at Inkpen, Berks., 1850.
The smaller village schools, usually erected by the church and suitable jobs for the early careers of the Ecclesiologist-architects, adopted cottage features as well. However, this did not mean the thatching or heavy bargeboarding of the earlier 'cottage orné' but neat contours, reduction of decorative features and a reliance on the colour contrast of cheaper materials, such as brick and flint.

Street made use of 'cottage' features.[28] The rediscovery of the cottage as a feature of picturesque landscape in the 1790s had continued to influence architects of the early nineteenth century, and, as we have seen, cottage elements were to be found in designs for Early Victorian churches, although not, oddly enough, on their auxiliary buildings. A certain ecclesiastical symbolism was expected of vicarages and schools designed in the forties, and the cottage as a possible type was not mentioned. In the fifties, with the general decrease of emphasis on symbolism, the cottage-type gained more importance and more country vicarages and country schools were executed in the cottage-revival tradition.

Street's remote country schools at Inkpen[29] [Plate 18] and Eastbury[30] in Berkshire, designed at the beginning of the fifties, show the re-appearance of cottage traits: a dominating roof, with the upper storey, as it were, reaching into it; and all features simplified, with hardly any cut-stone detail or tracery. Yet there is no 'roughness' of the earlier 'cottage' stereotype, with its widely overhanging and bargeboarded eaves; Street goes back to the neater old models, the effect is reduced to the contrasts of the materials, tiles, brick and flint.

Street's vicarage at Cuddesdon,[31] a sandstone building of 1852, has traceried windows and elaborate carving; his vicarage at Colnbrook (Bucks.)[32] [Plate 19], built of brick in 1853, has very simple windows

19 G. E. Street, Colnbrook, Bucks., vicarage, 1853 (Courtesy Paul Joyce). The coloured decoration seems to become more independent of the arrangement of the building, cf. the white stripes and their relationship with the windows.

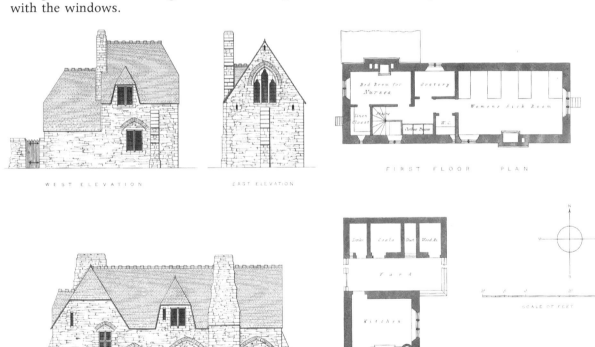

20 G. E. Street, model design for village hospital (from *Instrumenta Ecclesiastica* II, 1855, 63, 64).

and only a few white bricks as decoration. Aside from considerations of cost the difference of form seems the result of the choice of materials. Slightly less elaborate than Cuddesdon is the vicarage at St Ebbe's, Oxford, of 1852.[33] The most characteristic example of the 'cottage' is perhaps the model-design for a village hospital which Street published in *Instrumenta Ecclesiastica* in 1855[34] [Plate 20].

Other, more ambitious, projects show an increase in 'modern' features. The big, only partly executed design for Bloxham School[35] [Plate 21] is characterized by ingeniously calculated contrasts between long horizontals, unbroken wall surfaces, and a long series of repetitive features, such as the windows in the court, and, on the other hand, strongly irregular accents such as the porch. The same was true, on a much smaller scale, of the Adderley Park Institute, at Saltley (Birmingham) of about 1855 (recently destroyed).[36] It differed from the country

21 G. E. Street, Bloxham School, design, 1854 (Courtesy Bloxham School, Oxon.).
This partly executed design shows the increase of the tendencies first noticed at Milton (Plate 15): concentration of openings in order to contrast them with large amounts of blank wall surface. There is also a greater emphasis on the continuity of horizontals. Whereas Pugin demanded variety in outline as a result of the variety of function, Street turns the argument round: 'I think the medieval builders strove as much as they could to simplify their plans. . . . The consequence is that in old designs one sees long lines of roofing and no attempt at a display of gables, except when they are positively necessary.'

buildings in so far as the street-front was no longer gabled, but had eaves parallel to the crested ridge of the roof; the adjoining dwelling had gabled fronts. The layout and treatment of the houses adjoining the church at Boyne Hill is very irregular.[37]

More remarkable is the project for the Oxford University Museum of 1853 [Plate 22], which Street published together with an extended version of his article of 1853 on domestic architecture.[38] This is again a very orderly and regular layout, with few irregular accents. Some rich sculptural decoration was to be contrasted with long spaces of blank wall surface. In his pamphlet Street speaks of this decoration in Ruskinian terms: 'the function of architecture is . . . to tell about nature,'[39] which he relates to the contents of the Museum, namely natural history. Here Street paralleled what Woodward was doing at the same time in Dublin, and, indeed, anticipated what was to be done

22 G. E. Street, proposed Museum for Oxford, 1853 (from his *An Urgent Plea for the Revival of the True Principles of Architecture in the Public Buildings of Oxford*).

Shortly afterwards, in 1854, Deane & Woodward obtained the commission for a University Museum (Plates 123–4).

23 W. White, St Columb Major, Cornwall, rectory, 1850 (from the *Ecclesiologist*, 1851, 235).

Street and White, who knew each other since their time in Scott's office, had many commissions in Cornwall in these years, due to patrons who were enthusiastic supporters of the Society. White's buildings must be compared with his design-recommendations (Plate 13).

a few years later, as we shall see, when the Oxford Museum was actually built from Woodward's designs.

From about 1854 onwards Street made greater use of constructional polychromy, especially at Boyne Hill. This aspect will be gone into in Chapter 5, with Street's work from 1855 onwards when he had finally worked out his ideas and started applying his principles on a much larger scale.

William White and others

In White's buildings of these years, the same tendencies can be shown. Illustrations of his large vicarage at St Columb Major [Plate 23] appeared in the *Ecclesiologist* in the year of his 1851 lecture on design.[40] The layout resembles a college, with a quadrangle, but only the main front has any elaborate stonework; the others are more 'cottage-like'. The three elements recommended for the development of church design in those years can be found again: restraint in the use of buttresses, the uncluttered treatment of the roofline and tracery flush with the wall. The 'fire-proof' staircase is typical of White's practical-mindedness. Another, smaller vicarage in a more remote place, Ruan Lanihorne (Cornwall),[41] had more 'cottage' elements of the traditional type, especially large bargeboards and projecting eaves; the walls appear specially thick and massive.[42]

In the years following, White seemed at first headed toward what has been called 'rogue' design (see below) but the bulk of his work in the fifties falls under the head of brick and constructional polychromy (see the next chapter).

The wider range of Ecclesiologists' rustic churches in the early fifties can be suggested by the work of several men. Ewan Christian, the well known architect of the Church Commissioners, in the early fifties pursued a strong tendency to 'massiveness' and 'horizontality' and also towards the integration of tracery into the wall (St John, Kenilworth; St James, Leyland).[43] He, as well as John Piers St Aubyn (1815–95, whose churches at Godolphin and Halsetown (Cornwall)[44] are examples here) will also appear in the next chapter with their brick buildings. In the work of Henry Woodyer various tendencies can be found, a 'rogue' design at Tenbury, and 'massive' designs at Highnam and Tutshill (Glos.).[45] Even Richard Cromwell Carpenter (1812–55), who most closely adhered to Pugin's flint and stone manner, used severe horizontal lines (Hurstpierpoint College, Sussex [Plate 24], and his late church at Milton Gravesend, Kent).[46]

A remarkable instance of cottage features being engrafted upon a small country house is S. S. Teulon's Enbrook (Kent) [Plate 25] of 1853. There are no parapets or stone-framed gables, the roof is allowed to project over the walls, many gables are hipped. Enbrook may be compared to Pugin's own house 'The Grange' at Ramsgate

(1841) [Plate 1]; but Teulon abandoned the heavy bargeboarding of the gable in favour of neater contours.

Only three more widely employed church architects of these years can be mentioned here: Benjamin Ferrey, an early follower of Pugin and later his biographer, with most of his smaller churches of the fifties; Thomas Henry Wyatt, whose churches were mainly in the diocese of Salisbury, and Joseph Clarke, especially active in collegiate architecture, some of it treated as simply as Carpenter's.[47]

'Rogue' tendencies

More difficult to place is another trend in the architecture of these years, the 'rogue' architects, as Goodhart-Rendel has termed them.[48] He limited this term to a certain group, but instances of the trend can be found in the work of many architects in the fifties. Their main characteristic is not 'simplicity' but complication. In Street's church at Filkins, irregularity is carried to an excess, hardly any buttresses are in line or parallel to each other; the size and design of the windows change abruptly. Butterfield's supposed or real idiosyncrasies will be discussed in the next chapter.

White's church of All Saints, Talbot Road, Paddington, begun in 1852 [Plate 26] is extremely complicated in its arrangement as well as in its details. One has to look and think a good deal before one can perceive what the exact relationships are between nave, chancel, aisles, and transept.[49] Of the great variety of smaller details, perhaps

24 R. C. Carpenter, Hurstpierpoint College, Sussex, 1851–3.
Richard Cromwell Carpenter died young in 1855. His main works are the great Colleges of Sussex, Lancing and Hurstpierpoint. His quiet flint walls, broken by simple flush tracery, seem to derive from Pugin.

the most striking are the rudely notched capitals of the arcades of the third storey of the tower. These forms seem to derive from Cornish late medieval architecture,[50] and indeed White used more of that repertoire in some churches in Cornwall during the following years, of which St Hilary is the most important.[51]

The 'rogue' aspect is stronger in the work of Samuel Saunders Teulon.[52] Most of his churches of the fifties belong to this group. Complicated penetrations of space, great variety of arches, profiles, traceries, and concentrations of decorative sculpture are all characteristic of his churches, of which Holy Trinity at Hastings [53] and St Thomas's, Wells,[54] may be cited as the biggest and richest. Even greater than in the case of White is the contrast between these works of Teulon's and his others in a simple brick manner to be discussed in the next chapter.

The 'arch-rogue' is generally said to have been Edward Buckton Lamb.[55] His contrasting of very large and very small features, his complications of tracery, are even more unusual than Teulon's. Lamb built consistently in that manner, and perhaps the most important difference between his buildings and those of the Ecclesiologists, with whom he had nothing to do and who were usually rather hostile to him, was the repetition of the same kind of irregularity in every part of a building. But he, too, adopted some elements which were first introduced by the Ecclesiologists. He gave to his churches at Thirkleby (Yorks.),[56] of the late forties, and Englefield Green (Surrey),[57] of ten years later, low and massive contours; he used polychromy of a

25 S. S. Teulon, Enbrook House, near Folkestone, 1853 (from the *Builder*, 1854, 487).
The amount of 'cottage' features in this relatively large house is surprising for its date, especially the hipped gables.

26 (below) W. White, All Saints, Talbot Road, Paddington, begun 1852, interior (Courtesy Gordon Barnes).

In some of his works of that time White – like Butterfield and Street – was searching for complications, especially in his plans; this view is from the nave into the transept, which is screened off by the continuation of the nave arcade. The transept continues eastward, where it opens into the chancel with much larger arches, just visible on the right.

27 (opposite) E. B. Lamb, Eye, Suffolk, Town Hall, 1856 (from the *Building News*, 1857, 44).

The term 'rogue' has been loosely applied to the work of some church architects from the 1840s to the 1860s and Edward Buckton Lamb has generally been called the 'arch rogue'. The *Ecclesiologist* criticized him heavily: 'originality at the expense of standards of architectural style'. But Lamb was of an older generation, his picturesque was the picturesque of the thirties and forties.

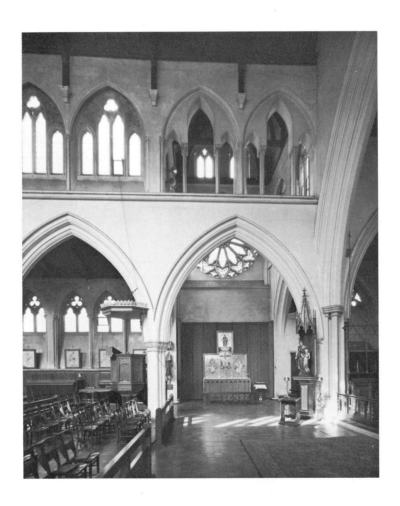

Puginian sort at Leiston Church[58] and at the Town Hall of Eye (Suffolk)[59] [Plate 27] in the mid-fifties. In this last building he used a mixture of classical cornices and Renaissance-type windows with a sense of plasticity which is premonitory of 'neo-baroque' massing of a much later time.

In a lecture of 1860 Lamb talked about his principles. They seem to belong to the thirties and early forties rather than to 1860. In fact Lamb was nearly a generation older than the younger Ecclesiologist architects. He had contributed elaborate designs of Perpendicular Gothic cottages to Loudon's *Architectural Magazine* in the thirties. His 'aesthetic' recommendations, as he calls them, belong entirely to the picturesque. He recommends 'a kind of rough building', with broken surfaces and especially irregular 'artistic jointing'. He attacks the forms of the young architects: unrelieved walls look as if they were 'of one stone perforated with openings'.[60]

Lamb continued to follow his principles, for example in two fairly

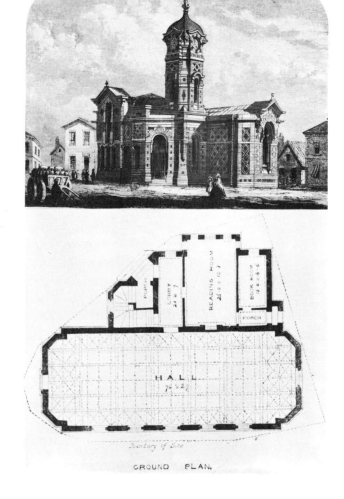

GROUND PLAN.

28 E. B. Lamb, London, St Martin's, Gospel Oak, 1866 (Courtesy National
Monuments Record).
A profusion of shapes and materials over a relatively simple plan.

wealthy churches, St Martin's, Gospel Oak, Camden, 1866,[61] [Plate 28]
and St Mary Magdalene, Addiscombe, Croydon, 1868.[62] As usual with
Lamb the plans are Broad Church rather than High Church, nearly
centralized in fact. The skylines are extremely varied, and inside, the
vast roof spaces are filled with enormously complicated wooden
constructions.

The reaction of the *Ecclesiologist* to such work is predictable: the
arcadings of White's St Hilary are 'approaching to meanness'; the
aesthetic of the 'sublime' demanded on the contrary, solid and simple
forms. On the question of historical and geographical motifs, the
Ecclesiologists, as well as Ruskin, demanded more consistency, if not
in search and selection, at least in application. Street had said explicitly (in his lecture about regional architecture in 1850) that the
architect should not take up obscure regional forms if he knows
'better' ones, which might hint at a controversy on this point with his
'friend White'. Lastly the Ecclesiologists argued against 'originality'.
Again and again Lamb was attacked for 'originality at the expense of
standards of architectural style',[63] and in the case of St Hilary the
critic wrote of 'White's crotchets'. The architecture of the Ecclesiologists' group during the next few years, in fact, was of a very
homogeneous kind.[64]

Brick and 'constructional polychromy' in the work of Butterfield and White

four

Butterfield's architecture around 1850:
All Saints, Margaret Street

Only briefly touched on in the last chapter, we must now trace the use of brick and 'constructional polychromy' from 1850 onwards in more prominent examples. This means beginning with the most important building, the 'Model Church' of the Ecclesiological Society, All Saints, Margaret Street, St Marylebone, begun in 1849–50 by William Butterfield (1814–1900). The exterior was finished in 1853, and the church was consecrated in 1859 [Plates 30–2]. Although a biography of Butterfield has only just been published,[1] All Saints has been the object of several investigations.[2] Sir John Summerson's article 'William Butterfield; or, the glory of ugliness', first published in 1945,[3] is one of the first positive evaluations of a work of later nineteenth-century architecture, though from a Mannerist point of view. Subsequent investigations have attempted to discern the various sources of the design. Hitchcock tried to trace the influence of Ruskin[4] and Paul Thompson has given the history of the building and the actual influence of the patrons,[5] especially that of the President of the Society, Alexander J. Beresford-Hope (1820–87).[6] With our discussion of the church one has to bear in mind the theories of the Ecclesiologists between 1845 and 1850 (Chapter 1), and other works by Butterfield in these years.[7] For his early works in the mid-forties it must suffice here to refer to Hitchcock[8] and Thompson. Butterfield's contacts with the Ecclesiological Society were even closer than those of Street and White although he hardly ever contributed to its publications. Also, more than for Street, the less important interests of the Society, schools and vicarages and small secular buildings, had become a special concern for Butterfield.

In the later forties a trend towards complication can be observed in his layout of such buildings. The individual parts and rooms stand out more prominently and break the continuities of plan and elevation. Compared with the smooth outlines of his vicarage at Coalpit Heath in 1844,[9] and the school at Sessay (Yorks.) of 1847,[10] the school at Alfington (Devon), 1850,[11] is subdivided into a great and confusing number of parts. In accordance with the recommendations of the article 'Schools', 1847, the arrangement intends to show all individual rooms as independent entities from ground-level upwards. All the parts are of different height, arranged at right-angles to each other.

Another element of multiplicity is the use of very tall chimneys. The vicarage at West Lavington[12] shows a very complicated arrangement of roofs, especially over the outhouses. At St Saviour's Hospital at St Pancras (Osnaburgh Street) [Plate 29],[13] built about 1850 and demolished some years ago, the street front was broken only by smaller irregularities but the courtyard contained a multitude of receding and projecting parts, different roofs etc.[14] Other elements make clear that Butterfield also tended to adopt the 'cottage-type', the interference of the roof with the upper storey, as well as tile-hanging (Alfington)[15]. In their eastern parts, churches also provided occasion for complicated arrangements, as in the eastern tower for the project for a cathedral at Frederickstown (New Brunswick).[16] The more secular parts of the churches are developed in a very free and conspicuous way, for instance the chimney for the fireplace of the sacristy of St Ninian's Cathedral at Perth,[17] which nearly reaches the height of the ridge of the chancel.

The strong emphasis on the material purposes of the buildings is matched by a strong adherence to ecclesiastical hierarchy. In his churches Butterfield always retained a great deal of symmetry. His churches at that time had none of the wild irregularity of Street's Filkins. The long unbroken ridge-lines of Butterfield's colleges probably have to be understood in the same hierarchical way, as at

29 W. Butterfield, St Saviour's Hospital, St Pancras, 1850, demolished 1964, rear façade.
Extreme variety and irregularity in planning and elevation is characteristic of Butterfield's secular buildings in these years.

Cumbrae[18] and already in his first greater commission, St Augustine's College at Canterbury, begun in 1845.[19] The Ecclesiologists, however, liked the roof at Canterbury for formal reasons: 'a less bold and skilful architect would have feared to venture such an endless horizontal line as the unadorned crest of the roof.'

Every description of All Saints, Margaret Street, must start with the difficulties of the site: far too small (only 108 feet long) for a 'big' church and with only one front really visible. But Butterfield was well known for his ability to overcome problems of that kind: 'Mr. Butterfield always seems to build *con amore* when there are extraordinary difficulties,'[20] the *Ecclesiologist* said about St Thomas's, Leeds, 1850,[21] where also he had very little space available [Plate 33]. In the contemporary church, St John the Evangelist at Huddersfield,[22] the problem of sloping ground was overcome by a very complicated two-level arrangement of chancel, tower and sacristy. At Canterbury he had to respect medieval remains. One may perhaps say that in these instances the real opportunity for 'picturesque utility' could be found; as has been shown, the argument of utility could very easily be used for different formal solutions, but the difficulties of these sites required very special, irregular solutions, for which the aesthetic of Pugin was much more suitable than that of Durand. Naturally these problems occur haphazardly, but it was perhaps a 'typical accident' that it happened with the 'Model Church' of the Society.

As seen from the street, or south side, All Saints [Plate 30] is fronted by a small courtyard flanked by houses that are part of the design (on the right the vicarage, on the left the parish rooms), and the whole is dominated by the tall south-west tower of the church. Many elements described so far occur again: especially the complicated interpenetration of parts such as with the tower and the porch. A new problem is the four-storey height of the houses, which Butterfield treats with extreme verticality. In the court he varies the arrangement of windows to emphasize the individuality of the rooms; he avoids that continuity of horizontal openings advocated by Ruskin and Street and practised by Wild just then for St Martin's Schools[23] [Plate 145]. On the other hand, the interior of the church has the spaciousness and openness recommended by Benjamin Webb.[24] Butterfield followed the plan of the bigger church of *A Few Words to Church Builders* of 1841, but reduced the bays from six to three and omitted the transept. Compared with his churches at Huddersfield and Perth the height of All Saints might well be explained by the site.

The characteristic elements of churches described in the last chapter can be found in Butterfield's work as well. Reduction of buttresses at All Saints is, however, contrasted to decorative emphasis on the centre buttress of the south aisle. Simplification of lines where the roof meets the walls can be seen at Alfington, and tracery flush with the walls at West Lavington church and Cumbrae. Butterfield was

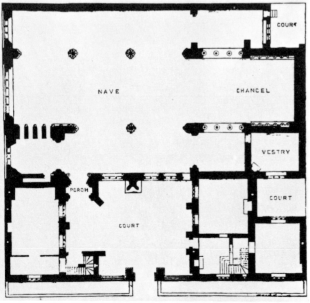

30–32 W. Butterfield, All Saints Church, Margaret Street, St Marylebone, begun 1849/50, exterior completed 1853, consecrated 1859: exterior and plan (from the *Builder*, 1853, 57, 58) detail of vicarage and interior (Courtesy *Country Life*). The model church of the Society, always considered as *the* monument of the Ecclesiological High Church Movement as well as High Victorian Gothic, with all the controversies that are bound to arise from such a difficult project. Apart from Butterfield it was A. J. Beresford-Hope, the President of the Society, who had a strong influence on the design, especially as he paid for most of it as well. First of all its very small and awkward site (108 feet long) was always considered a drawback; at the same time the ingenuity of planning was admired. Besides the

church there is the vicarage on the right and the parish rooms on the left; there are additional rooms underneath the whole of the courtyard. Butterfield's ideas of planning were extremely picturesque at this time anyway and, as the *Ecclesiologist* remarked, he took pleasure in solving the difficulties of each particular site. The other element is, of course, 'constructional polychromy'. At that time it was unusual to use brick for a rich building; Butterfield chose, however, not the common yellow London stock brick but a bright red one. The decoration with tiles, different

coloured bricks and stone was applied in many different ways, e.g. the houses are characterized by random treatment in contrast to the systematic patterning on the church. In the interior, where the usual white-wash was banned, there is a strict differentiation between pillars, archivolts and wall spaces. The laws of flat pattern decoration have been observed most radically. Finally, contrasting with the nave, the walls of the chancel – the site was too dark for windows – are covered with a rather earlier nineteenth-century kind of overall colour treatment.

especially strongly interested in flat surfaces.[25] There are no projecting stringcourses in the façades of the houses at All Saints, and also the spire begins without much horizontal division.

All Saints was not Butterfield's first design for brick: he had already designed one big church in brick, the Cathedral of Adelaide in Australia in 1847. Then the *Ecclesiologist* was not ready to see the positive value of brick, commenting: 'The building, though plain to excess and of a material so mean as brick, will be religious and imposing from its unusual height and marked outline.' Later Beresford-Hope said of the cathedral: 'it was intended to show at how cheap a rate the cathedral character might be given to a church . . . extremest simplicity, red brick with few mouldings, and the simplest tracery, but cruciform and lofty.'[26] Butterfield made an important formal element out of the blank surfaces and right-angles appropriate to brickwork, as with the angular buttresses at Leeds, and had more complicated forms executed in stone. Street, too, as has been quoted, was saying at the time that he would use brickwork 'on account of its superior smoothness and evenness of surface'. Yet Butterfield's external colour at All Saints [Plate 31] and St Thomas's, Leeds [Plate 33], tends to emphasize the surface, not the depth of the wall, as in later developments. The stone courses of the walls of All Saints are framed by dark bricks above and below and the black strings on the houses are mixed with patterns in which horizontals do not prevail. At Leeds, stone courses related to window-frames and tracery (see window over entrance-door) are not continued across the wall, but are clearly conceived as a surface decoration around the window. It is a polychromy of external skin only.

The coloured decorations of the interior of All Saints [Plate 32] have often been described, in their relationship to *The Seven Lamps* and to Matthew Digby Wyatt's publication of Cosmati mosaics in about 1849,[27] yet the relationship between the decoration and the building has not been gone into enough. Three elements may be distinguished according to the basic 'constructive' relevance of the parts of the building: wall surface, openings through the wall, and features such as arcadings, shafts, and corbels that are applied to the walls. The wall surfaces are covered with flat patterns following the Puginian anti-illusionistic principles. Roof supports are not carried down below clerestory level. The breaks through the wall, arcades or window-openings are treated in an entirely different way: their relationship to the walls Hitchcock described appropriately: ' . . . an all-over composition of decorative and flat patterns and then, cutting through, as by accident, an almost unrelated arrangement of plastic architectural forms'.[28]

A further formal characteristic might be noticed: the chancel is flanked by tripartite screens in openings that seem to continue the nave arcade; while the chancel arch itself springs from corbelled colonnettes that stop some distance above the floor – the latter a common feature in the fifties. Consequently, if one takes a section through the building below the chancel arch and the supports of the chancel vaults, as the plan in the *Builder* does[29] [Plate 30], the main divisions of the church cannot be perceived. The continuity of wall surface is, as on the exterior, strongly emphasized. Even in Pugin's buildings uninterrupted surfaces were given priority, but Pugin would never have separated the vaulting-system from the walls to that extent, or disregarded the vertical constructional unity of the interior. On the other hand, Butterfield did not allow Pugin's overall decorative patterning (as at Cheadle) to cover all parts of the interior at All Saints alike, preferring his own way of linking the decoration with the different 'constructional parts' of the building. But this was not the fully realized system of 'constructional decoration' either. Later, the wall and its openings were to be considered not as different constructional units, but as facets of one mass of masonry that is penetrated by multicoloured layers throughout.[30]

The question of deliberate ugliness in Butterfield's work has been debated by Summerson and refuted by Thompson. We have to recognize that the difficulty of the site and the squabbles between the architect and Beresford-Hope must have accounted for some of the less successful features of the building. Yet, the *Ecclesiologist* made

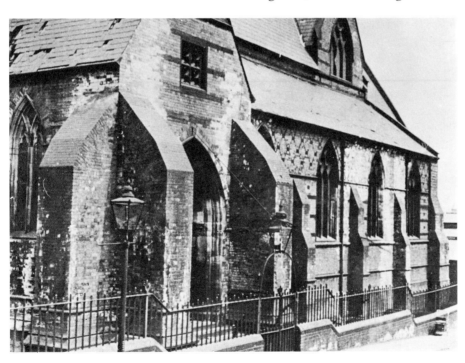

33 W. Butterfield, St Thomas, Holbeck, Leeds, 1850 (demolished) (Courtesy Sir John Summerson).
The same treatment as at All Saints: brick with reduced stone dressings.

use of the same characterization when the building was consecrated in 1859:[31] 'deliberate preference of ugliness'. This dislike for most of the design of All Saints was partly due to the fact that the *Ecclesiologist* by that time was very keen on stressing the changes in opinion and design since 1850, but this kind of criticism was also thrown at architects like Lamb, as we have seen. Another term used in a derogatory sense against Lamb and as reserved praise for Butterfield was: 'its coarse, but honest originality'. The problem can only be solved by a more meticulous investigation into the uses of these epithets, which cannot be done in this book.

A detailed and satisfactory assessment of the position of All Saints among the influences from Ruskin and other writers is hardly possible and is perhaps unnecessary. On the one hand, this church was part of the general tendency toward colour in architecture in these years; and on the other hand, nothing quite so complicated as All Saints had been undertaken so far. Surprisingly, Butterfield himself made little use of the richer kind of polychromy in the next few years.[32]

Butterfield's next large church, St Matthias, Stoke Newington [Plate 34], badly bombed in the last war, shows new trends though its design cannot date later than early 1851.[33] The arrangement is still complicated, for a tower is squeezed between nave and chancel, but Butterfield tried to clarify the total effect, where he was not restricted by the site. This can well be shown by comparison with a less bold, slightly earlier published design for the church.[34] There are fewer buttresses in the executed design, but they project more. What is important is again their close relationship with the wall surface: most of the corners have only one buttress which continues the surface of one of the walls; the buttresses of the west front continue the nave walls, those of the tower the (wider) transverse walls of the tower. These devices, as well as the continuation of tower windows into the east and west gables – the same device is adopted at the west front – not only give simpler and grander areas of wall, but also clarify the arrangement of the whole building in that everything is subjected to one line, the axis of the church. This characteristic is probably hinted at in the comment of the *Ecclesiologist* that 'the saddle-back roof of the tower is in line with the line of worship'. In the interior of the nave height and clarity are gained by the unusual height of the clerestory and the steepness of the aisle roofs.

Butterfield: the early fifties and the cottage-type

During the next years Butterfield was more concerned with domestic buildings, concentrating on the type of the small house and school, the 'cottage-type', which has already been dealt with in reviewing Street's work of those years. In 1853 two model-designs for village schools appeared in *Instrumenta Ecclesiastica*,[35] a bigger one

34 W. Butterfield, St Matthias, Stoke Newington, 1850–1, from the west.
In this case there were no restrictions and Butterfield produced a very
unified design with everything organized along the central axis. There
are no 'Italian' elements either, simple brick and conventional stone
dressings. The central buttress on the west front, reaching into the window,
was taken from Dorchester church which he was restoring at that time.

67

including a teacher's house and a smaller one without [Plate 35].
Butterfield still seemed to adhere closely to certain recommendations
of the *Ecclesiologist* article on schools of 1847. But the formal development seems to be in line with what has been observed in St Matthias.
Before and around 1850 Butterfield had, as for example in Alfington
school, subdivided his buildings in as many parts as possible, varying
in height and position from each other. Now he aimed toward an orderly
whole yet without sacrificing the individuality of the parts. In the
small school he continued complete separation of individual rooms
under different roofs and placed them wherever possible at right-
angles, but with a greater degree of coherence, especially by clarifying

35 W. Butterfield, model designs for a school, 1853 (from *Instrumenta
Ecclesiastica* II, 53).
As with St Matthias, Stoke Newington, there is a tendency towards clear
axial organization. Compared with Street's and White's schools of the
same time, Butterfield's designs, at least the ones for stone buildings,
appear more 'church-like'.

the main axes of the building and by a strict subordination of smaller to bigger parts. The porch and cloakroom on one side of the smaller school appear to be a lesser repetition of the arrangement of the schoolrooms. In the bigger school the house is treated as a separate unit and more as a coherent mass of the kind of Street's schools and houses. Butterfield also continues the purity of line and contour: the rooflines are reduced to simple rectangular edges, no parapets, no bargeboarding, and there are no buttresses. The treatment of details is differentiated most carefully according to their materials. The tracery of the smaller school, which is a stone building, is flush with the surface of the wall, but the tracery of the other school, a brick design, is slightly recessed and, being of wood, more angular in contour. A comparison with the nearly contemporary publication by Joseph Clarke, *Schools and Schoolhouses* (1852), helps to reveal Butterfield's personal method. Some of Clarke's designs are even simpler than Butterfield's without the rigid axiality. On the other hand Clarke supplied a great variety of designs, elaborate hewn-stone versions, as well as purposely primitive proposals; he still thinks in terms of the 'cottage orné', a tradition to which Gilbert Scott adhered even more in the elaborately bargeboarded cottages of his model-village at Ilam (Staffordshire) of 1854 – one of his few efforts in this category.[36]

In 1853–4 Butterfield was lucky in his commissions. The Yorkshire family of Downe, who had employed him earlier at Sessay, founded three parishes at Hensall, Cowick and Balne (Pollington) in the south of the county; for each Butterfield had the almost identical task of a small church with school and parsonage, to be built in brick.[37]

The overall layout of each parsonage is that of an L, also used in Street's and White's parsonages of that time. On the exterior, hall and staircase are revealed by a bigger window interrupting the storey division. At Balne [Plate 38], the arrangement is reduced to two simple rectangular blocks with steep roofs, put side by side, the fronts not quite in line, like two cottages linked together. There is no tracery, the window-frames are of wood, mostly painted white.

The churches for the most part correspond to the houses and schools; few buttresses, neat contours except in connection with the bell turrets, and very simple tracery, except in the west and east windows [Plate 36]. The practical element is emphasized by huge chimneystacks rising from the aisles. Inside, proportions are more vertical than was usual in smaller churches of these years.

Butterfield's interior roofs [Plate 37] appear to be a special field of formal experiment. He always keeps the roof members away from the walls, yet he takes complicated measures to interrelate these two main compartments of the interior space. His roofs are steep in section and divided inside into two horizontal parts, whereby the lower section, at a very steep angle, seems to continue from the wall underneath.

36 W. Butterfield, Hensall, Yorks., W.R., church, 1853.
In three almost identical commissions near Snaith in the south of Yorkshire, Balne (Pollington), Hensall and Cowick, all endowed by the Downe
family, Butterfield continued his preoccupation with brick in small
churches and simple cottages. The churches continue to rely on cottage
elements like the big roof, but there is no 'rustic' elaboration. On the
contrary, the details are sparse—flush tracery, except for the east
windows, sharp and simple contours. As usual, Butterfield enjoys
expressing the practical necessities of the building: cf. the chimney for
the fireplace in the aisle.

The transverse beams are in the upper section, whereas their supports
start off in the lower section, which serves to bridge over the angle
between the two sections. He makes a clear distinction between the
different parts of the construction, beams and rafters, none of which
is decorated. In tending to lighten the space in the roof he made
increasing use of white-plastered surfaces.[38]
   Butterfield built a similar group at the same time at Wykeham
(North Riding),[39] but using stone and stone dressings throughout.
The hierarchy of decorations is identical, but the material seemed to
suggest more elaborate forms, like tracery, for some parts of the
houses. Probably a few years later, but apparently during the series
of three brick groups, Butterfield built his last group for the Downes
at Baldersby St James [Plate 39].[40] The cottages – the other buildings
are to be described later – are even more simplified in arrangement and

37 W. Butterfield, Balne,
Yorks., church, interior, 1853.
In the interior of Butterfield's
smaller churches the roof
allows for a great variety of
forms and constructions.

38 W. Butterfield, Balne, Yorks., vicarage, 1853 (Courtesy Paul Thompson).
The schools and the vicarages of the three Yorkshire groups are treated
as simple cottages, in the case of Balne two small cottages joined together.

detail. They are perhaps the most characteristic example of the blending of rationalistic and aesthetic ideals which may be found in the architecture of the fifties, combining rational picturesque planning with clarity and simplicity of outline and surface. His practical reasons for this arrangement are emphasized in the comments which accompanied the designs published in *Instrumenta*: 'The special object of publishing this design is to call attention to the proper arrangements of a mixed school; each room having its own separate entrance and cloakroom and the offices for the boys and girls being not only kept away from the main building, but quite distinct from one another, with some intermediate building between them.' In the case of the teacher's house the practical-moralizing comment is extended to a more general social level: 'The amount of accommodation in the Master's House, looked upon as a cottage, is likewise of great importance, from moral considerations. This part of the design may furnish useful hints for cottage architecture, a practical branch of social improvement, which has hitherto been far too much neglected.'

With this last remark, Butterfield surely hints at neglect by the Ecclesiologists, a criticism in line with the remarks by White and Street. But in other architectural circles these questions had been

39 W. Butterfield, Baldersby St James, Yorks., N.R., cottages, c. 1855 (Courtesy Gordon Barnes).
In Baldersby the group of church, school and vicarage is supplemented by a number of cottages like a 'model village'. The picturesque and associational simplicity of the former 'cottage' was replaced by formal and moralistic simplicity. But this did not yet mean the creation of a 'garden city' in the later sense; cottages remained a subordinate type.

thought about for some years, concerning both town houses and the new social role of the 'ornamental' country cottage. Contemporary concern with housing problems does not belong to the present context, because the outcome was usually associated with buildings of a less advanced state of architectural theory, in classical or 'Tudor' or other forms typical of early nineteenth-century villas.[41] But the question of whether these church-cottages contribute to the general development of housing, that is to social solutions in architecture, remains to be answered. Simple cottages did have an important place in the architectural thinking of Butterfield, as indeed with many great architects since the end of the eighteenth century, but only in their place, as Paul Thompson points out,[42] at the lowest level of a social hierarchy, both in the Church and as secular remnants of feudalism. From here there is no direct way to the garden cities of the late nineteenth century. Architects were not ready yet to consider housing a suitable field for new architectural ideas. During the following years the importance of the cottage lessened in the work of Ecclesiologist architects, perhaps mainly with acceptance of Ruskin's pronouncement that unadorned buildings have little to do with 'art', and, moreover, as the practice of these architects grew, they were concerned with bigger and more remunerative jobs. Scott, who wrote a great deal about cottages in his book, *Secular and Domestic Architecture,* had little time for this sort of thing in practice. After the mid-fifties it was mainly William White who continued the 'cottage-type' with great zeal and also wrote about domestic architecture, as we shall see. Decisive social innovations, continuing the formal elements of 'cottage-architecture' of the fifties, lay in the development of the smaller house in the country or in the suburbs by a new class of bourgeois art-lovers; but this only seems to begin in the sixties and will be discussed briefly in the last chapter.

Butterfield: the later fifties

Butterfield's buildings of the next years are of less importance in this context. The reputation of All Saints grew but advanced architects had already developed their ideas further. His esteem within the Society had greatly suffered from the controversies about All Saints.[43] The Yorkshire buildings were not published; and also Butterfield did not take part in competitions, which brought so much fame to advanced architects in the mid-fifties.

His work shed the unity of the preceding years. One can distinguish four kinds of types and formal treatment. The first is the continuation of the cottage type.[44] The second is a series of bigger houses, treated rather richly, with ecclesiastical features such as tracery, or with rich timber framing (Alvechurch vicarage, Worcs., 1856, Baldersby St James, school and vicarage, c. 1856[45]). Milton

Ernest Hall (Beds.)[46] reminds one even more of convent buildings.[47]

The third type are some village churches, marked more playfully than before by special elaboration of plan and arrangement.[48] From Langley (Kent), finished in 1855[49] [Plate 40], to Milton-Adderbury (Oxon.)[50] [Plate 41] and Waresley (Hunts.)[51] begun in 1856, the tower changes its position each time; at the west end, between chancel and nave, and then again at the west, but on the side. The buttresses vary a great deal in form and in combination with the walls, towers, and staircase-turrets. There are also many variations of coping and tracery. The churches have hardly any 'constructional polychromy', but the treatment and variations of the surface are carried to a perfection hardly noticed before. At Langley, where limestone with a rough surface is used, the trim is smooth. At Waresley it is a finer limestone and the difference in smoothness between dressings and wall is less, but profiles are fairly complicated. At Milton it is sandstone with no difference between trim and wall surface – here the

40 *Opposite page* (left) W. Butterfield, Langley, Kent, church, 1853.
One of the stipulations of the Ecclesiological Society was to use local materials and that designs should differ accordingly. Butterfield's relatively simple small churches of the mid-fifties on closer observation reveal an astonishing variety in the treatment of surfaces and profiles.

41 *Opposite page* (right) W. Butterfield, Milton-Adderbury, Oxon., church, 1856. Cf. Plate 40.

42 (left) W. Butterfield, Holborn, St Alban's, 1860, destroyed in the last war and rebuilt (from the *Builder*, 1862, 443).
Only from the later fifties onwards Butterfield returned to polychromy on a larger scale. In the interior of St Alban's there seems to be a greater balance between the linear quality of the architectural members and the vivid flat pattern decoration than at All Saints, at least as seen in this engraving.

voussoirs of windows are varied slightly in colour. A similar treatment to Langley is shown in the later churches of Ashford (Middx.)[52] and Etal (Northumberland)[53] of 1858 and in the remote little church at Gaerhill (Som.).[54]

With his fourth group, after 1855, Butterfield joined in the latest development of brick and structural colour, to be dealt with in the next chapter. Continuous bands of different coloured stones can be found on the outside of Balliol College, Oxford,[55] and on the interior of the large church at Baldersby St James,[56] providing a certain contrast to the earlier treatment of All Saints, with courses shown both on the wall surfaces and on the splay of window-openings, as well as around the voussoirs of the arches. A similar treatment is shown on the exterior walls of the church at Landford (Wilts.).[57] St John the Evangelist at Hammersmith[58] is a big church, spacious, with a comparatively empty interior roof and little decoration. Equally spacious is St Alban's, Holborn[59] [Plate 42], largely destroyed in the last war but rebuilt. Also destroyed in the war and not rebuilt was St John the Evangelist at Newbury (Berks.),[60] begun in 1860. Both of these had vivid polychromy, though less vigorous and more finely patterned than Street's or White's churches of those years. In general, a new attitude towards constructional polychromy was to emerge, however, which did not concern Butterfield whose works of the sixties we shall return to briefly.

White's work of the later fifties

Of the other architects who worked in close connection with the Ecclesiological Society, and whose designs were regularly reviewed in the *Ecclesiologist*, William White had seemed in the early fifties uncertain of his direction, but from about 1853 onwards, he developed very clear conceptions of constructional polychromy and also tried to combine elements of the 'sublime' with the requirements of small houses. A building which seems to combine 'rogue' tendencies, west country local decorative motifs, and a very primitive country look is the church at Plymstock-Hooe (Devon)[61] with its rubble walls, nave pillars without capitals, and awkward forms of tracery. Yet these forms are laid flush with a continuous wall surface, as shown both by the plate tracery and the chamfers of the nave-piers. The interior roofing consists of simple boards.

The arrangement of the country vicarage at Lurgashall (Sussex) begun in 1852[62] [Plate 43] is very much the same as with Butterfield, a larger range containing the smaller rooms, and at right-angles a smaller range with the two main living rooms. This scheme is repeated in most of White's vicarages. But his general treatment of the exterior is simpler than Butterfield's. The roofs are nearly all of equal height, and so are the rows of nearly uniform windows. The general outline reminds one of Street, but White did not normally break his uniformity with little irregularities. The whole is decorated with alternating colours of stone, sometimes regularly spaced, sometimes irregularly. Holy Trinity vicarage at Halstead (Essex) of 1854[63] [Plate 44] is similar in the simplicity of its arrangement, but the material, brick, seems new for White. He expounds its decorative possibilities in an extraordinarily complicated way, to quote the *Ecclesiologist*: ' . . . red brick, covered with old tiles; with horizontal lines of heading bricks in black, and diagonal lines of white brick. There are also projecting strings of bevelled bricks.' He even used different mortars. More simplified are two brick buildings in Cheshire of the next year, the school and the teacher's house at Rhode Heath;[64] a house at Arley Hall[65] [Plate 45] is reduced to a simple gabled type, a form later chosen for the German estate development house of the twentieth century where a return to 'rural simplicity' was also advocated.[66]

43 W. White,
Lurgashall,
Sussex, vicarage
1852.
See White's com-
ments on design,
Plate 13.

44 W. White, Halstead, Essex, vicarage (Holy Trinity), 1854.
From the description of White's design in the *Ecclesiologist*: '. . . red
brick, covered with old tiles, horizontal lines of heading bricks in black,
diagonal lines of white brick, projecting strings of bevelled bricks. . . .'
The bay window was originally intended to be continued into the roof.

77

As has already been observed, the brickwork employed by the High Victorian architects allowed only simple features, blank surfaces, rectangular corners or simple chamfers. Dressings had to be of stone or, in the case of smaller houses, wood was much preferred. The wooden frames of doors and windows are again very simple, yet allowing for variations in treatment that characterized the approach of different architects, analogous to the varied interior roofs of the churches. The difference between Butterfield's and White's woodwork lies mainly in the relationship between the masonry and the frames. At Halstead the lintels of the window-frames are prolonged into the wall surface at either side, in contrast to Butterfield's wooden window-frames which appear more as slightly recessed infilling within the opening. Correspondingly, White often uses open porches of a simple rectangular framework, whereas Butterfield prefers neatly closed verandahs of a more complicated construction.[67] There are also characteristic differences between White's and Butterfield's wooden church fittings. White tends to use simple rectangular beams filled with flat boarding, only enriched with cut out circular holes; Butterfield, on the other hand, tends to use forms deriving much more from

45 W. White, Arley Hall, Cheshire, chaplain's cottage, 1854.
A very basic version of Ecclesiologist cottage architecture. The open porch on the left is characteristic of White.

stone architecture, which in the case of his restoration and refurnishing of Hathersage church (Derbys.), 1854, was severely criticized by the *Ecclesiologist*.[68]

White's main attempts in 'constructional polychromy' of the mid-fifties are three small churches, at Hatherden [Plate 46], Smannel (Hants)[69] and Hawridge (Bucks.).[70] Again, the contours are simplified as much as possible with little division between nave and chancel. Here it becomes specially obvious how far architecture had moved away from the principles of Pugin and the early forties. The material is brick, coated with flint on the outside, but the quoins at Hatherden and Smannel are of brick. The tracery, a kind of plate tracery flush with the surface, is of hewn stone with the simple brick insertions and brick jambs interpreted as parts of the wall. This is one of the most scrupulous examples of distinguishing various constructive members and it also achieves a maximum variation in colour by manipulating the different materials, an effect enhanced by making these all part of one unified outer surface. There are no projecting bases, capitals or mullions, so no shadow can disturb the pattern of colours.

Interiors are treated similarly. The brick piers at Smannel are square

46 W. White, Hatherden, Hants, church, 1856.
A superb example of High Victorian flushwork polychromy. Only the arches of the windows are executed in stone, their jambs are treated as parts of the wall carefully inserted into the surface decoration.

79

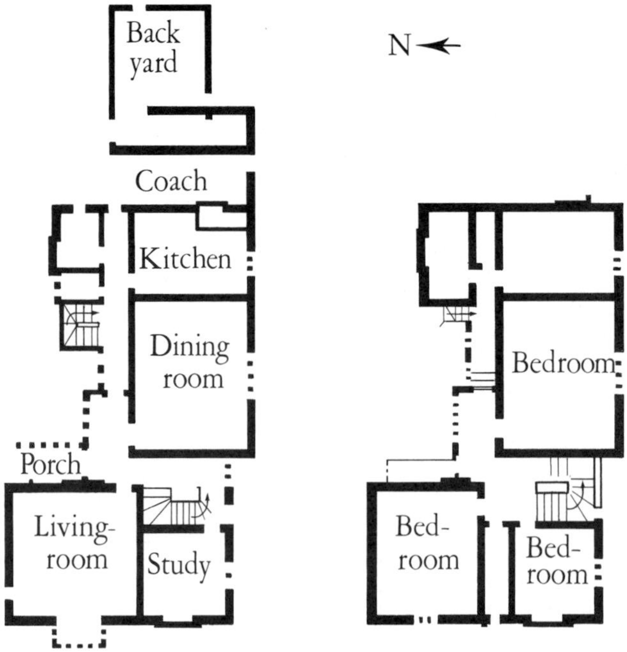

Back yard

N ←

Coach

Kitchen

Dining room

Bedroom

Porch

Living-room

Study

Bed-room

Bed-room

47 W. White, Little Baddow, Essex, vicarage, 1858, plan of ground floor and upper floor.

and unchamfered. The interior of Hawridge, however, is white-washed; the treatment of the chancel arch, where a wooden arch projects from the wall, was 'too domestic' for the *Ecclesiologist*.

White's houses from 1855 onwards can only be described briefly. There is a new tendency for massiveness in the sense that there is less angularity. Very often gables or dormers are hipped. Visually the roofs are extended down to the tile-hung upper parts of walls and gables. This applies to the school and master's house at Ramsbury (Wilts.), 1856,[71] and the parsonage at Coopersale (Essex), 1857,[72] and also to the convent-like building of St Michael's House at Wantage.[73] The long ranges of very small windows as well as the increased massiveness of the cottage-type building suggest an influence from Street's work of these years. Cottage elements appear on two other buildings for purposes quite unusual in the range of the Ecclesiologist architects: a row of houses with shops at Audley (Cheshire), 1855, (the shops lie behind an open arcading),[74] and a bank at St Columb Major, 1857.[75] Both these designs were for small towns, where White saw no reason to change his general manner of layout or detailing. (We shall look at the problems of town buildings in Chapter 7).

The vicarage at Little Baddow (Essex), built in 1857–8[76] [Plates 47–9] and excellently preserved, might be described as a model example of these houses of White's, and in a wider sense of the Ecclesiologists in general. The arrangement is L-shaped of the type described for Lurgashall or the Butterfield vicarages, but the individual rooms are more clearly distinctive and everywhere there is projection or recession of walls; the simple double-pile arrangement of rooms can be easily 'read' from the outside, unlike the earlier

48–49 W. White, Little Baddow, Essex, vicarage, 1858, garden front and entrance.
White has turned away from the massiveness of his earlier grouping (cf. Plate 43) towards an extremely lively plan and outline which meant a more direct expression of the interior disposition on the outside. Moreover, the different format of the windows expresses the different functions of the rooms behind (following White's complicated investigations on the fall of light in different rooms). The polychromatic treatment is hardly less complicated than at Hatherden, though arranged with an air of informality.

planning, as at Coalpit Heath or Lurgashall, where one can only guess from the arrangement of the windows what the interior division is like.

Once again there is also a material reason for this arrangement: all the rooms should get as much daylight as possible, but a different kind of light. In a lecture before the Ecclesiological Society 'On Windows in Domestic Architecture', in 1856,[77] White made use of very complicated psycho-physical considerations about the various kinds of light in which life's various activities should be performed: ' . . . in order to be most useful, light ought to fall so pleasantly as to induce the greatest composure of the nervous sytem.'[78]

The various kinds of light could be achieved by differing forms and positions of windows; and indeed at Little Baddow a great variety of forms of windows can be observed.[79] Externally the house shows again a complicated balance between picturesqueness and massiveness, interrelated with subtle polychromy in brick.[80]

The schools and vicarages of the next years continue the tendency towards massiveness (Chute, Wilts., 1858,[81] Andover, Hants, 1859,[82] Great Maplestead, Essex, 1860[83]). The intensity of polychromy seems to weaken in these smaller buildings; buildings in hewn stone emphasize the elaboration of details instead (Hinton Charterhouse, Som.,[84] Monkton Deverill, Wilts., both 1860[85]).

In 1859 White was given the chance to execute a major design, as many young Ecclesiologist architects were about that time. This was the church at Lyndhurst (Hants)[86] [Plates 50, 51]. The general layout is similar to that of White's first big church, All Saints, Talbot Road, already described as extremely complicated. One characteristic difference in detail must suffice here to indicate the change of attitude: although Lyndhurst church is generally richer than All Saints, Talbot Road, the archivolts of the nave are very much simpler, mainly rectangular in profile. Yet simple profiles were now contrasted with elaborate sculpture and members in other materials: the means used for rich effects have completely changed.

Teulon and others

Teulon, already mentioned for his churches in the 'rogue' group, made much use of brickwork. His St Andrew, Lambeth, of 1854[87] [Plate 52], damaged in the war and destroyed a few years ago, was a boxlike building of brick with horizontal stripes of stone, no buttresses, and thin tracery nearly flush with the wall. As a church for a rather poor district, it cost comparatively little: unbroken surfaces accorded with economy. Teulon's smaller schools and vicarages continue these tendencies. His large brick vicarage at Birch (Essex), probably built in 1849,[88] already included a small amount of coloured brick; the later schools and teacher's cottages at Angmering (Sussex)[89] and the school

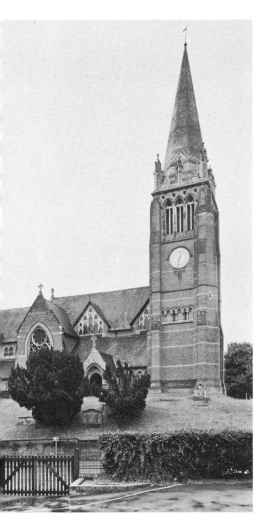

50 (above left) W. White, Lyndhurst, Hants, church, 1859 (Courtesy
National Monuments Record).
In this somewhat larger church White returned to the complicated plan-
ning of his early church, All Saints at Paddington of 1852 (cf. Plate 26).
A comparison between the two reveals the power of the impact of
'constructional polychromy' in the intervening years.

51 (above right) W. White, Lyndhurst church, interior (Courtesy National
Monuments Record).
View from the south aisle into the nave and transepts towards the chancel.
The stone sculpture is by G. W. Seale of Brixton, the painting on the
reredos by Frederick (Lord) Leighton (1864), the stained glass mostly by
Morris & Co.

at Ladywood (Birmingham), both from 1856,[90] are remarkable for their rectangularity. 'Mr. Teulon has judiciously avoided all projections,' commented the *Ecclesiologist* on the latter building. The church at Burringham (Lincs.) of 1856[91] [Plate 53] is also very much simplified: a low, broad south-west tower is merged in the single space of a short nave ending in a semicircular apse. The term 'tracery' can only be applied within, for the window-openings are seen on the outside as small cutouts in the wall – another radical example of the dissolution of the tracery into the wall. More elaborate devices of this kind can be found in the churches at Leckhampstead (Berks.)[92] and Silvertown (West Ham, Essex, now derelict) [Plate 54].[93] At Silvertown some of the tracery is reduced to plates of stone with rectangular cuttings into it. There is also much more brickwork colour in these two churches. St Thomas, Agar Town,[94] which was bombed in the war, was similar. An example of Teulon's exuberant striping with coloured brick on a large country house is Elvetham Hall (near Hartford Bridge, Hants).[95]

52 S. S. Teulon, Lambeth, St Andrew, 1854, destroyed (Courtesy National Monuments Record). Economy through High Victorian sharpness of contours and simple polychromy.

53 S. S. Teulon, Burringham, Lincs.,
church, 1856.

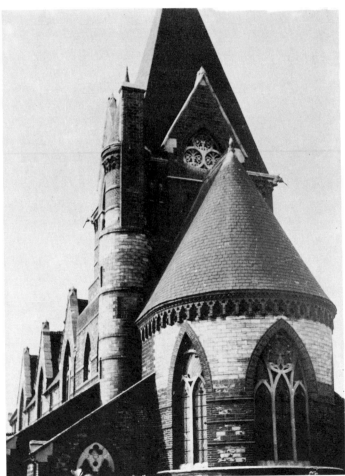

54 S. S. Teulon, Silvertown, West
Ham, Essex, church, 1859.
More complicated in its arrangement, the elements of decoration,
contrast of materials and simple,
sharp contours, remain the same.

55 R. J. Withers, Cardigan, Municipal Buildings, 1858 (from the *Building News*, 1859, 840).

One of the earliest examples of applying the Ecclesiological approach to the planning of a civic building. The exterior is only slightly more ornate than a large school (the execution is somewhat different from the illustration given here). At the back the upper market, which needs protection from heat and dust is surrounded by a massive unbroken wall (see Plate 56).

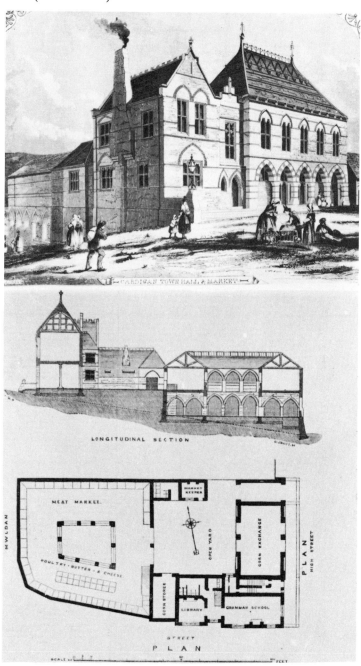

CARDIGAN TOWN HALL & MARKET

LONGITUDINAL SECTION

PLAN

In the years after 1855 Ewan Christian, who has been mentioned among the very 'rural' church architects, built a few churches in brick, ornamented with brick and flush stonework, as at Oakengates (Salop)[96] and Tiptree (Essex).[97] Tiptree is still low, in the 'rural' manner, with a very short unified interior under a light, open roof. The same kind of openness can be found in the big church at St Peter, Troy Town, Rochester.[98]

A combination of complicated plan and simple outline characterized the work of Robert Jewell Withers.[99] In his public buildings at Cardigan, designed c. 1856,[100] [Plates 55–6] he combined a corn exchange, grammar school, civic offices, clock-tower, and market hall in a closely grouped whole. The market extends to the rear, surrounded by a very massive unbroken wall. A typical example of the many churches he built at that time in remote places in the west of Wales, was the church at Llanllawer (Pembs.),[101] a little un-buttressed box, its tracery flush with the outer wall surface. A very typical example of polychrome brick inside and out is the little church at Little Cawthorpe (Lincs.).[102] The building for Lavers and Barraud's Painted Glass Works, Endell Street (1860), still standing, must also be mentioned for its absolute continuity of surface.[103]

Three more buildings built between 1853 and 1856 that received special credit as early examples of brick were built by architects not

56 R. J. Withers, Cardigan, exterior of market.

normally much concerned with this kind of design. St John's, Limehouse,[104] destroyed in the war [Plate 57] was by Henry Clutton, one of the most versatile architects of the time. Said the *Ecclesiologist*: 'Externally the church ... is a plain parallelogram, wears an air of great reality, from total absence of buttresses, which would not be needed from the material and construction of the roof.'

Henry Woodyer's 'House of Mercy' at Clewer (Berks.)[105] is a simple brick building without stone dressings, with unchamfered openings. Of this it was said: 'No other building shows greater pains and more workmanlike thought having been bestowed on its minutest details as on its general design.' 'Real progress' was also shown by St Aubyn's church of St John the Baptist, at Enfield (Middx.),[106] with its light coloured bricks and dark stripes, and its marked contrast between the stonework of the tracery and the rectangular corners of the brick masonry. In St John's, Limehouse, the ragged contour of the stone tracery in the brick walls was a point which the Ecclesiologists did not like, as is evident in another criticism of a brick church by Benjamin Ferrey at Fauls Green (Salop):[107] 'We prefer that in a brick church, where stone windows are inserted, they should be let in as panels, with the external lines of the stone work straight. ... ' Again a maximum of clear contrast was sought in the handling of the different materials.[108]

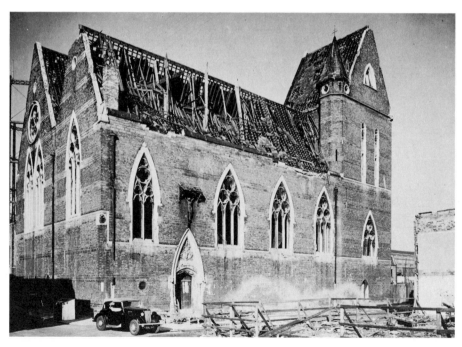

57 H. Clutton, London, St John, Limehouse, 1853 (destroyed) (Courtesy National Monuments Record).
An early example of flush tracery.

Butterfield and White in the sixties

From about 1856 onwards, the leadership of the High Victorian Gothic Movement passed into the hands of other architects, Street, Burges and Scott, to whom most of the next three chapters will be devoted. Naturally, no firm lines of division can be drawn but, with the exception of Clutton who will be mentioned again later, the later work of the architects dealt with in this chapter is of less interest in the context of this book. Butterfield and White and more especially Woodyer adhered to English motifs rather than the French ones which became common after 1860. Constructional polychromy, which began to be considered vulgar or at least superfluous by people like Burges and Godwin, remained an important factor in Teulon's work and especially in that of Butterfield. Neither did the latter subscribe to the doctrine of contrasting bare walls with concentrated pictorial effects in painting or sculpture. Butterfield's work was hardly reviewed in the *Ecclesiologist* and All Saints, Margaret Street, was considered old-fashioned at the date of its completion in 1859.[109]

Yet the later buildings of Butterfield show a greater degree of elaboration and perfection than it was possible for him to achieve in the fifties. Only a few can be mentioned here. It seems that Butterfield's work in the sixties becomes more individual. He continued the small, regular patterns of polychromy of his St Alban's, Holborn, for example on the classrooms for Rugby School[110] in 1860 and Winchester County Hospital (he was the architect in charge of St Cross) in 1863,[111] where he tried to combine his 'Gothic' forms with modern conveniences such as sash windows, and grouped the whole along an oblong that culminates in the chapel. His churches at Babbacombe (Devon)[112] [Plate 58] and Penarth near Cardiff[113] are characterized by strange motifs and vivid constructional polychromy. Other churches, especially the ones in large towns, such as Holy Cross at Openshaw (Manchester),[114] 1863–6, and later St Augustine's, Queen's Gate in Kensington, begun in 1865,[115] are relatively simple in plan with wide open spaces. Here Butterfield does share an idea propagated by the *Ecclesiologist* and especially by Beresford-Hope during these years— the 'town church'—as we shall see (p. 139).

Butterfield's *magnum opus*, Keble College, Oxford, was begun in 1868 [Plate 59].[116] The most striking feature in the arrangement of the whole is the predominance of the chapel over the residential buildings. The latter appear as endless successions of small motifs and long continuous horizontals are contrasted with groups of irregular ranges. The chapel is short and compact, four and a half bays long, and its windows begin at the height of the roofline of the dormitories. Constructional polychromy in brick and stone is the main element of decoration, in pattern the most vivid conceivable, horizontal stripes on the lower parts, mostly diaper-work above. The interior of the

58 W. Butterfield, Babbacombe, Devon, church interior, 1868–74 (Courtesy National Monuments Record).
Butterfield's churches in the sixties are characterized by an overwhelming richness of unusual decorative features which do not necessarily adhere to High Victorian laws of form any more.

chapel, including the stone vault, is decorated on similar principles.

William White's work in the sixties does not reach his standards of the fifties and can rarely be compared with Butterfield. There is, however, the outstanding church at Islington, Holy Saviour, Aberdeen Park [Plate 60].[117] The arrangement is as complicated as usual in White's bigger churches, narrow, small spaces contrasted with higher ones, low chancel arcades with the taller nave arcade, and so on. The polychromy is restrained: there is only the contrast between the

59 W. Butterfield, Oxford, Keble College Chapel design, c. 1867 (from the
Builder, 3 Jan. 1885).
The chapel is built into the north-east corner of the quadrangle but
surmounts it considerably, in fact its windows only start at the height of
the roof of the domestic wings. The main effect of the decoration lies
perhaps in the constant interplay between the restless surface pattern
with the repose of the main horizontals. Butterfield, like Burges, remained
faithful to this mode of design to the end of his life.

beautiful red brickwork and the stonework of the windows. But
internally the brick is laid in different ways, the joints forming many
different patterns. By a singular device these walls are covered by
strongly conventionalized floral patterns applied in thin paint as a
kind of see-through lace. Although perhaps not 'High Victorian' in all
its elements, White's Holy Saviour church is one of the most perfect
examples of the exploitation of brick in these decades.[118]

60 W. White, Islington, Holy Saviour, Aberdeen Park, 1866, interior
(Courtesy Gordon Barnes).
White had often experimented with brick (cf. Plate 44) but nowhere does
he give more variety than in this relatively remote London church. White
also adheres to his complicated spatial arrangements of high and low
arches.

Street and others from 1855 to 1860

Most of the buildings of the fifties described so far were rather small commissions. With a few exceptions, White's, Butterfield's and Teulon's work stood outside the really important jobs of the time. Butterfield refused to enter competitions as a matter of principle. But it was in a series of important competitions that the young architects of the new Gothic movement made themselves known.

The series began in 1854 when Benjamin Woodward won the competition for the Oxford Museum, as we shall see (Chapter 7). In 1856 William Burges, then completely unknown, together with Henry Clutton, won the international competition for the cathedral at Lille, with Street second; only the third prize went to a Frenchman, J. B. Lassus.[1] The competition for a Crimean Memorial church at Constantinople, the terms requiring a form of 'gothic' adapted to a southern climate, had already been influenced by the movement, and it was not surprising that the first three prizes were won by the new young men, Burges, Street and Bodley.[2] None of these designs for the two churches was executed; Street built a smaller version in Constantinople in the sixties. In the Government Offices Competition of 1856–7, the Gothic designs by Scott, Street, Woodward and others attracted great attention and led to the widely publicized battle of styles during the following years.

On balance, one might side with the *Builder*, which in 1855 called Street a 'leader',[3] largely on the strength of his publications: his lectures (those up to 1853 have been dealt with in Chapter 3) and his book *Brick and Marble in the Middle Ages, Notes of a Tour in the North of Italy*, published in 1855.[4]

For Street writing about architecture meant reporting his journeys on the continent. He travelled fast by making full use of the new means of transport, the railway. 'At Erfurt [in the middle of Germany] it was late in the evening when I left the Domplatz, but I saw hurriedly the exterior of some eight or ten pointed churches. . . .'[5] And by the next morning he was at Marburg, about a hundred and twenty miles away. He even acknowledged the influence of the faster means of transport on the knowledge of architectural history, in his view another argument in favour of 'eclecticism' (see above, Chapter 3).

On the other hand, he said explicitly that what he had found bore out his previously enunciated principles. Like many other travellers, he found what he looked for. In his book *Brick and Marble,* describing his tour in 1853, he remarks: ' . . . nor is this feeling the result only of what I saw with my own eyes in Italy, for so long ago as 1852 I ventured . . . to point out . . . the natural and proper mode of attempting any improvement upon, or development from, our present position in regard to architecture.'[6]

Street was exclusively interested in buildings of the twelfth to fifteenth centuries. He chose and described details irrespective of their decorative value to a building as a whole and usually preferred the simpler ones. There is little about building types and no plans. A few derogatory remarks on buildings from other periods occur: 'S. Andrea [at Mantua is] a hideous classic edifice tacked on to a most beautiful brick campanile.'[7] And his illustration shows as little of Alberti's façade as possible. Much of his text falls into the class of traveller's chat. Germany he found less rewarding, liking best the brick churches of Lübeck on which he held forth in 1855.[8]

Most of the Italian buildings Street singled out in his book were well known through Benjamin Webb's and Ruskin's writings, but there is more emphasis on Veronese Gothic, especially that of the church of Sant'Anastasia.[9] His earlier aesthetic principles continue: 'breadth', 'unbroken surfaces of wall', variations on 'plate tracery'[10] and so on. Windows and their subdivisions ought to be part of the wall. He strongly criticized some windows on the west front of the Duomo at Verona: ' . . . [the] enclosing arch . . . is again surrounded by a square line of moulding. The effect . . . is exceedingly unsatisfactory, as it appears to make the window with its arch and tracery quite independent, constructively, of the wall in which it is placed, and, as it were, merely veneered on the face of the wall.'[11] Simplicity of layout and construction was commended, in one case, for a 'certain air of openness and clearness', in another for 'simplicity of groining'.[12]

But more than anything else Street was fascinated by materials and their colours, as the title of his book indicated. Much of his final chapter is devoted to 'Italian Brickwork' and 'Colour in Construction'. He insists on pure red brick: 'Italian brickwork is remarkable as being invariably composed of nothing but red brick.'[13] In some cases where more complicated forms occur, he thinks stone ought to be used instead, but he advocates simple forms in the case of stone, too, in order not to disturb its inherent colour. Referring to the monument of Mastino II at Verona he said: 'The architect had to deal with a material which best takes its polish and exhibits its beauty and purity when used in flat surfaces and shallow carving, . . . of the science of moulding [it is] valueless, there is absolutely no moulding upon it; why should there be?'[14]

Like Ruskin, Street hesitates a little whether to recommend incrustation or layers of various stones in the masonry, but tends to prefer the latter mode. He summed up the problem in a lecture on colour to Worcester Diocesan Architectural Association in 1885:

The whole building is composed of a succession of horizontal layers, one over the other. The horizontal line is therefore eminently the line of construction, and if in using the materials of your walls you so dispose a coloured material as to lead the eye in any other than this line, your coloured material at once ceases to give the idea of anything constructional, i.e. being an integral part of the fabric.[15]

From 1855 to 1858, Street published very little: he was too busy with his competition entries. In 1857 he was still advocating more study of building materials – 'architects must think more of their materials, not only of their designs' – and recommending attention to the contents of the Museum of Economic Geology.[16]

In his buildings there are two themes to be pursued, closely interlinked: 'constructional polychromy' which in Street's work of 1855 is not yet handled quite in the way *Brick and Marble* would suggest, and the development of 'massiveness', the emphasis on flat wall surfaces and the horizontal line.

In some of Street's earlier buildings, as we saw in Chapter 3, coloured materials were used.[17] The earliest was presumably the school of 1850 at Inkpen [Plate 18]. Yet the polychromy here is of a different kind: brick, contrasted with the flint walls, only occurs as trim around windows and corners, not as an element embedded in the wall.

The several courses of white brick which run around the walls of the vicarage at Colnbrook of 1853 are perhaps the first instance of this developed polychromy. Much stronger polychromy is used on the exterior of the church at Chalfont St Peter (Bucks.),[18] begun perhaps in late 1853, after the Italian journey. Courses of stone and black brick diapers leave little of the actual red brick wall showing. The houses at Boyne Hill have equally vivid black patterns, and the church there on both inside and outside walls has horizontal strips of stone flanked by strips of coloured brick, still emphasizing surface in the manner of All Saints, Margaret Street, but separating more clearly the stone tracery of the windows from the brick walls.[19]

The tendency for 'massiveness' was continued by Street on a larger scale in his competition entries of the next two years. The cathedral for Lille [Plates 61–2, 64] was to be armed with an enormous number of buttresses of broad and simple shapes, even for the upper walls. Nevertheless the main horizontals were hardly disturbed by this, with rooflines emphasized by broad parapets. At the west front the system of buttresses was further complicated by towers, but still there was a tendency to simplify surfaces and to provide horizontal lines wherever possible. For example, the gables over the west doors were to be flush with the front face of the buttresses, which were to terminate just below the main cornice of the façade below the octagons

of the towers. A characteristic contrast was made between richly
sculptured areas and plain wall surfaces, as between the portals and
the neighbouring wall face. The decorative element was mainly
confined to courses and dressings in hewn stone, to be irregularly
spread over the whole building. (Street was one of the very few
competitors who took up the suggestion to use brick.) It is useful at
this point to contrast Street's design with the third-prize design of
Lassus [Plate 63]. On the whole, Lassus' design (as that of an archaeologist and Gothicist, Viollet-le-Duc's predecessor), in the eyes of
an Ecclesiologist architect, comes under the head of 'meagreness',[20]
which at that time was still the rule on the continent. Lassus' endless

61 G. E. Street, project for Notre Dame de la Treille, Lille, 1855 (Courtesy
Archives Diocésaines, Lille).
During the years 1853–4 an increase of constructional polychromy and a
more sophisticated handling of massiveness could be observed in Street's
works and projects (Plates 16–22). From 1855 a series of competitions
provided ample opportunity for thinking out these problems. Street was
second after Burges in the Lille competition. To design a fully developed
Gothic cathedral cannot have been an easy job for the young Ecclesiologist architects. But Street manages to employ the complete apparatus of
flying buttresses and at the same time remains faithful to his principles of
'repose', his unbroken rooflines, large expanses of quiet roof surface,
brick and stone dressing plus horizontal stripes (Cf. Plate 83).

62 (left) G. E. Street, project for Lille Cathedral competition, west façade, 1855 (from the *Builder*, 6 Feb. 1858).

63 (below) J. B. Lassus, design for Lille, 1855 (Courtesy Archives Diocésaines, Lille, Charles Handley-Read).
With Clutton and Burges first, Street second, only the third prize went to a Frenchman, the highly thought-of Gothicist Lassus. No doubt, from the English point of view the French design was much inferior, more schematic and without any 'innovations'.

64 (above) G. E. Street, design for Lille Cathedral competition, 1855, interior of chancel (Courtesy Archives Diocésaines, Lille).
Street's interior is treated as his exterior in brick and stone polychromy. Street like Burges, won his prize largely on account of the elaboration of his fittings (see Chapter 6).

65 (opposite above) G. E. Street, design for Constantinople, Crimean Memorial church competition, 1856–7 (from the *Builder*, 1857, 163).
For Constantinople (again he came second after Burges) Street chose a much simpler plan, that of a large chapel. The exterior again contrasts simple and elaborate parts, verticals and horizontals, decorative spikiness and plain wall surface.

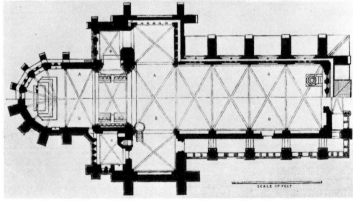

66 G. E. Street,
design for Con-
stantinople
Memorial church
competition,
1856–7, plan
(from the *Builder,*
1857, 162).

subdivisions and finely carved ornaments are entirely lacking in Street's project. Another solution was that of Burges, as we shall see [Plates 83–4].

For the Constantinople competition [Plates 65–6] Street chose a simple plan with a crossing: the nave, including the crossing, was to consist of five oblong bays, the transept arms of one square bay each, and there was to be a short polygonal chancel. Two slender towers rising from side chapels east of the transept, were not apparent as such on the plan. The elevations are handled in a very unusual way. The nave is characterized by a large amount of roof surface. Beneath the main roof the space between the buttresses is bridged by smaller roofs and an ambulatory opened to the exterior carries another roof, reaching to the sill of the nave windows. In contrast, transept and chancel were lofty, huge walls and small slender windows with sills far above the ground. The buttresses are more slender and vertical than at Lille. Horizontal emphasis is restricted to continuous coloured bands. This design, as illustrated in the *Builder*, could be described in its links with the traditions of the 'picturesque' and 'sublime' as well as for its 'dynamism'. Its 'external plastic mass' has been aptly compared with Butterfield's 'flat ornamented surface planes'.[21]

The Lille exterior design, in spite of a complicated system of construction, is characterized by a horizontal continuity of surface. In the interior [Plate 64] the constructive system was made much more apparent. A framework of thin supports in groups of small slender shafts outlined large openings for windows and galleries, although larger areas of wall surface showed the external mode of brick with horizontal stripes. On the whole Street's interior was to be much more like Lassus' framework rationalism. Here Burges' solution, with a predominance of horizontals and the reduction of columnar supports to short, stout shafts, was to be the more influential.

Street's next big project was for the Government Offices [Plate 67]. Only one view of his design is known.[22] The roof is a predominant feature, with few gables – a domestic element that he tended to avoid in town buildings – but contrasted with tall slender towers and spires. The layout of the whole was to be asymmetrical, as aggregation of a few individual blocks which in themselves were very unified as he suggested in his earlier article on domestic architecture: 'various buildings brought together, that they form a more imposing mass'.[23]

Yet another unexecuted project by Street dates from the same year, 1857, for a rebuilding of St Dionis Backchurch in the City of London [Plate 68].[24] In a plan carefully adapted to the irregular site and to Wren's foundations, large and small parts alike were to be reduced to blocklike, striped forms.

The role of smaller buildings in Street's work was much reduced in these years.[25] A few of those built should be mentioned for their relevance to the greater designs. 'Constructional polychromy' in the form of irregularly spaced horizontal stripes of stonework can be seen in the church at Pokesdown (Bournemouth),[26] on the exterior as well as in the interior. The small church of Firsby (Lincs.)[27] [Plate 69] is a freestone building without polychromy. Here Street introduces a semicircular apse, not as a simple geometrical form as in Teulon's church at Burringham but as a piece of massive walling. An example of massiveness in a brick building is Christ Church School at Burton-on-Trent;[28] in its plan hardly more than a simple parallelogram, it has a large hipped roof.[29]

From 1859 Street built a series of lavish churches. St Peter's at Bournemouth is a large town church with a complicated building

67 G. E. Street, design for Government Offices competition (Foreign
Office etc.), 1857 (from the *Illustrated London News*, 1857, II, 412).
'Orderly monumental design in terms of function' (Hitchcock). It would
have been unthinkable for Street to arrange this big complex into one
vast symmetrical structure, as the classical competitors proposed and
among the Gothicists Scott and Woodward (see Plates 125 and 130).

68 G. E. Street, London,
City, unexecuted project
for St Dionis Backchurch,
1857 (from the *Ecclesiologist*,
XXI, 1860, 88).

history lasting through the sixties into the seventies.[30] A smaller church, of the type with a low clerestory, was begun in 1858 at New Bradwell (Bucks.).[31] Two small but very rich churches were begun in 1858–9 at Whitwell[32] and Howsham (Yorks.) [Plates 70–1].[33] At Whitwell, 'massiveness' is effected by deeply-sunk windows. At Howsham, flat surfaces seem the main formal element, with some windows reduced to small holes in the wall, and buttresses treated as simple projections from the wall with the plainest possible outline; horizontal courses of coloured stone dominate: they even run across the nave wall containing the chancel arch. Again, the emphasis of the horizontal is at the west front, where the short columns carry flat-headed arches with the aid of impost blocks treated as part of the wall. More variation in window treatment was proposed for an unexecuted church at Cowley.[34]

At about this time, in May 1859, the two most important churches of these years were announced: St James the Less, Westminster, and St Philip and St James at Oxford. The tower of St James the Less,[35] [Plates 72–3] in its isolation and 'sturdy squareness', may well be the best Ruskinian tower ever built. The plate tracery at the east end, consistent with its well-like character, is bent with the curve of the

69 (above) G. E. Street, Firsby, Lincs., church, 1858.

70–71 (opposite) G. E. Street, Howsham, Yorks., church, 1859, exterior and interior (from the *Civil Engineer and Architect's Journal*, 1861, pl. 9 and 13).
One of the most successful combinations of simple massiveness and rich polychromatic decoration.

apse. The interior brickwork is contrasted with a great variety of materials. The roof of the nave is panelled as a high curved space with smooth surface while the chancel is vaulted with low, heavy arches. St Philip and St James[36] [Plates 74–5] is somewhat different in plan and material, though hardly in general approach. The tower is now over the crossing. The material is Bath stone which meant less colour but more texture. One interior feature must be mentioned: the chancel and crossing are narrower than the nave, so that the arch which divides nave and crossing is cut through a wall that projects further inward than the nave arcades and clerestory walls. This eastern wall of the nave and aisles (which can be seen as another example of emphasis on wall surface against the principle of framework, as at Butterfield's All Saints) cuts off part of the easternmost arch of the nave arcade, which runs dead against the wall, without responds. But more surprisingly, the nave-clerestory walls themselves are slightly bent inward so that the nave narrows towards the crossing and the angle is not marked by any architectural members. There had been rounded compartments in such a position in Baroque architecture, but those resulted from a sophisticated use of architectural members, pilasters and cornices, in combination with circular or elliptical

CHURCH OF ST JOHN
HOWSHAM

THE EVANGELIST
YORKSHIRE.
G.E. STREET, ARCH.T

72 G. E. Street, Westminster, St James the Less, Thorndike Street, 1859
(from the *Builder*, 1861, 411).
Street's most important executed work so far. Following Ruskin's
recommendations about the Campanile (cf. Plate 12) in many ways,
Street does not isolate the tower completely, but apart from linking it
with the church door carefully joins it to the boundary of the site, whose
fences enclose the spaces in between the schools and the church. The
schools differ considerably in their execution.

73 G. E. Street, Westminster, St James the Less, 1859, interior (Courtesy Gordon Barnes).

Two tendencies seem to prevail: the rambling plan and an emphasis on height and spatial clarity, something that was to be superseded by different solutions very soon. Otherwise we see again the contrast of materials increased by the vaulting in the chancel, and, in this exceptionally well endowed church the pictorial decoration; the fresco is an early work by G. F. Watts, the carving is mostly by T. Earp.

74 G. E. Street,
Oxford, St Philip
and St James,
1859 (from the
Building News,
1861, 713).

variations of ground-plan geometry and these variations could never
entirely free themselves from the basic classical motifs. Later Soane
had tried other possibilities of curved walls, but they remained within
exact geometrical definitions.[37] In the case of St Philip and St James,
the wall is treated as a mass of masonry which may freely be bent
like any plastic mass, a general trend of great importance in the later
nineteenth century.

Street continued designing big churches in the sixties, which we
shall mention, but he can no longer be called the 'leader' of the
movement.

George Gilbert Scott had actually preceded Street's book with a
lecture 'On the Pointed Style of Italy' in 1855,[38] but drawing attention
to different aspects of north Italian Gothic architecture. There is less
emphasis on materials or on flat surface and plate tracery. What

75 G. E. Street, Oxford, St Philip and St James, 1859, interior (Courtesy National Monuments Record).
The vigorous build-up over the east meant heavy support in the interior. The rather spacious nave was terminated by a wall supporting the western part of the tower. In a curious fashion the nave walls are canted as they approach the eastern wall and the angle is not indicated or strengthened by any additional feature. Since stone is used throughout there is less variety of colour but vivid contrast of surfaces.

mattered for Scott – in his use of constructional polychromy too – were detached monolithic shafts for arcades and for window decoration, as in the cathedral at Genoa. He seems to have employed this system in 1854, in a round-arched addition to Camden Church at Camberwell (destroyed in the last war) [Plate 127].[39] However, Scott's main contribution of these years belongs into the context of the next chapters, under the headings of public buildings and the development of church planning.

John Pollard Seddon (with his partner John Pritchard) was diocesan architect in the diocese of Llandaff (Cardiff). They joined the Street-Scott 'line' with several secular designs, beginning with a project for the Government Offices in 1857. Their country house, Ettington Park (War.), begun in 1858 [Plate 76],[40] is one of the most elaborate examples of the more informal kind of constructional polychromy, in brown and grey stone. John Loughborough Pearson started as a close follower of Pugin in the early forties, and from the early fifties tended towards massiveness and simple treatment of the 'lancet style',[41] but in his churches from c. 1856 he adopted an arcaded manner like Scott's, at first, it seems, in a small church at Scorborough (Yorks.).[42] Then on a lavish scale at Dalton Holme [Plate 77] nearby, begun in 1858,[43] there are interior walls lined with richly detailed detached arcades and on the exterior a rich assembly of rather freely distributed decoration. Two smaller churches continue these devices into the beginning of the sixties, Titsey (Surrey) and Daylesford (formerly Worc., now Glos.); and in 1860 Pearson designed the far more important church of St Peter's, Vauxhall, to be discussed under the development of 'town churches'.[44]

In 1857 Pearson built Quar Wood (Glos.)[45] [Plate 78], a moderately sized country house, now radically altered, in which he used some of the 'Gothic' features of Dalton and Titsey. At the same time this house has a remarkably simplified roof, really a 'cottage' roof, with projecting eaves.

76 J. Pritchard & J. P. Seddon, Ettington Park, War., 1859 (from the *Building News*, 19 Feb. 1869).
A superb example of constructional polychromy in brown and grey, arranged in a random manner.

George Frederick Bodley[46] takes part in all the stages of the movement. His earliest known building, the school at Bisley (Glos.),[47] the larger school (Normal School) at Cheltenham[48] [Plate 79] and the church at Llangrove (or Long-grove, Herefs.),[49] all of 1854, show influences of Street's earlier churches and schools, especially in the concentration of openings contrasted with continuous wall surfaces and variations in the use of buttresses. All this applies to the somewhat bigger church at France Lynch (Glos.) of 1855,[50] where high, sloped bases for the buttresses and parts of the walls increased an impression of massiveness. The interior contains coloured shafts with rich carving, and on the reredos a kind of intarsia with various coloured stones in the form of a cross, perhaps the first example of this jewellery-like decoration later to be found in Street's and Pearson's churches.[51] Bodley's most important contribution of these years must have been his project for Constantinople,[52] for which he won the third prize. Unfortunately no pictorial record has so far been found. Yet from the descriptions there is enough information to say that St Michael and All Angels at

77 J. L. Pearson, Dalton Holme, Yorks., E. R., church, 1858 (Courtesy Gordon Barnes). Pearson, an early follower of Pugin in Yorkshire after the mid-fifties, quickly caught up with the new tendencies: contrasting bare and ornate parts, small and large decorative features. He also takes up continuous arcading, especially the interior.

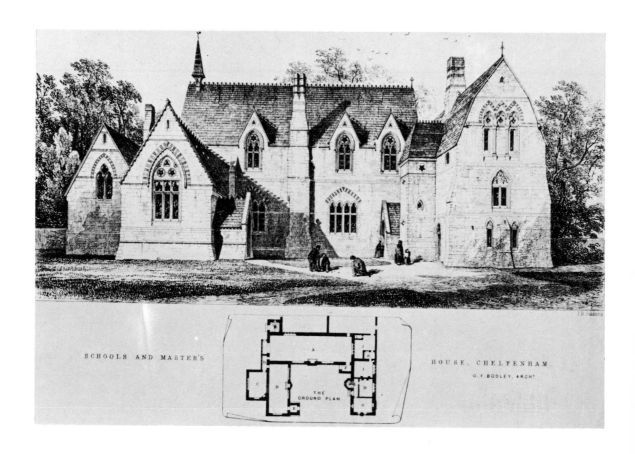

SCHOOLS AND MASTER'S HOUSE, CHELTENHAM
G. F. BODLEY, ARCH.T

THE GROUND PLAN

78 (opposite, top) J. L. Pearson, Quar Wood, near Stow on the Wold, Glos., 1857 (from C. L. Eastlake, *A History of the Gothic Revival*, 1872). The introduction of 'Gothic' here does not so much mean a variety of elaborate High Victorian features taken from church architecture, but the careful juxtaposition of openings and plain surfaces, as well as a cottage-type roof, reminiscent of Teulon's Enbrook (see Plate 25) and premonitory of the development of domestic architecture in the sixties and seventies (see below, Chapter 6). Unfortunately this house has lately been altered beyond recognition.

79 (opposite, below) G. F. Bodley, Cheltenham, Normal School, 1854 (from the *Civil Engineer and Architect's Journal*, 1858, 317).
Bodley was, like Street and William White, a pupil of Scott. His contribution to the High Victorian Movement is only a preliminary stage in his work. In his preference for battering he seems to be influenced by earlier tendencies, such as Truefitt's treatment of the exterior of his churches (cf. Plate 14).

80 (below) G. F. Bodley, Brighton, St Michael and All Angels, 1859 (Courtesy National Monuments Record).
The higher nave on the right was added by William Burges (planned in the late sixties). Bodley's first larger church: church building remained his main activity. It is another case of extreme simplification of details, the square profile reigns supreme.

81 G. F. Bodley, Brighton, St Michael and All Angels, interior, 1859 (from the *Building News*, 1864, 695).

Brighton, designed in 1858 [Plates 80–1],[53] (later added to by Burges), basically repeated the Constantinople project. This was a very simplified Basilican plan, no transept, no towers, no apse. (An 'engaged' tower at the west end of the south aisle had been planned for Constantinople.) 'The plan almost errs on the side of simplicity,' said the *Ecclesiologist*. The rectangular section was pursued with great zeal at Brighton: in the window-frames, the geometrical patterns, in the 'plate tracery', and the interior arches. We shall be discussing Bodley's work of the sixties below.

William Slater was assistant to R. C. Carpenter and took over his office when the latter died prematurely in 1855.[54] But Slater did not continue Carpenter's manner of design. The interior of the small

82 W. Slater, Basseterre, West Indies, St Kitts, 1856 (from the *Ecclesiologist*,
XXI, 1860, 142).
The church is designed to keep out the heat and to meet the danger of
earthquakes. It is a truly 'tropical' and 'speluncar' design; earlier on
climatic reasons had been a pretext for heavy forms.

church at South Tidworth (Hants)[55] is decorated with coloured shafts
and naturalistic carving, his 'tropical' design for St Kitts at Basseterre
in the West Indies [Plate 82][56] is highly polychromed, his cathedral
at Honolulu[57] is a good example of overall massiveness. (We shall come
to an iron church by Slater below.) Philip Boyce's church of St John's
at Barnsley (Yorks.),[58] with its massive piers and bold shafts supporting
the chancel arch, belongs in this context, as do the richly decorated
churches at Welsh Bicknor (Herefs.) and Greetland (Halifax) by the
very little known architect T. Henry Rushforth.[59] Arthur Blomfield,
a very active church architect of the seventies and later, also started
practice in the early sixties.[60]

six

New tendencies in the late fifties and sixties

France

'France' instead of 'Italy' became the new battlecry among some Ecclesiologist architects in about 1858. In Charles Lock Eastlake's *History of the Gothic Revival* of 1872 a good account of the developments in the sixties can be found. He sums up the main characteristics:

> Artistically considered, the examples of modern Gothic might be said to approach a more archaic type than previously. From a constructive point of view they were pronounced, in the professional slang of the day, more 'muscular'. The small and intricately carved foliage of capitals which had hitherto been in vogue gave place to bolder and simpler forms of leaf ornament. The round abacus was superseded by the square. In place of compound or clustered pillars plain cylindrical shafts were employed. Arch mouldings grew less complex. Crockets and ball-flower enrichments were reduced to a minimum.[1]

One may add that this new attitude was also reflected in the simplicity of church planning. Furthermore – and this Eastlake does not emphasize sufficiently – the bareness of the building was matched by special efforts in figure sculpture and painting, strongly linked with the ideas of Ruskin and of William Morris' circle.

'France' did not necessarily mean, or at least only to a very small extent, the influence of Viollet-le-Duc or other French archaeologists or architects. Viollet-le-Duc's publications and restorations could, of course, hardly fail to attract attention in England. In fact, he and Lassus (who died in 1857) had become honorary members of the Ecclesiological Society much earlier, in 1850, when they reported on their restoration of the Sainte-Chapelle.[2] The *Dictionnaires* found a wide readership in England. The article on military architecture from the *Dictionnaire raisonné de l'architecture française* was translated into English in 1860.[3] It was generally agreed that England had no architectural historian on the Middle Ages to equal Viollet-le-Duc. In 1864 he received the RIBA gold medal.[4] Later, his *Entretiens sur l'Architecture* and other books were translated.[5] Yet, whether English architects found models for their own buildings in his research is a different question. At times their views about the Middle Ages do appear to be very similar, especially in the case of Burges, who had by far the most intense contacts with France, as we shall see. The first volume of the *Dictionnaire du mobilier français* seems to have been especially influential: this was devoted to furniture, and came out during 1855–8. It must have been a mine of information for Burges, Street and others, who had laid so much emphasis on the fittings in their designs for Lille. But on the whole one must assume that although Viollet-le-Duc might have initially directed attention to this or that French building an English architect did not have to rely on his guidance to the buildings he himself visited, sketched and described. Street, for instance, quotes the *Dictionnaire* at length about Laon Cathedral as a product of a more democratic society than other cathedrals, but as far as Street's observations are concerned this is quite pointless: for him, Laon derived its special character from the influence of the Rhenish Romanesque churches which he had seen on previous tours.[6] One aspect of French archaeological activity – restoration – was most fervently opposed by the Ecclesiologists. Street had already written in 1857 about 'Destructive Restoration in France',[7] and in a long discussion in 1861 the Society proposed an official protest (not in the end pursued) against the French restoration movement.[8]

Which, then, were the important steps in the development of English knowledge of French medieval architecture? Only a brief survey can be given here, although some details follow with discussions of the work of the architects themselves. Street had strongly recommended what little he seems to have seen in France in 1850 (see above p. 40); Scott drew attention to French features when he discussed the cathedral of Genoa; in his chapel at Exeter College, begun in 1856,[9] he took certain elements from the Sainte-Chapelle, but generally he was interested in mixing 'styles' so he never spoke very strongly in favour of French Gothic alone. The most detailed book on French medieval architecture was of course Petit's *Architectural Studies in France* of 1854, which, however, only dealt with Romanesque churches in south-western France. Yet his emphasis on simple, rough massiveness and the omission of constructional colour must have helped to turn some people's eyes away from Italy.

The Île de France, Picardy and Champagne became the most relevant areas for English architecture in the years which followed, partly because architects in England were taking a greater interest in sculpture. Not only Burges but also Philip Webb and William Morris made enthusiastic journeys to Amiens and other places. Burges published many articles on church-fittings and iconography; Street, as usual, gave accounts of his journeys. Also the competition for the cathedral at Lille in 1855–6 must have incited the study of French Gothic architecture. Norman Shaw's *Architectural Sketches from the Continent* of 1858 included illustrations of French buildings. In 1861 and 1862 two large comprehensive English publications on French

Gothic architecture appeared: R. J. Johnson's *Specimens of Early French Architecture* (1861–4) and W. E. Nesfield's *Specimens of Medieval Architecture* (1862). They both specialized in buildings from the Île de France and Champagne around 1200; they both preferred the simpler buildings, the smaller churches or the simpler parts of the cathedrals. Johnson included only a little sculpture, whereas Nesfield provided many sketches of capitals in a rather Burges-like manner. In 1865 Robert Edis provided a long series of similar illustrations for the *Building News*. But in the same year, Street published *Some Account of Gothic Architecture in Spain,* and the interest of architects was again directed towards other areas, Spain, Germany and back to England.

Another important general trend which must be mentioned here was the growing distaste for constructional polychromy. In 1858 several voices protested against too much use of it. This was partly because the scraping of old church walls in order to reveal the surfaces of the material very often meant the destruction of remains of old wall paintings. T. Gambier Parry of Highnam in Gloucestershire (whose important collection of Italian 'Primitives' has recently been acquired by the Courtauld Galleries) wrote a long series of articles entitled 'Whitewash and Yellow Dab' from 1858 onward.[10] Another reason for the reaction against structural colour was that it was 'wanting in repose'.[11] Although by no means given up entirely, it was seldom now discussed in Ecclesiologist circles. In 1864 Burges denounced it: 'No-one is satisfied until the building presents a most piebald appearance.'[12]

William Burges

Burges is by far the most important figure in this context. His activities are, however, much more complex than those of Street or Butterfield. Burges was deeply involved in many crafts besides architecture, and was also widely conversant with mythology and romance. In this many-sidedness he must be compared with Pugin and Morris and, to a lesser degree, with Viollet-le-Duc. But Pugin and Viollet-le-Duc, as well as Ecclesiologists like Butterfield and Street, who designed a great deal besides buildings, held some orthodox ideas of constructional morality which they thought applicable to all crafts. Morris, on the other hand, was more literary-minded until the seventies, when he became more interested in the essential nature of each individual craft. Burges, closer to Ruskin's earlier outlook on art, stood in the middle, combining in his sumptuous buildings and fittings overall style and 'disegno', the different crafts concerned with various materials, and romantic subject matter. Here we look at his architecture briefly, and refer to his other activities later in this chapter.

There is no full-length biography of Burges but a number of articles by Charles Handley-Read provide a great deal of information and criticism.[13] Little is known about his beginnings as an architect and archaeologist. Before 1850 he spent some years in architects' offices, first in that of Edward Blore, who specialized in country houses, then in that of Matthew Digby Wyatt, who was conversant with many aspects of decorative design. In the early fifties Burges travelled on the continent, and in 1853 helped Henry Clutton with illustrations for the latter's book, *Remarks with illustrations of the Domestic Architecture of France,* a series of picturesque views of mostly minor late-medieval French secular architecture. In 1855 Burges began to publish articles and lectures on various crafts and iconographical problems; in 1855–6 he designed, with Clutton, the prize-winning entry in the Lille Cathedral competition. It seems difficult to determine how much interchange there was between Burges and Clutton: the design for Lille, however, seems largely by Burges.[14]

Burges only occasionally touched on architecture proper in his writings. His ideas about it are clearest in his architectural drawings. He despised perspectives and kept to a linear pattern without shading, modelled on those of the thirteenth century, especially Villard de Honnecourt, whose sketchbook in an edition prepared by Lassus was brought out in England in 1859.[15] Burges, who had studied the original himself, commented: 'the manipulation of the line is curiously in unison with the stern severe local character of the thirteenth century architecture of Flanders and Picardy.'[16]

In the following year he gave an illustrated lecture on architectural drawing in which he repeated his views.[17] In a later lecture, in 1864, he went into more detail on architecture, pleading for simple massing, balance in the general composition, bold unchamfered corners and especially continuity of horizontals:

> . . . to get the same strings running uninterruptedly through.
> The eye always requires a line, either real or imaginary,
> to mark the springing [of the arches]; put this line a little
> below, and it does not much matter, as in the case of the
> best French examples, where the arch is always slightly
> stilted to allow for the portion taken off by the projection
> of the abacus.

That is, seen from below, the uppermost member of a capital should not hide the springing of the arch.[18] He emphasized that he preferred French architecture, 'the sterner French type, such as Chartres and Laon',[19] and that he strongly disliked Early English which 'was supposed to survive more starvation than any other' (he meant, of course, the meagre 'lancet-style' of the 1840s).[20]

Burges' Lille design of 1855 [Plates 83–4] rather seems to adhere to the 'First Pointed' of the late forties, such as Scott's more elaborate

117

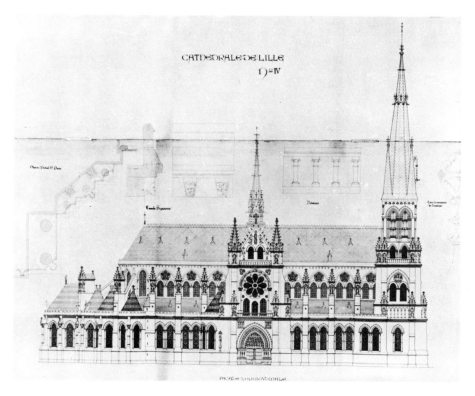

CATHEDRALE DE LILLE
I)ᵉ IV

83–84 W. Burges, designs for Lille Cathedral, 1855 (Courtesy Archives Diocésaines, Lille, Charles Handley-Read).

Before William Burges joined the movement with his spectacular success in the Lille competition (together with Henry Clutton) he was hardly known. Burges shows more severity of form than any of the other architects. What is the origin of this trend, soon to be labelled 'Early French' or 'masculine'? Burges was familiar with all aspects of the arts, historical, contemporary, technical, literary. He had a keen interest in the 'Primitives' and medieval manuscripts which he was obviously taught to see by the Pre-Raphaelites as well as German Romantic illustrations. It seems probable that his 'primitivism' in architecture can be related to these modes of representation. Burges also knew Villard de Honnecourt's thirteenth-century model book on north French architecture, which for him showed the right way of representing architecture. At least 'the stern severe local character' of French Gothic around 1200 was 'in unison with the manipulation of the line' in that book. Burges never resorted to the usual way of representing his buildings in pictorial perspectives (at least in his own drawings) – something that Street understood so well. In the event, Burges did not build Lille Cathedral, but the design was entrusted to the local architect Leroy, with some of Burges' features; it is still unfinished today.

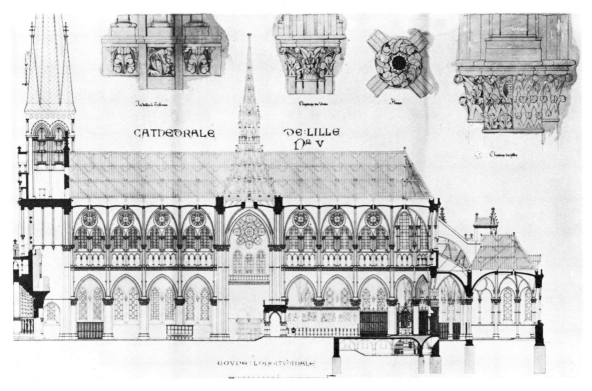

CATPEORALE   DE:LILLE
Nº V

COVPE:LONGITVDINALE

versions of that style (to which we shall refer), but enriched with French late twelfth- and early thirteenth-century features. The *Ecclesiologist* criticized the 'ungainly and undeveloped forms where some clearer adumbration of the beauties of the more advanced Pointed style would have been . . . expected'.[21] Yet Burges' 'primitivism' did not mean an adherence to Petit's geometrical forms. In fact, the constructive system seems as accomplished as one would expect from a Gothic cathedral of about 1200. The numerous supports of the stone vaulting are clearly emphasized with their series of shafts and pillars. A recurrent feature of the exterior is the canopied covering for statues where both horizontals and verticals are clearly accentuated – an element perhaps influenced by Viollet-le-Duc. Yet the design shows some familiar High Victorian characteristics: especially its emphasis on the horizontal; its 'low and heavy appearance' being not so much the result of proportions, which hardly differ from Lassus' design – but of the priority given to horizontal lines. Equally High Victorian seems the character of the flat plate tracery in the clerestory and the continuity of wall surface in many parts of the design. Examination of the fittings – the most admired part of the whole design – bears out the character of the architecture. They are exceedingly heavy; note for instance the font, where, perhaps for the first time in High Victorian design, stumpy columns appear with the shaft measuring little more in height than in diameter.

In the Constantinople design,[22] [frontispiece and Plate 85] Burges

85 W. Burges, competition design for Crimean Memorial church, Constantinople, 1856–7 (from the *Building News*, 1857, 356). Cf. frontispiece.
Burges' plan differs radically from Ecclesiological practice for medium-sized churches: he adopts a reduced cathedral plan with a tall spacious nave accompanied by very subsidiary aisles, separated by a very narrow arcade. There is also a prominent clerestory and a regular crossing. 'Constructional polychromy', however, is the exception rather than the rule in Burges' work.

again chose a cathedral system, though somewhat reduced and with less emphasis on the horizontal. He added some constructional colour – while simplifying his details: 'colour in a building or moulding, not both', as Burges himself put it. There were no groups of shafts in the interior; the crossing piers were elongated box-like shapes with only the indication of a shaft at the corners. Even the soffits of the crossing-arches were broad, flattened bands. The buttresses were no longer battered but treated like pilaster-strips. The crowning turrets, treated like steep-canopied groups of columns gave the impression of heavy little shrines. The contrast between broad, coloured wall surface and the small shafts was most striking at the west front. In 1858 Burges designed a reduced and even more sturdy version of the project [Plate 86] but his designs were never used.

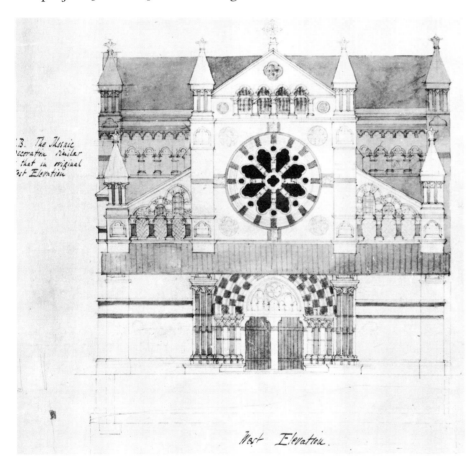

86 W. Burges, second design for Constantinople, 1858 (Courtesy RIBA Drawings Collection).
Burges' personal manner is easily to be recognized in this reduced version of the Constantinople design: symmetry, continuity of horizontality, especially in the arcades, rose windows, small, stumpy shafts.

121

New tendencies in the late fifties and sixties

The Constantinople project was Burges' last major venture in constructional colour. The next years were devoted more to art-historical research than to designing buildings. But the project for Brisbane Cathedral, probably dating from 1859 [Plate 87] and also unexecuted, carried his ideas further. The exterior was to be very plain, the clerestory windows were plate-traceried roses; inside, he accentuated the contrasts of wall areas, vertical shafts and horizontal stringcourses. At Waltham Abbey, which Burges restored from 1859 onwards,[23] the east wall contained short shafts with heavy shaft-rings and wide-branching capitals, together with rich sculpture. At last, from 1863 onwards, Burges was allowed to carry out one of his cathedral designs at Cork, St Finn Bar's Anglican Cathedral [Plates 88–9].[24] In plan, the building is very similar to the Constantinople

87 W. Burges, design for Brisbane Cathedral, 1859 (from the *Building News*, 1860, 991).

*New tendencies
in the late
fifties and sixties*

88 W. Burges, Cork, St Finn Bar Anglican Cathedral, begun 1862–4 (from
R. P. Pullan, *The Architectural Designs of William Burges,* 1883, 10).
The only major church Burges was able to execute. It is typically High
Victorian in combining splendour with simple, massive features. The
fittings, all designed by Burges, are extremely rich and varied.

123

*New tendencies
in the late
fifties and sixties*

design – a short nave, transepts, and apse with semicircular ambulatory. It has a large crossing tower and two west towers. On the whole, the exterior is rather more elaborate than the earlier designs in its profiles and vertical accents, although still, like the Brisbane design, severe in contour. The Cork interior is striking with its extremely vertical proportions and the insistence on square sections, again and again interrupted by the equally stern insistence on carrying through the horizontal divisions.

For the small brick church at Fleet (1860), Burges also adopted a very flat relief and square sections. Another small church by him at Lowfield Heath of 1867,[25] is simple and massive in its arrangement and elaborate in its sculptural enrichments. Cardiff Castle, begun in 1865,[26] one of his largest works, summed up his military Romanticism

89 W. Burges,
Cork Cathedral,
1862, interior
(Courtesy Charles
Handley-Read).

in its exterior as well as in its interior [Plate 120]. During this time, Burges tried out his ideas about simple massiveness in two secular buildings, St Anne's Court model lodgings and a warehouse in Upper Thames Street, which are discussed below, as is his design for the Law Courts [Plate 143].

On the whole, Burges remained faithful to the characteristics described here. He continued his severity and ornate 'Gothic' into the seventies when most other architects took to the less dogmatic 'Queen Anne Revival'.

Godwin, Nesfield and Shaw

For other architects such as Nesfield and Shaw, High Victorian Gothic of the sixties meant only the beginning of their careers. Edward William Godwin is also better known for his work for Whistler and Oscar Wilde in the late seventies and eighties, for his manifold connections with the art world and the 'aesthetes'. However, his 'Gothic' beginnings and early works up to the seventies are equally outstanding. Godwin read Ruskin in the later fifties, and though working at first in Bristol, he became friendly with most of the protagonists of the movement. It is said that he was most impressed when he first met Burges in 1858, and saw his design for the Gloucester Fountain,[27] and in the early sixties his own pronouncements sounded identical to those of Burges.

Godwin's first major work was Northampton Town Hall [Plate 90] of 1861. In its general design it follows the pattern which Scott had initiated for official buildings with his Hamburg Town Hall design in 1854:[28] two storeys of Gothic arcades and a central tower. The Town Hall at Congleton (Cheshire) [Plate 91] followed three years afterwards.[29] The design had to be simpler than that at Northampton for this smaller community. A tendency towards massiveness is expressed by the way in which the ground floor arcade appears to be cut into the solid masonry, and there are fewer of the small, repetitive decorative features. The machicolation of the tower was not in the manner of Scott's rich elaboration but of Burges' plain style. In the interior of both town halls we find the same simplicity: bare masonry and plain woodwork prevail.

Perhaps the most striking example of Godwin's tendency towards solidity and repose is the block of two 'Gothic Cottages' at Northampton [Plate 92].[30] They appear to be entirely symmetrical, wall openings are few and small, and the emphasis is on the horizontal – for example, the imposts of the arches are continued by stringcourses, perhaps a direct hint from Burges. Later, in 1870–1, he devised in his design for Bristol Assize Courts[31] a short, symmetrical street front with very rich decorations. However, the back shows a much freer treatment in composition and again more emphasis on heavy walls

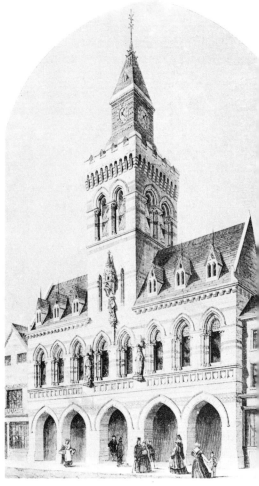

90 (above left) E. W. Godwin, Northampton Town Hall, 1861 (from the *Building News*, 1861, 893).
Godwin, famous for his contributions to the Aesthetic Movement in later years, began his career under the influence of Burges and Scott.

91 (above right) E. W. Godwin, Congleton, Cheshire, Town Hall, 1854 (from the *Builder*, 1864, 529).
A simpler design for a smaller town.

92 (opposite above) E. W. Godwin, 'Gothic Cottages', Northampton, St Martin's Villas, 43–4 Billing Road, 1865 (from the *Building News*, 21 July 1865).
An extraordinarily formal design for this informal type of building.

*New tendencies
in the late
fifties and sixties*

with low-arched openings. The whole design, especially the tower
with its machicolations, is again very much reminiscent of Burges –
one only needs to compare it with Cardiff Castle which Burges was
rebuilding at that time. Godwin's designs for Dromore Castle
(Limerick) in 1867[32] [Plate 93] are more unified. There is the same kind
of bare wall throughout, basement batter, simply shaped battlements,
and simple geometrical tracery mostly flush with the wall. In his
Gothic Revival (1872) Eastlake comments: 'This tendency to shun the
minutiae of decorative details, to aim at sturdy masses of unbroken
wall space, and artistic proportion of parts is perhaps the main secret
of Mr. Godwin's artistic power.'[33] Later, in an article on the 'Queen
Anne style', Godwin himself speaks in similar terms about the 'careful
adjustment of solids and voids'[34] which, as he says, has nothing to do
with historic periods of decorative detail applied to the façade. But
Godwin does not mean this in the neo-classical sense that symmetry
is enough to achieve beauty: his 'solids and voids' are arranged in
a free, asymmetrical way, no two arrangements alike. Godwin's
starting point is not a system of symmetry and proportion, but a given
area of smooth masonry surface and its interruption by recesses. In
1879 he even provided an example of this approach in a classical
design for the Brompton Oratory.[35] In some measure these principles
seem to be behind Godwin's special kind of interior domestic design
which he evolved in the later sixties, briefly discussed in the Epilogue.

William Eden Nesfield[36] can be called a gentleman-architect
of country houses. His father, William Andrews Nesfield, was
a famous landscape gardener and watercolourist. Very little is known
about the son's life since he refused to have his designs published

127

New tendencies
in the late
fifties and sixties

93 E. W. Godwin, Dromore Castle, Limerick, 1867 (from the *Building News*, 1 Nov. 1867).
There is a delight in military features, obviously deriving from the earlier 'castellated' mode; on the other hand the layout is more simple.

94 W. E. Nesfield, Combe Abbey, War., East Wing, 1864 (Courtesy Victoria & Albert Museum).

Nesfield who is, like Godwin, better known for his contributions to the Queen Anne Revival, specialized in country houses from the beginning of his career. He combined Burges' and Street's severity with the convenience of the large Tudor-type window.

in the architectural journals. In his early years he published *Specimens of Medieval Architecture* (1862) which has already been mentioned. He tried to combine Burges' strictness of contour with picturesque sketching. His two great early houses, an addition to Combe Abbey (War.) [Plate 94] and Cloverley Hall (Salop),[37] have been for the most part demolished. Both had a certain Gothic heaviness, although he used very large transomed windows. From the mid-sixties, Nesfield moved away from High Victorian 'Gothic' towards a new, free interpretation of the classical manner.

The contribution of Richard Norman Shaw[38] was much greater. In 1858, the year in which he published his *Architectural Sketches from the Continent*, he succeeded Philip Webb as chief assistant in Street's office and remained there until 1862. There are many open questions in his career as well. From 1862 to 1868 he shared an office with Nesfield, and a competition entry for the Manchester Assize Courts had already been sent in by 'Shaw and Nesfield' in 1859. No pictorial evidence of this design is known, and a description in the *Building News* gives little idea:[39] apparently there was quite a strong contrast between 'plain and solid' parts and highly ornate ones; and it had some high arches on short thick columns.

Apart from a couple of pieces of furniture which Shaw designed in the Webb-Burges manner in the early sixties, the first architectural designs date from 1864. Fortunately the drawings for Shaw's Bradford Exchange project have been preserved [Plates 95–6].[40] In one way this design is strikingly different from the manner of Burges and Godwin, as it is wildly asymmetrical in nearly all its parts. For the roughly triangular site Shaw pushed the tower into one corner.

129

New tendencies
in the late
fifties and sixties

95–96 R. N. Shaw, unexecuted design for Bradford Exchange, 1864
(Courtesy RIBA Drawings Collection).
Shaw, a pupil of Street and influenced by Burges, made a few very
personal contributions to High Victorian architecture. His Bradford
design is unsurpassed in the irregularity of its elevations, conditioned by
the irregularities of the site and the varying size of the rooms. Yet, at the
same time, the treatment of details and masonry shows an imposing
heaviness, especially the Burges-like wide arches on low supports.

*New tendencies
in the late
fifties and sixties*

Cross Section on line N - O.

Longitudinal section on line P-Q

However, the most striking irregularities occur in the elevation – one hesitates to use such a word. The roofline is relatively quiet as is the main division of the storeys, but the walls are broken up by an astounding variety of doors and windows: varying in size, in position, and in shape, rectangular windows alternating with semicircular or pointed ones. On the Market Street side the main hall 'breaks through' with large windows. Yet the actual wall surface level varies little and, although it is so much broken up by openings, conveys a very strong feeling of heaviness. This is achieved by the typically High Victorian way of making the frames of the openings part of the wall. Many of the arches are 'top-heavy' to an extreme degree, in some cases three times as high as their vertical supports. Inside, the main hall's transverse arches, high and pointed, rest on a series of low, massive spurs of wall at right-angles to the long axis of the room. Later, Shaw's great hall at Adcote (Salop) in the seventies is faintly reminiscent of these arches, without the spur walls. It is regrettable that Shaw's

131

*New tendencies
in the late
fifties and sixties*

Bradford Exchange design was not executed, although Lockwood and Mawson's pile in Scott's manner certainly looks effective.

Less unusual in nature is Shaw's church at Bingley (Yorks.) of 1864 [Plate 97].[41] In plan, nave, aisles and chancel it does not differ from what the Ecclesiologists had been doing since the fifties. A feeling of spaciousness is given by the open roof and the width of the arcades. The walls of local stone are left uncovered in the interior as well and there is no mortar. The exterior is less usual in that Shaw reverts to the very plain 'lancet style' of the forties. The upper part of the very high tower that rises between nave and chancel was redesigned by Shaw in 1869 to improve on his earlier stumpy proposal not unlike his design for the Bradford Exchange tower. The 1869 version is

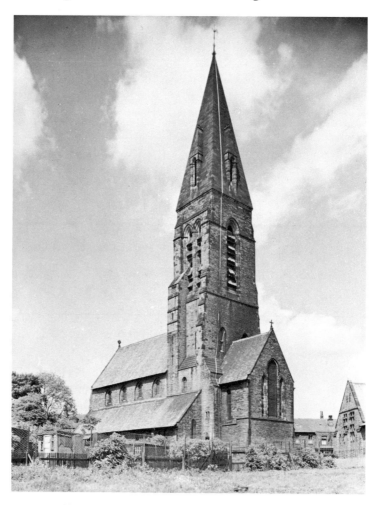

97 R. N. Shaw, Bingley, Yorks., church, 1864, tower, 1869 (Courtesy National Monuments Record).
In its arrangement strongly reminiscent of Butterfield's St Matthias, Stoke Newington (see Plate 34), the spire with its free, not geometrical contour is more reminiscent of Street.

superb: it wholly dominates the church and seems to combine several hints from Butterfield. Its oblong shape and relationship to nave and chancel remind one of St Matthias, Stoke Newington, and the combination of buttresses and stair towers and the tapering off of the latter are reminiscent of Butterfield's work in the later fifties.

At about the same time Shaw started to build the English Church at Lyon[42] [Plate 98] – perhaps one of the most interesting of the great number of Anglican churches abroad, although Street's later churches in Rome are the most famous. Shaw had to cope with a very small site enclosed on three sides, so he ingeniously combined the gable of the short, high nave with a saddleback bell turret, and, correspondingly, the aisle with a porch. Yet at this very time he was giving up

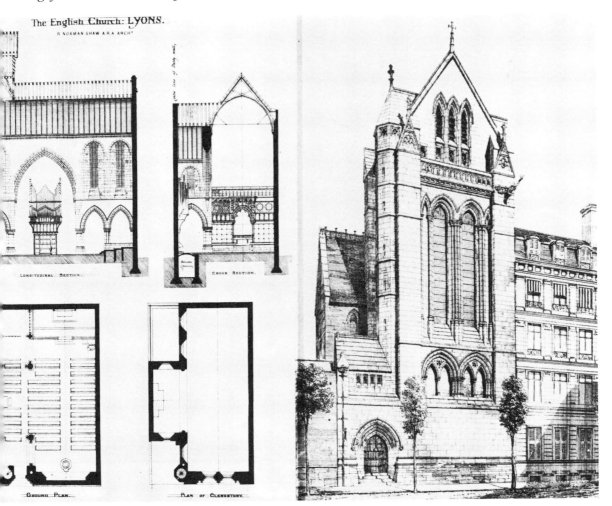

98 R. N. Shaw, Lyon, English church, c. 1869 (from the *Building News*, 1873, I, 42).
A clever piece of planning in Gothic, at a time when he had given up this style for all other types of buildings.

133

*New tendencies
in the late
fifties and sixties*

this manner for secular buildings – the Bradford Exchange had already shown signs of this – and turned to something then called 'Old English', briefly to be discussed in the last chapter.

Street and others in the 1860s

Street's contributions to the themes discussed here are not very great. In 1858 and 1859 he reported on a short tour to northern France, 'certainly the richest field for the study of our art in Europe'.[43] His predilections become very clear in comments like the following about Rheims Cathedral, typical of the judgments made under the influence of the aesthetic of the sublime: 'It lacks the stern character of Chartres, there is enrichment of every inch of detail.'[44]

During the next years he made extensive journeys to Spain and in 1865 produced *Some Account of the Architecture in Spain*. The more Street tried to satisfy his hunger for architectural history, the more he believed in 'eclecticism'; his work never achieved the 'stern' character of that of Burges or Godwin.

Of Street's churches of this period, All Saints at Clifton [Plate 99],[45] destroyed in the last war, was perhaps the most remarkable, at least in this context. The interior was illustrated in very effective perspective in the *Building News,* very much the *avant-garde* organ of these years. The nave was now much more dominating, the chancel smaller, leaving much of the eastern nave wall blank, and the aisles reduced to passages covered with transverse pointed tunnel vaults, supported towards the nave by very stout pillars that were alternately round and octagonal, while the roof was a smoothly boarded barrel. St John's at Torquay (1868)[46] and St Saviour's at Eastbourne (1865)[47] appear more conventional, save the east end of the nave of the latter church which ends in two canted walls forming an intermediate funnel space between the nave and the narrower chancel. One of Street's sturdiest designs was for the Crimean Memorial church actually built in Constantinople, begun in 1864, a much scaled-down version of his earlier second-prize design.[48] In 1865 a large complex was started at East Grinstead, St Margaret's Convent,[49] established earlier by John Mason Neale, one of the founders of the Ecclesiological Society. Here, as in the Law Courts Competition as well as in his church St Mary Magdalene, Paddington, begun in 1867,[50] as we shall see, Street turned to something more quiet, less grandiose in arrangement and surface treatment.

Among other architects, John Seddon took a somewhat different line in his vast Castle Hotel at Aberystwyth, which shortly afterwards became the University College of Wales [Plate 100].[51] Its great number of high turrets with conical roofs are obviously influenced by French Renaissance châteaux. John Francis Bentley, who became famous

New tendencies
in the late
fifties and sixties

99 G. E. Street, Clifton, All Saints, 1864, destroyed (from the *Building News*, 4 Aug. 1865).
Cf. Street's churches from the late fifties (Plates 70–75).

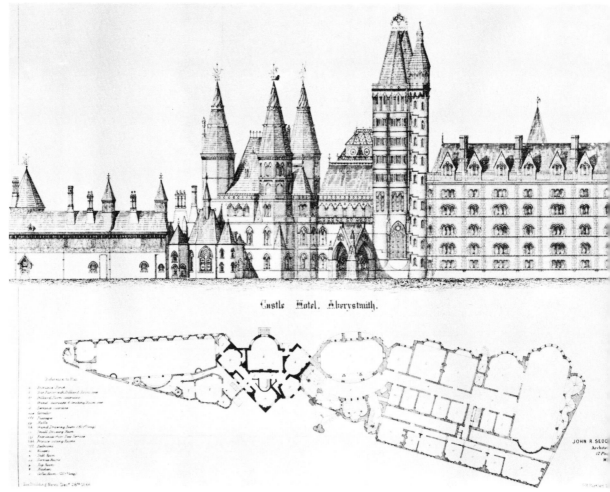

Castle Hotel, Aberystwith.

JOHN R SEDD
Archite
12 Pa
W

100 J. P. Seddon, Aberystwyth, Castle Hotel, now University College (from the *Building News*, 26 Dec. 1866).
One of the largest hotels of its time (it cost c. £100,000 to build) but was sold to University College before it was finished; it is hardly conceivable that its picturesque and turreted expression was considered suitable for its new purpose.

much later with his Westminster Cathedral, designed the remarkable Baptistry Chapel to St Francis of Assisi at Notting Hill in 1860,[52] with typical short shafts, wide capitals, and shaft rings. An early example of 'Early French' is E. R. Robson's St Cuthbert at Durham of 1858:[53] the south aisle covered by the low-sweeping roof of the nave, the broad apse at the east end, slender lancet windows and the saddleback roof of the tower.

Pearson, apart from his big church at St Peter's, Vauxhall, which is described in a different context below, produced Appleton-le-Moors (Yorks.) in 1864,[54] [Plates 101–2] a very typical example of the

101 J. L. Pearson, Appleton-le-Moors, Yorks., church, 1864 (Courtesy Gordon Barnes).

Another very typical example of 'primitivism'. It is not, however, the cottage vernacular of the forties (cf. Plates 4, 5), but a vernacular based on closer archaeological investigation into the simple churches of north France which was soon to lead on to another archaeological vernacular, 'Old English'. How much the clumsiness of the west front is the result of deliberation is shown by the fact that the interior is very elegantly proportioned.

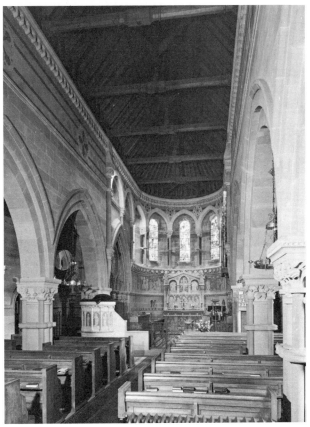

102 J. L. Pearson, Appleton-le-Moors, church interior (Courtesy Gordon Barnes).

*New tendencies
in the late
fifties and sixties*

'Early French' tendency of the early sixties. Aisle and nave are under one roof, making the church look very low and massive from outside, especially from the west. Buttresses are carried up the west wall and terminate just below the gable. The treatment of details is rather bleak, and even the rose window looks heavy. Later, in 1865, Pearson built a similar church at Freeland (Oxon.),[55] with broad low interior and a vaulted chancel. Both chancel interiors are richly fitted with paintings and sculpture. The west front of Appleton is perhaps the most telling example, apart from Nesfield's and Johnson's illustrations, of what the architects were looking for in the Île de France: the small village church of the early thirteenth century, where the elements of Gothic architecture were clumsily reduced to the barest essentials. Although in many ways similar to the rough 'rural' church propagated in the 1840s, or the cottages of the 1850s – obviously the sublime is a common denominator – the new 'rural' tendency differs in other respects: it was not just meant to be 'primitive' but primitivism is now linked with a historical 'style', a distinct foreign style, and thus a matter of serious research; the 'Early French' mode seems to be one of the signs of a more 'stylistic' vernacular revival in architecture, which began in the field of domestic architecture at about the same time.

Lastly, Bodley must again be mentioned. His St Michael's and All Angels at Brighton, designed in 1858, showed 'Early French' features remarkably early, especially the squat nave columns with their simplified leaf decoration. These tendencies were continued in his large spacious church, St Martin's on the Hill at Scarborough, in 1861.[56] Most of the windows are either simple lancets or 'plate' with circular holes in it. Characteristic for Bodley is the saddleback roof of the tower. The small church at Selsley (Glos.) [Plate 103],[57] of the same years, was very similar. His early design for All Saints, Cambridge [Plate 104], of 1861 shows a very massive tower, with a broad and massive spire continuing the buttresses, underneath a vast roof covering nave, chancel and aisles, and a very broad sloping base.

Yet, what is more interesting about Bodley's work at this time is that he departed radically from this manner and adopted English motifs of the fourteenth century. All Saints at Cambridge, as he built it from 1863 [Plate 105],[58] has a nave and an aisle of nearly the same height, a small chancel, and a short battlemented tower rising between nave and chancel, and carrying a long octagonal spire much narrower than its square support. The interior is entirely devoid of elements active at Scarborough: no feeling of a 'compact' space around a central axis. One might well assume that Bodley wanted to go back to the forties and early fifties, to Pugin's one-aisled churches, such as Ramsgate, or, closer to Cambridge, the Catholic church at Marlow (Bucks.) or even Scott's churches of the early fifties, such as Holy Trinity at Marlow. But during the years which followed Bodley does not seem to return to the extreme irregularity of All Saints. His church at Haywards Heath,[59] with its more regular plan and sharper contours, to some extent adheres to High Victorian modes. In his very rich church St John's, Tue Brook, Liverpool (1867)[60] Bodley is again more strictly 'English'; as at All Saints, Cambridge, an essential element here is the all-over stencilling, painting, and stained glass by Kempe and by Morris – Bodley was one of the first to employ Morris' firm.

'Town churches': Pearson and Brooks

Aspects of Ecclesiologist building types have been discussed in the first chapter in their functional traits as well as results of the aesthetic preconceptions of the forties. Little has been said so far about changes in planning. By the early sixties a change in the general arrangement of churches was imminent. In order to understand how this change came about, some features of the development in the fifties must be described again. As will be remembered, massiveness and simplification of the plan were the main lines of development.

103 G. F. Bodley, Selsley, Glos., church, 1862 (Courtesy Gordon Barnes).

104 (above left) G. F. Bodley, Cambridge, All Saints, design, 1861 (Courtesy Rev. H. Hard, Cambridge). Cf. Plate 105.

105 (above right) G. F. Bodley, Cambridge, All Saints, begun 1863 (Courtesy C. Middleton).
Quite unexpectedly Bodley changed his design into something closer to Pugin, closer to English fourteenth-century Gothic than anything else (cf. Plate 1). Only in certain elements, such as the large space of blank wall over the porch (and more clearly in the treatment of the south aisle on the other side) the manner of the late fifties becomes apparent. Bodley, with slight variations, continued this manner, becoming more consistently 'English' in the late sixties. It has to be seen in the context of the development of a vernacular. As a writer in the *Ecclesiologist* put it in 1864, English Gothic is 'homely and sweet', in contrast to the grandeur of French Gothic.

The demand for low and massive churches was the first reaction against Pugin's complicated planning. Yet after Benjamin Webb had recommended a balance of proportions in 1845, the demand for simple interiors became frequent. The demand for interior height, too, can be regarded as a demand for clearer space. Another method of concentrating space was to put a crossing-tower on the eastern parts of the church. At first, this had more obvious effect on the exterior (Butterfield, Stoke Newington). Also there was a tendency to reduce the plan as much as possible to a plain parallelogram – Burges' second proposal for Constantinople reduced the transept so that it did not project beyond the aisles – with the proportions approaching a square. He also generally reduced aisles to very small annexes to the nave. Bodley and Seddon proposed an unusual solution for Constantinople: aisles without windows.

The simplification of plan can be found in many churches. Scott's big church, All Souls, Haley Hill, Halifax,[61] begun in 1856, still shows the familiar arrangement with transept and chancel of different heights, and the tower placed at the side of the west front. But in St Matthias at Richmond (Surrey), 1857–62,[62] a church of about the same size, he dispensed with a transept and terminated the chancel with a semicircular apse. Earlier, in 1852–5, he had already built a church with a crossing tower, and with transepts and chancel of equal height, at West Derby (Liverpool). Here he was probably influenced by St George at Doncaster, a Gothic church he rebuilt at that time and his earlier Nikolaikirche in Hamburg, begun in 1844.[63] Many smaller churches by Scott of the later fifties show a big central tower terminated by a high octagon, such as Ranmore (Surrey)[64] and Leafield (Oxon.).[65] A special case is the chapel of Exeter College, Oxford,[66] where the simplicity of the plan was conditioned by the collegiate type. Street's demand (in his Town Church article) that the roofline should continue uninterruptedly over nave and chancel was only occasionally followed in smaller churches before 1860, least of all by Street himself. Another element of spatial unification was the tendency for apsidal terminations of the chancel. Here Scott started remarkably early, with Bradfield (Berks.)[67] of 1848 and Camden Church, Camberwell, of 1854 [Plate 127].[68] The designs for the Constantinople Competition in 1856–7 hardly made use of the apse; it became a common feature only in about 1858–9 (Street, Firsby). Probably the most important element for the development of interior space was the roof, with room for great variety. Two tendencies prevailed at the end of the fifties: to get rid of heavy beams altogether and to use light and smooth boards and to use stone-vaulting for the richer parts of the churches, especially chancels (Street, 1859, St James the Less, London, but cf. Scott at Bradfield, 1848). Only a few of the proposals for Constantinople planned stone vaulting (Burges, Street, White, and R. P. Pullan).

141

*New tendencies
in the late
fifties and sixties*

All this is exactly what A. J. Beresford-Hope, the president of the Ecclesiological Society, demanded in a book entitled *The English Cathedral of the Nineteenth Century* in 1861. The book contains much else (especially discussions of 'style', in which Beresford-Hope sides with Scott's 'eclecticism'), but its main point is a formal one: advocacy for the large, spatially unified church. He does not use these very words, but he means it when he speaks of 'breadth', i.e. general spaciousness, 'length', and 'height' when he describes individual features: the nave should be broad, aisles narrow; whereby he is very careful not to appear to advocate the state of affairs of twenty years earlier, when 'to build narrowly' meant 'to build meanly'. Finally he said that aisles could be omitted altogether, the nave should have a tall clerestory, it should be terminated by an apse, and the best covering for the nave was stone vaulting.[69]

Beresford-Hope tried to fortify his architectural reasons with religious and liturgical ones. In contrast to the liturgical debates of the forties, a concern with liturgy was at a low ebb in the fifties. This is perhaps best shown in the conditions laid down for the Constantinople Competition, prescribing considerations for 'style', climate and material but leaving open the type of church. So everybody took the type that appeared to suit his own aesthetic preferences: Burges a small cathedral, Bodley a simple parish church, Street a large chapel, Slater a 'collegiate church', White a complicated large parish church, and so on. Beresford-Hope's religious argument in his book centred around the evangelization of the populations in large towns. He thought that the parochial system was not enough, but whether it was an argument of Church policy or of architectural aesthetics (in his introduction he claims his book to be an 'architectural' one) that conditioned his view of how such a church should look, remains a question. 'The religious institution which will undoubtedly grow out of rational and business-like endeavours to evangelize large populations, whether it is called so or not, will virtually be a cathedral, and it had therefore best be moulded openly and honestly into a cathedral shape . . .'[70]

Pearson's church, St Peter's, Vauxhall, designed in 1860 [Plates 106–7],[71] seems to have been the first church to embody all these concepts. It consists of a very large and high nave, narrow aisles and an apse which is carried up to the full height of the nave. There is a slight division between chancel and nave apparent in the lower parts of the interior; the roof carries through with little interruption. The church is vaulted throughout, with stone ribs and brick infilling; on the other hand, one cannot speak of a vaulting system of a developed, rational Gothic type. The supports of the arcade are cylindrical columns, 'Early French' of course, which carry a blank wall with the main vaulting shafts only starting at the level of a stringcourse above. Apart from these new elements – which also include the 'convention-

*New tendencies
in the late
fifties and sixties*

106 J. L. Pearson,
Vauxhall, London,
St Peter's, east
end, designed
1860, and school,
built 1860.

alized' sculpture of the capitals – the church continues the trends discussed in Chapters 4 and 5. Except for vaulting ribs, tracery and some minor dressings, it is entirely of brick, with brickwork's characteristic continuous surfaces, simple contours and general impression of heaviness. This is especially true of the east end; the semicircular apse which, as with Teulon's and Street's small churches earlier, grows out of the rectangular part of the chancel without any division and is carried up to the triforium again without any subdivision, is perhaps the most impressive piece of High Victorian massiveness. Inside, the blank walls at triforium level in the nave were meant to carry mural paintings, but only those in the chancel were executed. It was not before the late sixties that Pearson was commissioned to build churches of this size again, when he proposed slightly different solutions, to be discussed below.

The greatest exponent of this architecture of the sixties was, without doubt, James Brooks. Little is known about him before he started the first of a long series of churches in and around London, St Michael's, Shoreditch.[72] It has some features in common with St Peter's, Vauxhall: a small tower attached to the west end and a

143

107 J. L. Pearson, Vauxhall, St Peter's, interior (Courtesy National Monuments Record).

The 'town church' was the most important issue in the Ecclesiological Society in the early sixties. It was not only an administrative problem, but first and foremost a formal one: unified space as against the earlier rambling plan of the Eccesiologists (cf. Plate 73). St Peter's, Vauxhall, was greeted as the first completely satisfactory solution: hardly any division between nave and chancel, great height, small aisles (Burges' influence, cf. Plate 85), an apsidal east end and, very rarely used, stone (i.e. brick) vaulting throughout – the latter feature became a speciality of Pearson's larger churches later on.

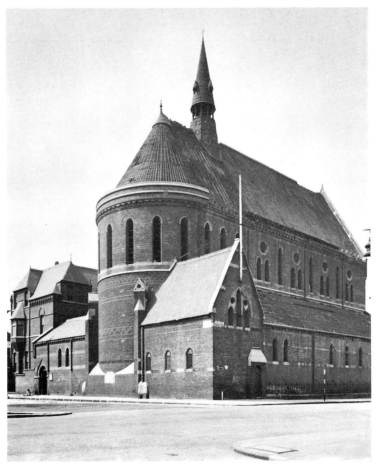

108 J. Brooks, London, Shoreditch, St Saviour's, Hoxton, 1864 (Courtesy National Monuments Record).

James Brooks, with Bodley and Pearson the third of the distinguished group of later Victorian church architects, began his career in the early sixties with a number of large town churches, some of them situated in the same relatively poor district of Shoreditch; they are all of brick, with simplified tracery and 'conventionalized' foliage, with a certain amount of painted and sculptural decoration.

narthex, but it does not yet continue the essential element of St Peter's, the continuity and simplicity of overall shape. This he approaches in his next church in the same poor district of London, St Saviour's, Hoxton, in 1864 [Plate 108].[73] Here the roof and walls of the exterior are carried through without interruption but the treatment of the interior and the clerestories differ. In St Andrew, Plaistow (Essex),[74] he squeezed a massive tower between nave and chancel. St Columba, Kingsland Road [Plate 109],[75] has a nearly regular crossing. Here the eastern parts are stone-vaulted. Like Butterfield in the fifties, Brooks gives many variations to his wooden roofs of the naves of these churches; in St Chad, Nichols Square, Haggerston [Plate 110],[76] several tiers of flat panelling approximate to barrel-vaults, their angular section contrasted with stilted arched braces. Brooks' church at Chislehurst (Kent) is similar, whereas at Christ Church, Clapton,[77] (not built) [Plate 111], nave and chancel were completely integrated and the only division was marked by small projections relating to the aisle, which continued round as an ambulatory, and the slightly raised floor. Otherwise the very open arcading on cylindrical shafts, a feature common to most of these churches, and

145

the clerestory with narrow repetitive windows, continue all around the east end. The carefully rounded wooden barrel-vault, a semicircle smoothly meeting the walls underneath, ends in a half-dome over the east end. Nearly all these churches were built of brick, with a decreasing amount of polychromy. Brooks continued this kind of design without much change into the 1880s.

A later example of the large, tall and bare brick church in a populated town district, St Bartholomew's at Brighton [Plate 112], was built by a local architect, Edmund Scott.[78] It is most impressive in its dimensions and proportions, but without Brooks' refined treatment of surface.

The discussion about 'town churches' went on. In 1864, at the twenty-fifth anniversary meeting of the Ecclesiological Society, Beresford-Hope[79] again recommended more consideration of that

109 J. Brooks, London, St Columba, Kingsland, 1867 (from the *Building News*, 28 Feb. 1873).

type. He now demanded width instead of length: one should think of centrally planned churches, 'magnificent in point of form, more convenient for preaching'. He even ventured to recommend galleries, as useful for coping with large numbers of people, a subject which had been anathema to the Society since its beginnings, and which even then nearly all the members of the discussion disliked. The concept of the centrally planned church was echoed to a certain extent by Burges ('we want . . . something like Angevine churches, with great thick walls, domed or vaulted') and Street ('domical churches . . . vast circular naves'). However, they seem to have had very little practical influence; one might perhaps cite such features as the east end of the nave of Street's church at Eastbourne, or later, in 1870, the domical termination of the nave of his St John the Divine at Kennington. Another recommendation of Beresford-Hope's might have been

110 (above left) J. Brooks, London, St Chad, Haggerston, 1868 (from the *Building News*, 9 Sept. 1870).

111 (above right) J. Brooks, design for London, Christ Church, Clapton, 1870 (from the *Building News*, 5 Aug. 1870).

112 Edmund Scott, Brighton, St Bartholomew, 1874 (from the *Builder*, 1874, 909).
Perhaps the most impressive of all 'town churches' by its size and proportions, although its poly-chromy must have been considered rather old fashioned at that time.

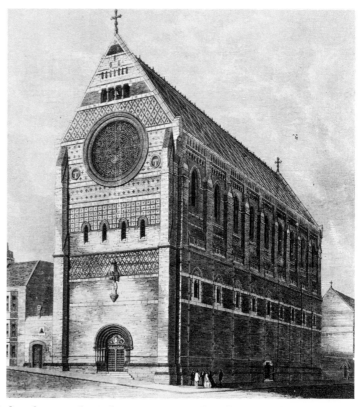

more influential: the Ecclesiologists were familiar with the first ecclesiastical works of the Dutch architect P. J. H. Cuypers; these were going up from the late fifties onwards. They praised them highly, and thought them better than anything else built on the continent at that time. Beresford-Hope actually praised the Posthoorn church at Amsterdam [Plate 113], built in 1860–3,[80] for the fact that it had two tiers of vaulted galleries. No example of a prominent church with a gallery can be found in England in these decades, yet Pearson – whose Vauxhall church is mentioned approvingly alongside Cuypers – introduced a sort of triforium in several of his large churches in the seventies, probably first in St Augustine's, Kilburn, perhaps his most famous church, begun in 1871 [Plate 114]. From then onwards, Pearson tended to vault all his larger churches; and he returned to a rational demonstration of the vaulting system as something related to the plan by shafts from ground level, consequently there was a much greater emphasis on continuity of the vertical. There was a general return to slender verticals, another example being St Augustine's, Pendlebury, near Manchester, by Bodley, also begun in 1870. Certainly the influence of Cuypers must not be overstressed; yet, if one looks back to St Peter's, Vauxhall, one realizes that continuity of wall surface, not of the vaulting system, was important there. By about 1870 this eminently High Victorian feeling for construction had definitely come to an end.

113 P. J. H. Cuypers, Amsterdam, 'Posthoorn Kerk' (O.L.Vr. Onbeflekt Ontvangen), 1860–3 (from *Het Werk van Dr P. J. H. Cuypers*, Amsterdam, 1917).

This church was recommended by Beresford-Hope in 1864 for its proportions, its vaulting and its galleries. It might well have been of some influence for Pearson's later church, St Augustine's, Kilburn (see Plate 114). For the Ecclesiologists Cuypers was by far the most important of all continental Gothicists. His background in the early fifties has not yet been clarified. He seems to have drawn from many sources, Germany (Cologne), Viollet-le-Duc and England.

114 J. L. Pearson, London, St Augustine's, Kilburn, 1871, interior (Courtesy Gordon Barnes).

Most of Pearson's later churches are large, spacious and stone- or brick-vaulted. But High Victorian massiveness and sturdiness has given way to slender and elegant forms which, as far as the vaulting is concerned, underline the verticality of the system, cf. Pearson's St Peter's, Vauxhall, from the early sixties, Plate 107.

*New tendencies
in the late
fifties and sixties*

Roman Catholic churches

It is here, for their share in the intensive search for new planning solutions within the High Victorian architectural movement, that we need to look at English Roman Catholic churches. Except for the works of Pugin, we have been talking only of Anglican church architecture. Although there had been a 'Catholic Revival', drawing from the same sources as the Oxford Movement, there was much less drive in the development of church building. By 1850 the influences of Pugin's earlier works had been absorbed and there was little difference between Roman Catholic architects and those of the Church of England, except those of the highest rank.[81] Many Catholic architects showed 'rogue' tendencies, including Pugin's son, Edward Welby Pugin.[82] There was a growing tendency to bring the altar nearer to the congregation, especially in large churches in working-class suburbs, where, in fact, most Roman Catholic churches tended to be. Joseph Hansom,[83] one of the most active Roman Catholic architects, hardly ever adopted the elder Pugin's maximum subdivision of space in churches. He rather continued a pre-Victorian wide, low space, such as in St Walburga at Preston, 1852.[84] Towards the end of the fifties Edward Pugin found a solution which was remarkably similar to that

115 E. W. Pugin, Liverpool, Vauxhall Road, Our Lady of Reconciliation, 1859.
Roman Catholics adhered to simpler spatial solutions out of liturgical reasons, but in this case the similarity to Pearson is also a result of economy; Pugin's son was usually much more ornate.

*New tendencies
in the late
fifties and sixties*

which the Ecclesiologists were trying at the same time: nave and chancel were united into a high and unified space, to which all other parts of the church were subordinated. His big church at Liverpool (Vauxhall Road), Our Lady of Reconciliation, built in 1859 [Plate 115],[85] actually preceded Pearson's St Peter's, Vauxhall, London. Yet the simplicity of its exterior is the result not of a desire for flat surfaces but of lack of funds. In the Cathedral of St Peter and St Paul at Cork[86] a similar arrangement can be seen, but with much exterior decoration with gables and pinnacles.

Probably the most able and widely active Roman Catholic architect of the later fifties and the next decade was George Goldie who had started in the firm of Weightman, Hadfield and Goldie, working chiefly in the north-east of England. St Peter at Scarborough, begun in 1856,[87] is remarkable in being rather short and fairly high, terminated by a polygonal apse. Goldie's two major churches in the sixties, St Wilfred's Cathedral at York[88] and Our Lady of Victories at Kensington[89] (Pro-Cathedral before Westminster was built, and destroyed in the last war) [Plate 116], followed the theme with more elaboration. E. W. Pugin was generally ornate,[90] whereas Hansom in the late sixties took to more unusual forms, at least in spatial arrangement of the east end. He was probably influenced by Street, if not by his churches then by his book on Spanish architecture (at Arundel, and Holy Name of Jesus, Manchester).[91] Henry Clutton must also be mentioned here, although he did not exclusively build for Roman Catholics and generally seemed to be much closer to the Ecclesiologists. His St Peter's, Leamington Spa,[92] has been cited as a typical example of spatial unification, but Clutton does not seem to have carried on with this theme. As another device of spatial openness, one may cite St Mary's at Woburn,[93] a hall-type church (the aisles of the same height as the nave) and vaulted throughout.

An exceptional design, not only for Roman Catholic church building, but also for the whole of English architecture of the decade, was the church Cardinal Newman had built by his architect, J. Hungerford Pollen, at Dublin, begun in 1855 (University Church, St Stephen's Green) [Plate 117].[94] Its motifs are not 'Gothic' but 'Early Christian': round arches, incrusted walls, and a big, simple rectangular space. Nevertheless, the principles of planning are Pugin's, with free asymmetrical placing of the furnishings and the galleries, and marble slabs according to Ruskin's descriptions, especially from some chapters of the second volume of *The Stones of Venice*.

The 'art-architect'

In the years from 1855 onwards Street had done comparatively little lecturing and writing. In 1858 he struck a note, the tone of which was all the more significant. His lecture 'On the Future of Art in England'

*New tendencies
in the late
fifties and sixties*

116 G. Goldie, Kensington, Our Lady of Victories, 1867 (destroyed) (from
the *Architect*, 2 Oct. 1869).

117 J. H. Pollen, Dublin, St Stephen's University church, 1856 (Courtesy R. Dawson, Dublin).
Cardinal Newman, who had this church built when he was professor in Dublin, did not favour Gothic. John Hungerford Pollen, who also was a convert and who had worked for Butterfield in the late forties (Merton College Chapel decoration), chose Early Christian, combining Pugin's free arrangement of fittings and Ruskin's slabs of marble.

153

*New tendencies
in the late
fifties and sixties*

at the anniversary meeting of the Ecclesiological Society[95] greatly surprised the reader of his previous writings. An opening excuse makes clear what Street now wants: ' . . . for few artists can or ought to be able to speak or write of art so well as work on it' – which rather contradicts his activities in that field so far. Street talks about the 'artist'. But 'art' now had little to do with architecture: 'We must all believe entirely that we should be better artists and greater men if we did a little less in architecture and a little more in painting [for] three-fourths of the poetry of building lay in its minor details.'[96]

The most important question for the architect was therefore how to promote painting and sculpture in architecture. According to Street, very little had so far been done in sculpture. With regard to coloured decoration, he acknowledged the value of the new feeling for colour, but argued that the aspect of representation was much more important, both in wall-painting and in stained glass. He pointed to the endeavours of the Arundel Society,[97] which was concerned with the publication of medieval paintings, and cited the Oxford Union, where a group of very young painters, including Morris and Burne-Jones, had painted on the walls in 1857.[98] Again and again he drew attention to the Pre-Raphaelite Brotherhood. Of course his remark that the 'Pre-Raphaelite Movement is identical with our own' can hardly now be taken as the truth; on the contrary the fact that he now recommended it so forcefully and that it had been mentioned so little by the *Ecclesiologist* before, suggests that the Ecclesiologists were only now taking over some of the principles of the PRB.[99]

Most of the principles current in architectural discussions of the time were not mentioned by Street at all: no rational considerations, nothing about 'constructional polychromy', no general demand that architects should respond to modern requirements, etc. Altogether the liberal atmosphere seems past. But perhaps most surprising are Street's remarks on the most discussed architectural question of the time and on those years. After describing discoveries of various elements in French and Italian medieval architecture, he said: 'No doubt men who speak as I do will be charged as mere medievalists. I dispute the adjective but accept in its fullest sense the substantive part of the charge. We are medievalists and rejoice in the name.' In the same year Scott had said, 'I am no medievalist,'[100] directed against classicists and liberals who charged him with antiquarianism.

Nevertheless, what Street was now advocating in 1858 had been for some time accepted in an advanced circle of young members of the Ecclesiological Society. William Burges seems to have been the first propagator of these ideas, which mainly stemmed from Ruskin's books, especially the later volumes of *The Stones of Venice*. Already in 1856 Burges had said that in the Middle Ages 'architecture was eminently an architecture of figures and subjects'[101] and in 1857 he wrote that architects should 'turn painters, figure painters'.[102] He

*New tendencies
in the late
fifties and sixties*

remained the most persistent spokesman of these concepts, in his antiquarian research as well as in his own work.

For an unbiased observer, Street's and Burges' remarks on the neglected state of architectural painting and sculpture and other decorations were not quite true. In fact, Beresford-Hope, who did not share Burges' extreme views, reviewed the situation of the applied arts and was very satisfied with their state.[103] From the forties onwards a considerable amount of thought and discussion was spent on these concepts. So far this survey has hardly touched on architectural decoration; the strict limiting of 'architecture' to function (Chapter 1) and to construction (Chapters 1–3), on which architects of the period themselves insisted, might seem to justify this. Yet hardly ever before, certainly not in the nineteenth century, were architects so much preoccupied with the decoration and internal fittings of their buildings. As was briefly stated in the case of Pugin, the concept of 'disegno', where the design mattered but the execution in various materials was of secondary importance, was now reversed. The materials themselves were now important, 'design' had to follow the material, and there were attempts to 'restore' individual traditions of craftsmanship. In England, and later in France and Germany, there were two sorts of people or bodies that tried to reform the applied arts on these lines: the churches, Pugin and the Ecclesiologists, and the Government's Reform Commissions and Schools. Only a summary of the Ecclesiologists' activities can be given here.

There was relatively little in the way of wall painting, probably because from the point of view of coloured decoration, 'constructional polychromy', or the 'permanent polychromy' inherent in materials seemed to offer a much better alternative. Also there seemed to be a general resignation after the not very successful attempts to create a school of fresco painting in England in the forties, for the decoration of the Houses of Parliament.

In contrast, the use of coloured stained glass was strongly recommended with its important principle of being anti-naturalistic, emphasizing colour and outlines with no shading. Imported German and Belgian stained glass was severely criticized, for failing to obey this principle.[104]

As for sculpture, the main question was 'conventionalization' – the right compromise between representing nature and adapting the design to the abstract contours of the building. Several writers and 'designers' specialized in this problem. One of the best known in the architectural field was James Kellaway Colling, also the influence of Richard Redgrave and Owen Jones from the Schools of Design was considerable.[105] As a source, there was the Architectural Museum,[106] installed in the early fifties to provide material for study. It was thought that the knowledge of architectural history should not be limited to those who could afford to travel or buy books, but should

*New tendencies
in the late
fifties and sixties*

be available to everyone concerned with building, including the masons and carvers. Thus it was a movement parallel to, and closely connected with, the founding of the Schools of Design in the applied arts. The Museum provided a collection of casts of ornaments of all kinds and periods where an eclectic need to choose from far-flung sources could most conveniently be satisfied. In the later fifties, the study of plants rather than historic forms was encouraged, also as a possibility to avoid question of 'style'. It was here that Ruskin's thoughts on the representational aspects of sculpture and on the freedom of the workman found a field of influence. Woodward's Oxford Museum, sponsored by Ruskin, was the first famous example of the high respect for an individual carver's work.[107]

Architects also took notice of a number of other crafts, such as metalwork and needlework; Street especially encouraged lay efforts in the latter craft. Soon the Ecclesiologists received international recognition in these fields: both Street and Burges won their Lille competition prizes partly on account of the completeness of their fittings. The greatest achievement in architectural decoration was, of course, the Albert Memorial which Scott erected in Kensington Gardens from 1862.[108] The architecture was only a thin framework – a combination of Veronese open-air tombs and Rhenish shrines – which was then decorated with forms carefully ranging from the 'conventionalized' to the 'naturalistic', in every material and every conceivable technique, executed by a vast number of 'artist-workmen'.

But this was not what Burges wanted. For first of all he insisted on stronger divisions between architecture and decoration: in 1862 he wrote: 'Another good sign is that our architecture tends to simplify itself . . . [and] the decoration is obtained by sculpture rather than by foliage; thus necessitating the massing of rich ornament, instead of spreading unmeaning leaves over the whole surface'.[109] He put the latter course even more drastically as 'the abuse of foliage, covering the building or object until it looks like a petrified arbour'.[110] And Street maintained that it was better to reduce the mass of sculptured decoration to the amount which could be designed by the architect himself. In pattern decoration a more lively representation of nature was opposed to geometrical treatment: 'the present popular "flat treatment" principles are opposed to pure art'.[111]

However, what mattered most in all this was that the sculpture, or the painting, should have a meaning and tell a story. Here again the influence of Ruskin and also the Pre-Raphaelites is decisive. The first link between the painters and the architects was probably the paintings of the Arthurian legend in the Oxford Union. The aim was, as Burges said later 'to make the building interest the spectator, and tell wondrous stories, without a moulding or a piece of foliage in architecture'.[112]

In his art-historical researches, Burges occupied himself more and

*New tendencies
in the late
fifties and sixties*

more with subject matter rather than with traditions of craftsmanship, although his concern with craftsmanship in his own designs was more intense than anyone's since Pugin. Burges lectured on such subjects as 'What we learn from the Chertsey tiles', 'French Portals', or 'Paganism in the Middle Ages'.[113] Just like the Pre-Raphaelites themselves, he fused romantic religious enthusiasm with medieval and classical romance.

Again, there can be no account of the outcome of that movement here. There seem to be only few instances of painting directly applied to the walls, e.g. the 'murals' in St Peter's, Vauxhall, and Leighton's frescoed reredos in White's church at Lyndhurst, dating from 1864. With regard to stained glass, the new principles meant less emphasis on glowing colours and more figure drawing in lighter hues. William Morris' firm[114] became the chief exponent of this style from the early sixties onwards, employed by such Ecclesiologist architects as Street and Bodley. All Saints at Cambridge is one of the first full examples. Greater efforts were made in sculpture. Certain sculptors worked with certain architects, such as T. Earp with Street, as in St James the Less, Westminster, and Thomas Nicholls with Burges.

Perhaps the most remarkable outcome was the painted furniture of Burges, Morris, Webb and Norman Shaw and others.[115] It was an unusual type of furniture: 'Another novel feature . . .: painted furniture . . . full of pictorial art, of colour and gold, combined with simple forms and often made of common materials.'[116] Burne-Jones and Webb and their circle had started making and painting furniture for themselves in about 1857; Burges followed soon afterwards, and they all exhibited at the 1862 exhibition. Burges' church furniture designs for his Lille project (1855) already showed the essential ingredients, especially his organ-case [Plate 118]. Although simple in outline and carpenter-like in construction, through indications of battlements and pinnacles these pieces of furniture seem to suggest shrines or castles, in which the painted stories are happening. In this they depart entirely from the Puginian rational principles that the architectural framework should be 'construction' or – in Ruskin's words – should be 'real' as distinct from the illusion of the pictorial representation. On the other hand, the representations themselves seem to be 'conventionalized' and the architectural details are adapted to the flat surface. Painted furniture seems to stem from complex ideas which should be investigated further, especially in relation to Pre-Raphaelite painting. A typical example of the way Burges saw architecture and legend woven together in a 'naive' way of representation is his drawing for the St Sabrina fountain at Gloucester of 1858 [Plates 119–20].[117]

A development of great consequence was the notion that there was a division between a 'professional' architect and an 'art-architect', a term which Burges actually used in 1864. Already in 1857 Street had

118 (above left) W. Burges, design for organ, Lille Cathedral competition, 1855 (Courtesy Archives Diocésaines, Lille).
Probably this can be called the first example of 'painted furniture', or Art furniture, a field of design which brought architects and Pre-Raphaelite painters together. The actual furniture is simple but it serves as a framework for rich narrative scenes.

119 (above right) W. Burges, project for St Sabrina fountain at Gloucester, 1858 (from the *Builder*, 1858, 375).
Burges liked to design complete, stage-set-like historical set-ups or interiors; a 'Gesamtkunstwerk', a total work of art not dissimilar to the castles of Ludwig II of Bavaria.

120 (opposite above) W. Burges, Cardiff Castle, Banqueting Hall; rebuilding and interior decoration of the castle begun in 1865 (Courtesy National Monuments Record).
Cardiff Castle, largely paid for by Lord Bute, occupied Burges until his death in 1881. The Banqueting Hall was probably finished even later. To a greater extent than the other architects, with the exception of Butterfield, Burges remained faithful to High Victorian design – or his own interpretation of High Victorian Gothic.

warned: 'We architects are in great danger of endorsing the popular idea that we are "professional men" and not artists!'[118] In 1864 Burges stated, quite bluntly, two possibilities: 'The architect should either have learnt the figure or have gone into the patentee line.' Burges seems quite aware of Ruskin's doctrines about the pleasure the artist should derive from his work, which should carry more weight than the finished result and the success afterwards. As Burges put it: '...thinking less about ourselves and of our reputation and more of our work for its own sake'.[119]

The idea of artist-architects was not new; for example, Boullée claimed himself to be a painter and maintained that building itself is not 'architecture'. Later in the nineteenth century the 'artist-architect' point of view was linked with an 'arty-crafty' view of honesty in construction, which was in fact a preference for vernacular methods of construction. This combination was then, somewhat paradoxically, held to be in opposition to the modern, professional, science-minded architect, an attitude which was influential in England until the 1930s.

seven   High Victorianism – public and commercial

So far we have only dealt with the activities of a small group of architects. Although by the early sixties their principles had influenced most other church architects in the country, the Ecclesiologists had an air of exclusiveness, whether it was the group of 'devout church architects', with perhaps Butterfield as its most characteristic exponent, or Burges and his 'art-architects'. It seemed that this circle took almost no notice of the architectural world at large.

Many things had changed since 1840. Professionalism had manifested itself.[1] The number of 'architects' had risen enormously: not only were building-types increasing greatly, but many buildings previously 'designed' by builders using pattern-book decoration were now put up by much more qualified men, in the technical as well as in a humanist sense. The architects had to compete, in a commercial sense, with other architects, since the old static system of patronage had largely gone. Architectural education, qualification and communications between architects, had become a much more complicated matter. They became elements of professionalization. There were several attempts to establish systems of education and there were many specialized societies and events, such as the (Royal) Institute of British Architects, the Architectural Association, the Architectural Exhibition and the Architectural Museum (see above p. 155). There were the architectural journals, the most important of which were the two weeklies, the *Builder* from the early forties and the *Building News* from the mid-fifties.

The old hierarchy of decorum still reigned, but it became more complicated. New classes demanded expression of their wealth. Therefore public buildings had to become even richer; at the same time, in an era of growing wealth and as a sign of growing social responsibility, a certain amount of ornament was doled out to the lower classes.

New motifs of ornament developed, and the old consensus within a narrow range was replaced by a wide choice among a variety of 'styles'. By 1860 or 1870 these questions had reached the lowest levels of architecture. Any architect with almost any type of building could be faced with the question of 'style'.

Again, where did the Ecclesiologists stand in relation to all this? One recalls that in the question of style they had decided on one period with a range of variety within its limits. To a large extent, they believed in a hierarchy of decorum: country churches were generally less ornate than town churches. On the other hand, some concepts such as simplicity of surface diminished these differences; Ruskin's views also tended to upset this hierarchy. With regard to practical considerations of function and construction, the Ecclesiologists were as 'advanced' as anyone else at the time. They had explored the functions of the church and its related buildings in great detail and they continually thought of the process of construction, at least within the traditional materials. Only the impetus did not seem to come from pragmatic and practical reasons, but from moral and theoretical ones. Finally, as to 'professionalism', in spite of their criticism, the Ecclesiologists showed many symptoms of this development, with their specialization in one type of building and their specialized communication through the journal and in the meetings of the Society.

From about the mid-fifties onwards, the concepts of both Ruskin and the Ecclesiologists started to influence the general architectural world decisively. This was largely possible because of the fact that the Society itself and its members became less dogmatic about their own convictions, and the general architectural public relaxed some of its preconceptions. Another factor which must never be overlooked was the simple desire of the architects to extend their practice beyond the range of types of the Society

Before the work and opinions of various architects and the results and the problems of Ecclesiologist influence in various buildings can be discussed, we must look at the most important point of the controversy between the two factions, the question of 'style'. The 'style' controversy, which had been going on since the forties and was particularly strong around 1850, flared up in the mid-fifties, but with a general change in tone. Initially one of the main stimuli was the feeling of shame over merely imitating past styles. Now it became more and more accepted that new styles could not be created out of nothing, and that everybody had to start off by imitating some historic style which could then be 'developed' according to the requirements of the nineteenth century. At the same time the answer to the question of which style to start off with became more flexible. Combining motifs from different styles and countries became respectable. Street was the first member of the Society to put forward these ideas, in 1852 and more forcefully in his book *Brick and Marble* in 1855. In 1856 this more flexible attitude had to be defended against an attack from the French Neo-Gothic architect, J. B. Lassus. His nom-de-plume motto for his Lille design that took third prize in the competition (with Burges and Street taking the first two places) was 'L'Eclecticisme est la Plaie de l'Art'. He wrote a letter to the *Ecclesiologist*, demanding 'unity of style'. But he received little support from his English colleagues, with Street, Scott and especially Beresford-Hope fervently advocating Eclecticism.[2]

The same year saw another flare-up of the discussion among English architects in the columns of the *Builder*. Sir William Tite, one of the older architects and a strong anti-Goth, wrote an attack against the 'Gothic' school. Scott, Ferrey and others replied in favour of Gothic, but the *Ecclesiologist* did not bother much. William White stated his position in two short letters to the *Builder,* saying that 'Truthfulness has nothing to do with "style" as such'; 'the principles of art are independent of classic and gothic . . . only convinced by those [the principles] can one change.' Gothic merely appeared to have the advantage of a greater adaptability to various purposes.[3] Eclecticism on all levels of quality seemed to be the way out in these years. In 1858 the *Builder* published a project for the Chelsea Vestry Hall[4] – to cite an awkward example – a concoction of motifs from all conceivable periods, classical and gothic [Plate 121]. In the same year a most comprehensive book provided recipes for eclecticism – Scott's *Secular and Domestic Architecture,* which will be discussed below.

Yet the worst 'battle of styles' was still to come. The story of the designs for the Government Offices, the buildings of the Foreign Office and Home Office, is well known. In 1857 Scott put in an entry in the competition to design these offices, but did not win. During the years which followed he tried hard to obtain the commission. He succeeded, but in the end was not allowed to build 'Gothic' and had to prepare an 'Italian' design [Plate 131]. The story is told best if not impartially in Scott's *Recollections,* but more important are the numerous pamphlets written about the struggle and the countless articles and letters in the press. Most of the participants were in favour of Gothic. As an older critic summed up: 'Gothic is national, constructional, real, adaptable to all kinds of buildings, it is convenient, it is cheap because it can be either simple or ornate, whereas classical must be ornate or else it is not architecture.'[5] His adversaries replied that Gothic is not national, not practical, it is obsolete, just as the barbarism of the Middle Ages on the whole is most objectionable.[6] Here one is reminded of the discussions about the designs for the Houses of Parliament in the 1830s.[7] This in fact seems to provide a clue to the whole battle over the Government Offices: decisions were made and influenced by the taste and opinions of a generation before. The significance of the struggle in the fifties was that interest in the matter went beyond the small circle of connoisseurs in 1835 and beyond the closed circle of erudite Ecclesiologists into what one must call public opinion in a much wider sense. Again, in a context of eclecticism, it is to be remembered that 'style', as an expression of a period or of a country, did not matter so much any more, and as Scott himself stated later: 'the new design [was] even more suited to the Gothic style than the old one' [Plate 132].[8]

In 1860 another pamphlet on these questions received a great deal of attention: Thomas Harris's *Victorian Architecture: A Few Words to show that a national architecture adapted to the wants of the nineteenth century is available*. Nothing was new in this book: the idea of a new style suited to the nineteenth century; the kind of design advocated; brick, polychromy, the picturesque, the sublime, 'truth' in general, and the 'art-workman's' pleasure in his work. In fact, the *Ecclesiologist*[9] remarked that Harris had obviously taken over their

121 S. and H. Godwin, unexecuted project for Chelsea Vestry Hall, 1858 (from the *Builder*, 1858, 851).
'Eclecticism' seemed to be the way out of the dilemma: what style should we use? In many cases the combination of motifs from different countries and periods simply meant a compilation.

principles. Perhaps the only remarkable thing about the pamphlet
is that Harris manages to avoid mentioning any historical styles, but
even here he follows what Street and White had maintained earlier.

In fact, less was heard of the question during the next ten years.
In 1866 the famous Glasgow architect Alexander Thomson launched
a fierce attack against Gothic[10] (which coincided with the anger of
Glasgow architects at Scott's commission for Glasgow University).
Again the familiar arguments in favour of Gothic are repeated, this

122 B. Woodward (Deane and Woodward), Dublin, Trinity College
Museum, interior, 1852 (Courtesy the Hamlyn Group).
One of the first instances of 'constructional polychromy', still restricted to
arches, marble shafts and tiles. For the naturalistic sculpture Woodward
employed the O'Shea brothers, who followed him to England.

164

time by the *Ecclesiologist*.[11] In the next major competition, for the
Law Courts, styles other than Gothic were hardly taken into consideration. So it seemed that Gothic had finally succeeded. By that
time, however, some of the best Gothicists were already thinking of
abandoning Gothic in favour of another version of eclecticism: 'Old
English' or 'Queen Anne', as we shall see in the next chapter.

Benjamin Woodward

Benjamin Woodward (1815–61), an Irishman who worked in partnership with Thomas Deane (1792–1872),[12] was already influenced by
Ruskin to some extent in his first building, the Museum of Trinity
College, Dublin [Plate 122].[13] It was a museum and institute for
different branches of science like the Oxford Museum and was begun
in 1852. The arrangement of the building (for which the architects
were not wholly responsible) shows a strong influence of the club-
houses of Charles Barry. The rooms are grouped around a big hall with
a staircase – covered by a glazed roof – which became a common
feature in Woodward's architecture. The elevations show round-
arched windows of the kind at the back of the Travellers' Club. What
is new is the bold exposure of freestone, especially in the interior,
with interspersed coloured marble shafts. Rich, naturalistic carving
is contrasted with this stonework, which also marks the beginning
of the career of the carvers James and John O'Shea, whose precision
in the rendering of plants and animals was only equalled by Pre-
Raphaelite painting.

In the Oxford Museum, begun in 1855 [Plate 123–4] and finished
around 1860,[14] the unified arrangement is loosened. A large quadrangle is surrounded by ranges treated as separate parts. The main
front, however, has a hip-roofed tower in the centre, contemporary
with Scott's Hamburg project of 1854. Demands for 'realism' were met
by a slightly asymmetrical arrangement of the windows following the
irregular interior division. The inner yard with its seemingly endless
uniform arcades is a more truly Ruskinian feature. As has been
mentioned, Street's proposals for the Museum had repeated Ruskin's
demands that decorative sculpture should 'tell' the purpose of the
building. Now with the help of the O'Sheas and other sculptors and
Ruskin's own advice, an enormous sculptural programme of plants
and animals was started (and never wholly finished).[15]

Woodward's work is small. In some buildings he comes nearer to the
Ecclesiologists, as in the Union building at Oxford (now the Union
Library, 1856–7),[16] which with its wooden roof is little more than a
big schoolroom. His project for the Government Offices Competition
of 1857 [Plate 125][17] is characterized by endless, unbroken cornices
and arcades; but at the corners some horizontals are interrupted by
the slopes of the staircases. As in the Oxford buildings, an enormous

programme of 'story-telling' decorations was envisaged. Woodward's country houses of the later fifties recall Pugin's houses of the forties, with irregular planning, chimneys breaking through the rooflines, and no 'cottage' elements (Llysdulas, near Llanwellwyfo,[18] Anglesey, and Tullow, Clare).[19]

Woodward's last work (he died in 1861) was the Kildare Street Club in Dublin [Plate 126],[20] begun in 1858, using low segmental arches, which appear squeezed into the brick surface, throughout. We shall be mentioning his Crown Life Office in the context of commercial buildings [Plate 146]. In the sixties his partner Deane continued Woodward's style in another Crown Life Office (Fleet Street, 1866).[21]

123 B. Woodward (Deane and Woodward), Oxford University Museum, begun 1854 from NW (Courtesy National Monuments Record).
The Oxford Museum competition was the first in a series in the mid-fifties where the winning designs focused attention on High Victorian Gothic. Woodward groups his buildings around a large square court (see Plate 154). Only the range on the west side is treated symmetrically with a central tower squeezed into the façade, carrying a hipped roof, a common feature in public buildings for many decades to come. There are, however, some slight irregularities in the grouping of the windows in the ground floor.

124 B. Woodward, Oxford Museum, detail of elevation (from the *Building
News*, 1860, 715).
A typical piece of High Victorian elevation: string-courses and capitals
projecting from the plain wall surface, flush bands of coloured stone with
varying relationships with the openings and monolithic shafts in the
windows.

George Gilbert Scott

Scott's work at this time is of major importance.[22] His book of 1858, *Remarks on Secular and Domestic Architecture, Present and Future* (written in 1857 and earlier), is in many ways a repetition and a compromise of opinions already cited.[23] There is rationalism in the field of planning and construction, and the aesthetic of the 'picturesque' and the 'sublime' each get their share – not without contradictions. Principles of decorum are held up, as well as the stress on the importance of following the new requirements of the age, and regard for the field of social responsibility. Scott stressed the symbolic national importance of Gothic motifs as well as their rational connotations.[24]

In 1855 Scott preceded the publication of Street's book *Brick and Marble* with his lecture 'On the Pointed Architecture of Italy'.[25] But he was not interested in the same historical examples or the same

125 B. Woodward, design for Government Offices competition, 1857 (Foreign Office etc.; from the *Illustrated London News*, 1857, II 348). An imposing mass with square contours, broken at the corners by the expression of the staircases.

principles as Street. There was little emphasis on flat surface or on plate tracery. What interested him was the manipulation of detached column-shafts in arcades and as decorations of windows and as aspects of structural colour. In *Secular and Domestic Architecture*, 1857, Scott discussed at great length the distinction between 'structural' and 'decorative' columns and arcades, and in this he follows the traditional discussion in Classic and Gothic rationalism:[26] ' . . . wall arcading should be either purely decorative, in which case it should be so light as to forbid the thought of its separate existence; or else so clearly a constructive portion of the wall, and so intimately united with it, that the two evidently constitute a single structure.'[27]

The most important parts of his book are probably those where he deals with lower categories of buildings which have not before been dealt with at such length in books comprising the whole of 'architecture'. Scott propounded the aesthetic of the 'sublime' and straightforward treatment of material. Simple outline and simple plans can

126 B. Woodward, Dublin, Kildare Street Club, 1858 (from the *Building News*, 1860, 49).
High Victorian design, polychromatic stripes, window decoration, coloured shafts etc. do not necessarily mean pointed arches as well.

be adapted to everything and can be combined with most other principles. Scott thought that regularity and symmetry could give the greatest effect in important public buildings, but that they conform to demands of economy as well. In his chapter on 'Commercial Buildings etc.', Scott looked at town buildings in the way in which simple buildings in the country were looked at earlier, regardless of what their builders had had in mind. The late medieval Mauthalle at Nuremberg excels through 'straightforward, massive and natural treatment . . . grandeur of effect and noble character'.[28] He even mentioned an anonymous contemporary building, the big warehouse in the Goods Station at Nottingham, which for him had the same qualities. From that time onwards, again and again, simple buildings of the Industrial Revolution have been admired, regardless of the fact that their lack of decoration was a result both of cheapness and of a low position in the hierarchy of 'decorum'.

Yet it seems that Scott's respect for plainness was mainly part of the polemic against richer *classical* motifs. 'Architecture' for him, too, started with added decoration. He concluded: 'Yet it would be well that a caution, a precept or a promise should occasionally catch our eye in the midst of our everyday employments, and that the sculpture or painted decorations of our houses should, here and there, contain an allusion to the faith we profess to hold.'[29] On buildings of lesser standing, such as factories, he has very little to say, and in fact he finds that the big windows 'rather detract from dignity'.[30]

In his buildings, more numerous than with any other architect of the Gothic Revival, he had himself used detached shafts and arcades in the forties in his churches of the 'lancet' and 'Early English' type, mentioned above. But if we compare one of these earlier works, such as Holy Trinity at Halstead (Essex, 1843),[31] with the Camden Church at Camberwell of 1854 (damaged in the war and pulled down later)[32] [Plate 127], one observes in the latter that the shafts are more clearly separated from the walls, are more clearly shown as supports to the arches, and the whole appears to be more constructional in the sense of a rationalist framework. Street, who used arcades and shafts fairly often, too, remained much more at the Halstead stage. Scott's little brick church near Crewe (Cheshire)[33] shows a very rich treatment with arcades; again they seem to be linked with the masonry in a more constructional way. The same arcades are used in his project for the Town Hall in Hamburg[34] and in the first Government Offices project.[35] In the first case they do not project from the wall surface, in the second they come very close to a classical arcaded façade.

Scott was less devoted to dogmatic ecclesiology than Street, White or Butterfield. He therefore obtained more and more lavish commissions from those who were not particularly 'high' (or 'low'). Thus he built many churches with a large amount of decoration, mostly with naturalistic carving for which the many capitals of his arcadings

127 G. G. Scott, London, Camden Church, Camberwell, 1854 (destroyed)
(from the *Builder*, 1854, 363).
The consistent treatment of the arcade in relation to the wall – either
clearly detached or an integral part of it – was one of Scott's main concerns. With this he stands firmly within the tradition of classical-gothic
rationalism; at the same time he uses the arcade as it had always been
used, as a feature of decorative splendour. The polychromatic treatment
of the arcade is much more important to Scott than the polychromy of
wall surfaces.

171

provided ample space. Constructional polychromy he used much less, and when he did, always in regular patterns.

However, the most important element in Scott's work at his time is the element of the 'sublime' in planning, linked with elements of rich decoration in buildings of higher importance. The contrast between the new elements of the 'sublime' and his earlier 'picturesque' manner is much stronger than in Street's case. In 1852 Scott built a row of eight terraced houses next to Westminster Abbey in Broad Sanctuary [Plate 128],[36] with an astonishing variety of gables, parapets, bay windows, buttresses and so on. The front shows more variety than the rear on Dean's Yard. But the unexecuted project of 1854 for Hamburg [Plate 129] is completely symmetrical with a uniform treatment of the elevation; there it was the main front that had the greatest amount of regularity, while the rear part had a more lively outline. The same applies to the project for Halifax Town Hall,[37] of 1857, the year of the Government Offices competition [Plate 130]. The repetition of elaborate decoration increases the impression of

128 (below) G. G. Scott, Westminster, Broad Sanctuary, 1852 (from the *Builder*, 1854, 114).
A terrace of private houses and offices treated as a unified but picturesque group. Cf. Plate 129.

129 (opposite, top) G. G. Scott, unexecuted design for Hamburg Town Hall, 1854 (from the *Builder*, 1856, 63).
There is an abrupt change in Scott's work from the earlier picturesque rambling to imposing symmetry, heavy cornices and endless repetition of arches, common features in almost all of Scott's secular works from that time onwards.

130 G. G. Scott,
design for
Government
Offices competition, 1857
(Foreign Office
etc.; Courtesy
RIBA Drawings
Collection).
Cf. Plates 67 and
125 and see p. 162.

131 (above) G. G. Scott, London, Foreign Office, 1861 (Courtesy National
Monuments Record).
The final outcome of the competition and the 'battle of styles', a Renais-
sance design dictated by Palmerston. Cf. Plate 132.

132 (opposite above) G. G. Scott, Diploma Design for the Royal Academy:
'Gothic' version of his final design for the Foreign Office, 1861 (Courtesy
Royal Academy of Arts).
With his tongue in his cheek Scott presented this version to the R.A.,
representing what he would have liked to do for the Foreign Office. At
the same time it served to underline his belief, that the difference between
the styles is not really so great. As he himself wrote, the Foreign Office
in its executed design was 'even more suited to the Gothic style than
the old one' (i.e. the 1857 design, Plate 130).

uniformity. The 'sublime' is here linked not with 'economy', as in
Teulon's St Andrew's, Lambeth, but on the contrary with richness
and importance of status. The first Government Offices design can
also be seen in the context of the then emerging 'Second Empire'
mode, which was basically a picturesque variation on the classical,
as we shall see below. The mansard roofs of the corner pavilions
respond both to the desire for larger roof surfaces and to the demand
for strong horizontal divisions. All the same, Scott remained Ruskinian
in many ways. One need only observe the 'unclassical' treatment at
the angles of the Government Offices project: the octagonal projections cannot entirely be seen as vertical frames, because of the
horizontal sculptured bands which carry on without interruption.

In two big country houses, Kelham Hall (Notts.) [Plate 133][38] and
Walton Hall (Warwicks.),[39] both begun in 1858, all the elements of

133 G. G. Scott, Kelham Hall, Notts., 1858 (Courtesy National Monuments
Record).
Scott's rigid façade treatment linked with free domestic planning.

Scott's architecture so far discussed are fused into characteristic wholes. Here, too, symmetry can be found, but as Scott could never have built a completely symmetrical country house, it is restricted to parts of the buildings, which are then grouped freely. Scott again differed from Street, whose individual 'blocks' are subdivided asymmetrically [cf. Plate 67].[40] Scott carries his horizontals through the whole of the building uninterruptedly, although this does not mean that a big hall and its chimneystack are not allowed to cut through the horizontal divisions in the Puginian way. At Kelham, where he used brick with stone dressings and stone shafts, there is a very complicated yet convincing system combining these elements; the various hewn-stone features differ strongly in treatment as well as in the relationship to the brick walls. The vertical parts, nearly always shafts, never project from the wall surface as the horizontal parts do, but appear to be firmly contained within the wall. Other dressings fit neither category; these include the framing of arches and those parts which contain additional sculptural decoration, clearly attached to the surface of the wall. This system can be contrasted with the mode in which Street treated his elevations, with openings apparently cut out of the wall, as for instance, in the designs for the schools near St James the Less [see Plate 72]. On the other hand, Scott's framework is not the self-supporting framework of the earlier Gothic Rationalists and all in all, the decorative value of the materials, especially of colour contrast, is predominant.

How consciously Scott applied all these methods is shown by the treatment of Walton Hall, which offered an alternative in the choice of material: here he used two kinds of stone with very little difference between them. There is hardly more than one type of window, square in form, framed by sunk mouldings. The window-openings all recede from the exterior surface, which is decorated by horizontal bands, arranged symmetrically and linked with the window-frames. It is the treatment of Kelham, however, which prevails in nearly all of Scott's larger secular buildings of the next decade.

As for medium-sized public buildings, the Town Hall at Preston (1862)[41] has been lately destroyed, and the Brighton Baths (1866) [Plate 134][42] also no longer exist. Both were similarly arranged, combining regular arcading with irregular corner accents. The Town Hall showed a marked differentiation of ornament and composition; the Exchange was given richer treatment and a cornice marked the parts containing the town offices. The Brighton Baths were specially remarkable inside: the swimming bath was a vast circular space, surrounded by two rows of more or less continuous Ruskinian arcades and covered with a slightly pointed dome, which opened into a lantern. The dome was constructed of iron, with beams curving upwards without interruption and filled in with coffering-like framework. Scott had referred already in *Secular and Domestic Architecture* to the dome as the most beautiful architectural feature. Later in his *Lectures* he was to describe the basic principle of the dome: 'covering of a circular space produced by the revolution of an arch round its central axis'.[43]

A more utilitarian work was the big Infirmary at Leeds,[44] completed in 1867 [Plate 137]. It is a combination of three parallel ranges, connected by lower buildings. The middle range contains a larger rectangular space covered by an iron and glass roof. Similarly, the University of Glasgow, begun in 1868,[45] is a rather low, spread out complex, but largely symmetrical with a big hall, now vaulted over several aisles, and a tall steeple in the middle. Apart from the familiar motifs of decoration there are some features, strong circular turrets and stepped gables, which look like concessions to 'Scottish Baronial'. Scott continued this kind of design in the seventies: another example is the vast (unexecuted) symmetrical and domed design in the first competition for the new German Parliament at Berlin in 1872.[46]

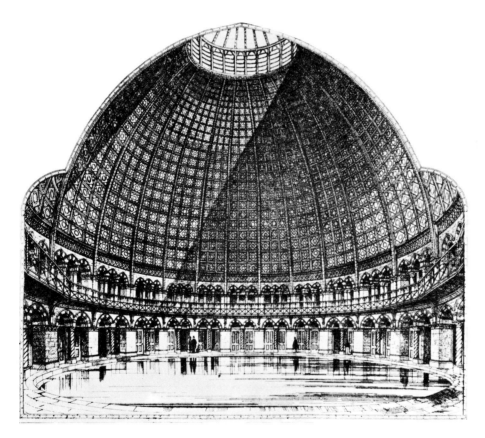

134 G. G. Scott, Brighton, Brill's Baths, 1866 iron dome (destroyed) (from the *Civil Engineer and Architect's Journal*, 1866, pl. 38). Scott, with his preference for simple shapes, thought the circular dome one of the most grandiose architectural features.

135 G. G. Scott, London, St Pancras Station Hotel, view from SW (Courtesy National Monuments Record).
It is impossible to convey the spatial quality of the exterior in a photograph. It is largely due to the ingenious handling of the situation that the two parts of the façade of the building do not run parallel to each other.

However, his most popular building, and probably also his most ingenious, is St Pancras Hotel, now occupied by British Rail [Plates 135–6].[47] Two elements were involved, the rigidity of the decorative system and the freedom and irregularity of planning. The plan was conditioned by the space left between Barlow's train shed – which had been finished by the time Scott started to build (but which already contained a few decorative Gothic features, even the pointed arch) – and the Euston Road. These two lines were not parallel, as in fact no corner of the site was right-angled. Also a great ramp was required, to lead from street level up to platform level. Scott arranged this ramp in such a way that it took up most of the frontage of Euston Road, and thus the long range of the building lies back from the road. This range runs parallel to the shed frontage and consequently not parallel to the road; only the smaller projection at the west end of the hotel has a frontage parallel to the road. It is this divergence, seldom consciously noticed, which gives St Pancras its overpowering sense of contained space, especially when seen from the western part of Euston Road. Again the strong plasticity of the horizontals helps to confine the space, both the continuity of the arcades with their polished shafts and the heavily machicolated cornice. St Pancras is perhaps the greatest masterpiece in the long

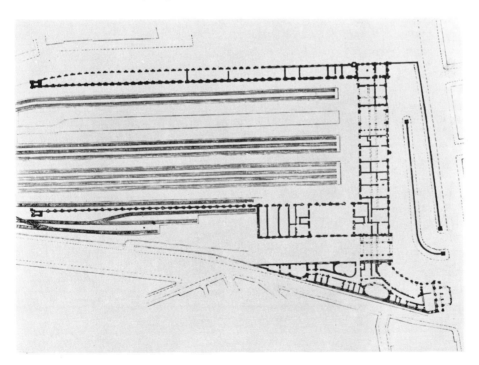

136 G. G. Scott, London, St Pancras Station Hotel, 1867 (the shed was by the engineer W. H. Barlow, begun in 1866) (from the *Engineer*, XXIII, 1867, 482).

179

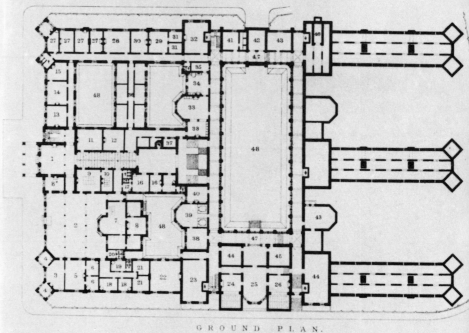

GROUND PLAN.

Reference.

1. Entrance Hall. 2. Out Patients Waiting Room. 3. Physician's Room. 4. Private Room. 5. Surgeon's Room. 6. Surgeon's Private Room. 7. Dispensary. 8. Laboratory with Cellar under. 8* Porter's Room. 9. Weekly Board Room. 10. Secretary's Room. 11. Library. 12. Students Waiting Room. 13. Assistants' Sitting Room. 14. House Surgeons Sitting Room. 15. House Surgeons Bed Room. 16. Accident Rooms. 17. Nurses Room. 18. Dressing Room. 19. Womens retiring Room. 20. Men's retiring Room. 21. Baths. 22. Mattress Room. 23. Linen. 24. Museum. 25. Dead House. 26. Post Mortem Room. 27. Bed Rooms for Assistants. 28. Common Dining Room. 29. Matrons Sitting Room. 30. Matrons Bed Room. 31. Matrons Stores. 32. Servants Hall. 33. Kitchen. 34. Scullery. 35. Stores. 36. Pantry & Larders. 37. Offices. 38. Flour. 39. Bake House. 40. Bread. 41. Beer & Wine. 42. Wood. 43. Cellars. 44. Engine House. 46. Ice House. 47. Corridor. 48. Open Court. † Water Closet. ‡ Lift.

SCALE OF 10 0 10 20 30 40 50   100   150   200 FEET

137 G. G. Scott,
Leeds Infirmary,
1864 (from the
Building News,
1867, 461).
Scott adhered to
the customary
separation into
different blocks.

tradition of combining neo-classically inspired uniformity of decorative detailing with irregular planning – which as usual turned the awkwardness of the site into successful irregular massing, or in other words, the ultimate combination of Pugin's picturesque and Ruskin's sublime.

Scott's influence on secular architecture was enormous. For example, Seddon's Government Offices project[48] of 1857 was influenced by Scott's Hamburg Town Hall project of 1854. One only has to mention such devout classical architects as Lockwood and Mawson in Bradford, who in their Exchange in 1864 and Town Hall[49] turned to Scott's Gothic, but at the same time found it possible to retain classical features such as rustication and coffering. Another success of Scott's Gothic, the first major one outside Britain, was Thomas Fuller and Charles Jones's Ottawa Parliament House, begun in 1859 [Plate 138].[50]

138 Fuller and Jones, Ottawa, Canadian Parliament, 1859 (from the *Building News*, 1859, 1063).
Cf. Plates 129 and 130.

Alfred Waterhouse

The best known of all the architects who concentrated on civic and commercial work was Alfred Waterhouse.[51] In the beginning his practice was based on the great demand for town architecture in Lancashire. In his first buildings of the later fifties he had already left behind the classical-Renaissance tendency of the day. His Fryer and Binyon warehouse [Plate 148][52] was an extreme case of 'Ruskinism', that is, the application of Venetian motifs, which we shall look at under commercial buildings. In his Droylsden Institute (Manchester)[53] as well as in his own house at Fallowfield (Manchester, now destroyed) in 1858,[54] he combined coloured brick, segmentheaded windows, and a cottage roof. In 1859 he won a major competition, the Manchester Assize Courts [Plate 139].[55] Here he took

139 A. Waterhouse, Manchester, Assize Courts, 1859 (destroyed) (from the *Building News*, 1859, 427).

over Scott's symmetry and scheme of side and centre projections, covered by high roofs. On the other hand, the treatment of the elevations is less unified and principled than that of Scott. In the executed design he followed Scott more closely, for example in the arcades of the upper storey and the roofline. In his Royal Insurance building in King Street, Manchester, in 1861[56] (destroyed) he again insisted on rigid symmetry, but varied the form of arches, round, pointed, segmental-headed. But Waterhouse did not adhere to symmetry, or to compositions based on a small set of regular units, as Scott did in his asymmetrical designs. Waterhouse's mature style was fully developed in a series of well known buildings begun in the later sixties, Balliol College, Oxford;[57] Gonville and Caius College, Cambridge;[58] Manchester Town Hall[59] [Plates 140–1], the additions to Eaton Hall (Cheshire), Lime Street Station Hotel, Liverpool,[60] and his project for the Law Courts in 1867. His buildings are composed of a variety of small parts, recesses and projections, different forms and sizes of windows. In Manchester he exploited the completely irregular site – there are no right-angles – by using an extremely lively exterior. He increased the irregularity of odd angles instead of disguising them as did for example J. Oldrid Scott, G. G. Scott's son, for the Manchester competition.[61] Yet Waterhouse's plan on the whole is very clear and simple; Waterhouse's capacity for convenient planning was held to be supreme. He continued his enormous output until the beginning of this century. The influence on him of High Victorianism in a strict sense was relatively small. In some ways he continued Puginian and 'rogue' tendencies from the late forties and early fifties into the more picturesque later Victorian periods.

The Law Courts competition

In 1867 the victory of Ruskinian Gothic seemed to be assured. All the eleven entries for the New Law Courts[62] were Gothic. Most of the important High Victorian architects were brought together, the 'art-architects' as well as the middle-of-the-road men. It seems at least what Burges, Seddon and Street have in common is that they differ from the rest. The middle-of-the road group is easier to describe: they all adhere to a basic symmetry of façade, to Ruskinian heavy cornices, wall treatment by continuous arcades and little that seemed basically new. Deane repeated some features from Woodward's Government Offices project of 1857, Scott [Plate 142] combined features from Preston and Glasgow. Raphael Brandon, an architect best known as one of the closer followers of Pugin around 1850, Lockwood and Garling (the classical winner of the Government Offices competition in 1857) all followed Scott, as did E. M. Barry, the son of Charles Barry, in a typically eclectic design.

The 'art-architects', however, offered more individual solutions.

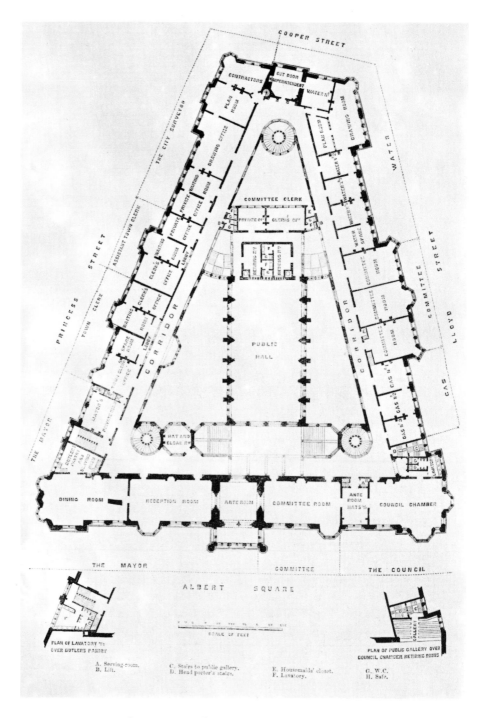

140–141 A. Waterhouse, Manchester Town Hall, plan and view of Princess
Street and Albert Square corner, 1868 (from the *Builder*, 2 May 1868).
Waterhouse, the most prolific architect of civic buildings in the later
Victorian period, soon turned away from the influence of Scott, as shown
in the Assize Courts, towards a more picturesque flexibility in planning
and elevation.

142 G. G. Scott, design for Law Courts competition, 1867 (from the *Builder*, 1867, 225). Cf. Plates 129 and 130.

143 W. Burges, design for Law Courts competition, 1867 (from the *Builder*, 1867, 311).

Seddon proposed a turreted building in the manner of University College of Wales, Aberystwyth, with the roof playing a more important role than usual. Burges [Plate 143] was by far the most asymmetrical although in many details, such as the continuous arcadings, he came close to Scott's group. On the other hand he offered the greatest massiveness, especially in his top-heavy towers, which he was soon to execute at Cardiff. It seems that on closer comparison Street's design [Plate 144] which won (Barry's plan was preferred) contained by far the most novel features. Although fairly

144 G. E. Street, design for Law Courts competition, 1867 (from the *Building News*, 24 May 1867).
Street's design differs from his competitors' designs as well as his own earlier models. The very unified block, strictly enclosed – with the massive Record Tower attached like a campanile – contrasts with the vivid detailing of the façades. Street has abandoned the coloured shafts and almost all other constructional polychromy. He seems to move into the 'English' direction like Bodley (cf. Plate 105). The building of the Law Courts through the seventies marked the ultimate achievement of Street's career. The difficulties during the execution – which differs considerably from the 1867 design – is said to have contributed to Street's relatively early death at the age of fifty-seven in 1881.

rigidly symmetrical in its layout, there was more variety on the
façades. He leaves large spaces of blank wall, contrasted with concentrated groups of windows of different sizes – a characteristic of
Street first noted at Bloxham School in 1854. Also he was getting
away from arcaded series of windows and prefers windows as
individual openings in the wall. On the whole, one is reminded of
St Margaret's Convent at East Grinstead: the design is much more
quiet with very little polychromy. Like Bodley, Street seems to lead
away from High Victorianism, perhaps more in this design than in
the actual execution of the Law Courts.

Commercial street architecture

There was no such thing before the early nineteenth century as the
office building as distinct from other town buildings.[63] With the
sudden increase of industry and commerce, there arose the need for
buildings more specially suited for office and warehouse purposes.
As a matter of course, increasing wealth was demonstrated by an
increase of stateliness and decoration. The status formula was the
palazzo-type. Innumerable palazzi rose in British cities from the
forties onwards, a particularly impressive development in northern
cities, especially Manchester and Liverpool, where few stately buildings of any type had been put up before.

The question here is how Ruskinian Gothic or High Victorian
eclecticism influenced this category of buildings in the 1850s and 60s.
That fact that it did have some influence must be seen as a remarkable
success for Gothicist propaganda. Some of the reasons were symbolic:
Ruskin had (in the second volume of his *Stones of Venice* in 1853)
described the domestic architecture of Venice in the Middle Ages, and
it was felt that the commercial world in medieval Italy corresponded
to the English set-up in the nineteenth century. But the old argument
that Gothic was the national style for northern countries played some
part as well. Street included a great deal of Italian civic architecture
in his book *Brick and Marble,* stressing Ruskin's point (see also
p. 42 above). Scott in his *Secular and Domestic Architecture* as usual
managed to stress both points and also advocated the large medieval
commercial buildings of Germany and Flanders. But his most appealing
argument as discussed above is his characteristic compromise between
simplicity, which in Gothic does not mean 'unsightliness', and decoration according to the standing of the owner.

Yet there were several practical matters as well, in which Gothic
seemed to be better suited to commercial architecture than classical.
Continuous arcading provided more window space (the arches did
not, of course, have to be pointed) than classical wall systems where
the size and number of windows often led to forced and mannerist
solutions. Another element was important: Ruskin had advocated that

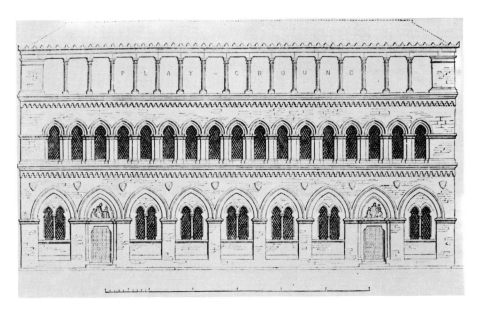

145 J. Wild, London, Holborn, St Martin's in the Fields, Northern
Schools, 1849 (destroyed) (from the *Builder*, 1849, 451).
Little is known about Wild (see above p. 42). Apparently under the influence of Ruskin's *Seven Lamps* he was the first to combine strict
horizontality with continuous rows of pointed windows. Soon the
building was considered a model for town architecture.

there should be as much independence as possible between the individual storeys of a building, and as a result there were no rules as
to the number of storeys, their individual height and their relationship
to each other. This was the other great problem with the palazzo
elevation, that the number of storeys was limited and there had to be
a certain succession of different proportions which it was difficult to
reverse [Plate 152].

Wild's St Martin's Schools [Plate 145], already mentioned, marked
the beginning of Ruskinian continuous arcading in 1849. Woodward's
Crown Life Office in the City (New Bridge Street, c. 1855, destroyed)
[Plate 146][64] gave an appearance of solidity with its semicircular
arches; at the same time the amount of window space seemed similar
to that of its Georgian neighbours. Prichard and Seddon's General
Post Office in Cardiff[65] seems essentially little different from any
simple Georgian façade, except for the arcaded ground floor, and its
details carefully executed in polychrome brick and stone. A young
Birmingham architect and strong supporter of Ruskin's doctrines,
J. H. Chamberlain, on his nos. 28–29 Union Street in Birmingham
[Plate 147],[66] enriched a cornice with a high parapet which, though
broken by small gabled dormers, emphasizes the block-like coherence
of the whole. Waterhouse's design for the Fryer and Binyon warehouse (1855) [Plate 148] differs from these others in its irregularity

189

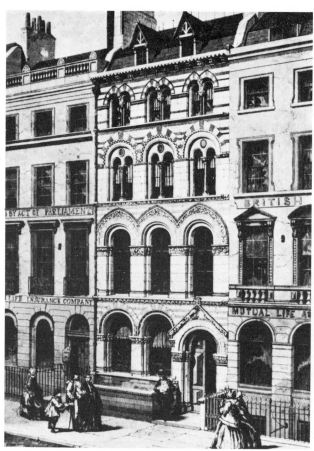

146 (above left) B. Woodward, London, Crown Life Office, New Bridge Street, 1855 (destroyed) (from the *Building News*, 1858, 723).
Round-arched version of the arcade with rich polychromy and sculpture by the O'Sheas.

147 (above right) J. H. Chamberlain, Birmingham, 28–29 Union Street, 1856 (destroyed) (from Thomas Harris, *Examples of Architecture of the Victorian Age*, Vol. I, 1862).
Ruskin and Scott railed against the common commercial shop fronts, where the whole ground floor was opened up with glass without any apparent support for the upper storeys, a flagrant breach of 'truth'. It was overcome by wide segmental arches, paradoxically constructed with the help of hidden iron ties.

148 (opposite) A. Waterhouse, design for Fryer & Binyon Warehouse, Manchester, 1856 (Courtesy Victoria & Albert Museum).
There is a direct inspiration from the Ducal Palace: the features, however, correspond to the internal use of the building, offices in the first floor and storage in the upper floor.

of composition indicating the functions of the different parts. On the
ground floor the two entrances are stressed, the first floor with a
continuous line of arcaded windows serving as an office or showroom,
while the upper floors, which serve for storage only, have very small
windows. In Smith's warehouse in Bristol (a town with several
distinguished architects developing a heavily rusticated style of
warehouse architecture), the young E. W. Godwin in 1858[67] combined
a gable with entirely flat surface and flush windows. A hipped gable
appeared on Crosby House in London, also noted for its large arcaded
windows (1860, by W. Wilkinson of Oxford).[68] A different solution
was provided by G. Somers Clarke in his premises for a publishing
and printing company in West Smithfield [Plate 149]:[69] the emphasis
was on verticals, with long brick piers ending in high pointed windows and surmounted by stepped gables. As on Withers' painted-
glass works in Endell Street of the same year (described in Chapter 4)
the surface remains flat and unbroken by any projections.

From the early sixties examples multiply. Buildings by Deane and
by Waterhouse have been mentioned. Godwin's best example, of
1864, is in Stokes Croft in Bristol,[70] where he dispensed with all

191

149 G. Somers Clarke, London, Printing and Publishing Company,
West Smithfield, 1860 (destroyed) (from the *Building News*, 1860, 895).
The basic subdivisions of this building are classical, the separated ground
floor, the main order comprising three of the upper floors, combined with
Gothic stepped gables. The treatment of the profiles, especially the fact
that there are no projections from the surface, is High Victorian.

detailed ornament. In the same year George Aitchison built what has generally been considered as the purest example of a Ruskinian arcaded façade, 59–61 Mark Lane in the City [Plate 150].[71] Three nearly identical storeys of a series of semicircular arches set on short columns and 'conventionalized' ornament inset in the surface.

These commercial buildings are exceptions in so far as this category of architecture generally was left to specialized local architects. For the 'higher' architects it was a field to which they occasionally condescended. Scott built very little in this category: Beckett's Bank in Leeds[72] of 1863 for his old clients the Denison family, was a rare example, modest in dimensions, little more than a town house and round-arched (destroyed recently). Burges ventured twice into these kinds of town architecture, in his Dry Salters' warehouse at 46 Upper Thames Street in the City [Plate 151][73] and his model lodgings in St Anne's Court, Soho,[74] both of 1866. For each he made use of his stern masonry; the warehouse was criticized for its small windows.

The effect of High Victorian Gothic street architecture must not be overrated. As an exercise in design this type of building remained too much of a 'façade'. The idea of a main cornice was never given up entirely, and the desire for decorative variety was never entirely suppressed. The High Victorian mode did not last very long; in the seventies it was rapidly forgotten and replaced by 'Queen Anne'. There were practical reasons for conservatism, however: although buildings in towns had generally risen above the traditional three or four storeys of the Georgian period, there was seldom need for more than five or six storeys, which could still, with some effort, be included in a conventional façade pattern. It must be observed that when the demand for more storeys arose in America in the seventies (plus the introduction of the passenger lift) architects continued the struggle with classical elevations. The solutions given by New York architects in the seventies (cf. Post's Western Union Building, 1873) seem far inferior to such buildings as Somers Clarke's Publishing Company, and inferior to the various designs proposed for the Record Tower at the Law Courts, which, although meant to serve storage rather than office functions, offered remarkable solutions for a higher type of building. But it took the genius of Louis Sullivan in 1890 to make the point about emphasizing the identity of office 'cells'.[75]

Related to the group discussed above but further remote from High Victorian Gothic and in many ways a continuation of Early Victorian tendencies is the 'Second Empire' mode. It derives its name from the architecture of Imperial France in the fifties and sixties, although, as Hitchcock pointed out,[76] the first examples can probably be found in England. Its main feature is the mansard roof. This must be seen as an element of grandiose domesticity which can easily be subjected to classical rigidity, as well as a useful tool of eclecticism ('northern

150 (above left) G. Aitchison, City of London, 59–61 Mark Lane, offices, 1864 (Courtesy RIBA Drawings Collection).
High Victorian continuous arcading was used to let in more light, but also by leaving out any superimposed order, to avoid the classical integration of the façade – a demand Ruskin made in the first volume of *The Stones of Venice* in 1851 (see above, p. 35). This meant that it was aesthetically possible to add as many storeys as would be needed. But in Britain, in those decades, there did not seem to be that need, whereas shortly later, in the USA, architects had to tackle the problems of a classical elevation again, until Sullivan solved the problem by the identicality of office storeys and continuity of verticals.

151 (above right) W. Burges, City of London, Dry Salters' Warehouse, 46 Upper Thames Street, 1866 (from the *Building News*, 1866, 780).
One of Burges' rare ventures into commercial architecture (very much altered today).

152 John Shaw, City of London, house in Threadneedle Street, 1854
(destroyed) (from the *Builder*, 1855, 97; shop on the left by H. Currey).
A building also remarkable for its disregard of the classical principles of
elevation, by an architect who adopted only polychromy from the range
of High Victorian forms.

Renaissance'). It created the impression (and reality) of more bulk,
just as the tendency in the treatment of the façades was a general
demand for stronger contrasts and more plastic forms.

One of the first to adopt these features in England, together with
some brick polychromy, was the London architect, John Shaw, in
his building ('house') in Threadneedle Street, 1854 [Plate 152][77] (which
also is remarkable in showing four storeys identical in height with
very little variation in detail) and his Wellington College[78] begun in
1856. Another protagonist was James Thomas Knowles senior (with
some assistance from his son of the same name). Knowles' office
building at the corner of Chancery Lane and Fleet Street (demolished)

153 J. T. Knowles Jr., London, Westminster, Grosvenor Hotel, 1860 (Courtesy National Monuments Record).
A combination of Ruskin's and Scott's horizontality and more literally classical motifs; the naturalistic foliage is Ruskinian; the mansard roofs are derived from the 'Second Empire mode', a kind of 'northern Renaissance' feature developed in France and England in the early fifties.

of 1854[79] is not very different from a common street façade of the time, except that the windows are round-arched and the upper storeys are left in London yellow stock brick. Knowles' son, familiar with Ruskin's writings, recommended a 'sober' and 'straightforward' treatment of commercial architecture, and truthfulness, 'cheerfully ornamented' – in essence the same as Scott. Knowles' main work is the Grosvenor Hotel,[80] begun in 1860 [Plate 153], with much Ruskin- and Scott-inspired sculptural decoration. Another example of this typically 'eclectic' attitude is the Langham Hotel (Portland Place, 1864, by Giles & Murray) which 'unites some of the leading forms of Italian with picturesqueness, the freshness, and variety of medieval work'.[81]

The 'iron problem'

In conjunction with the search for a 'new style' expressing the possibilities of the nineteenth century, most writers felt deep concern
about iron in architecture. For technical and economic reasons iron
structures were rising everywhere, especially in new types of buildings, such as railway stations.[82] By 1850 the stage arrived at which in
some buildings architects or decorative artists were called in to assist
the engineer, as in the case of Paddington Station.[83]

In many ways the Ecclesiologists were much more advanced in their
dealings with the problem – at least theoretically. Pugin, whose
principle it was to distinguish between the individual materials and
the way in which they had to be handled, devoted a section of his
True Principles to decorative ironwork. George Truefitt said in 1851:
'attempts should not be made to treat [iron-work] as stone, which
owes its effect to light and shade, for iron work, properly arranged,
trusts to its form only.'[84]

As already explained, by elaborating on the specific qualities of
stone architecture, Ruskin (above, p. 30) had to describe iron-
architecture at least negatively by stating that it is, or should be,
entirely different from stone. The discussion about the 'iron problem'[85]
went into a new phase, where it remained until the 1890s: the principle
of truth demanded that iron should be treated in accordance with its
material properties, but the forms which resulted were not liked
because they did not *look* solid.

In the mid-fifties, the High Victorian Gothicists tried to solve this
problem in two remarkable attempts. The courtyard of the Oxford
Museum [Plate 154], under the direction of Woodward had to be
covered by a large iron roof. The most surprising element is that this
roof is no utilitarian minimum construction, but rests on several rows
of rather narrowly spaced supports which form a series of aisles.
The supports and the arches themselves are carefully distinguished
by their treatment: the pillars are divided into several slender shafts,
whereas the arches are formed by double T-beams. All the iron
ornament appears to be clearly 'stuck on'. The contrast between the
ironwork and the masonry of the walls, brick and various kinds of
stone with continuous arcades and unbroken horizontals, is very
marked indeed. The difference from most earlier iron constructions,
such as Paxton's works, is analogous to the difference between
Butterfield's roughly contemporary iron gates in All Saints, Margaret
Street, and most earlier decorative cast-iron work: the whole appears
to be pieced together clearly out of parts of differently manufactured
iron, especially wrought and cast iron, with a clear differentiation
between the constructional frame and added decoration.

The Museum court was hardly begun when the Ecclesiological
Society itself made a proposal for a building totally designed in iron,

154 B. Woodward, Oxford, University Museum, court, 1855 (from the
Builder, 1860, 399; cf. Plates 123–4).
One of the most remarkable iron constructions at the time, not for its
economic constructional achievement, but for its formal treatment in
relation to the material. There is a clear differentiation between the
different constructional parts and the added ornament.

the 'Iron Church'. The designs by William Slater were published in 1856 in *Instrumenta Ecclesiastica* [Plates 155, 156].[86]

There had, of course, been examples of iron churches before, those by Samuel Hemming of Bristol[87] being the best known. Their purpose was to provide a cheap, practicable substitute for stone churches in distant parts of the Empire. In their design they were strictly utilitarian. It was for this purpose that the Iron Church of the Ecclesiologists had also been designed; there had been an earlier design for a wooden church by Carpenter.[88] But the main aims with this design were higher: 'The problem to be solved is how to employ iron for an ecclesiastical building in accordance with the qualities and conditions of the material,' as it says in the explanations which accompany the drawings. The design on the whole is similar to that of the iron portions of the Oxford Museum. To quote from the more technical parts of the description: 'The external walls are a framework of cast-iron, so arranged as to have the interstices faced internally and externally with corrugated plates, and packed between these plates with felt and sand. The arches (lateral and transverse), the framework of the roofs, and the girders of the aisles are formed of iron-castings riveted together.' The few areas of surfaces left in the inside, T-framed, are relieved as much as possible with openwork decoration. The demands of prefabrication are taken account of: 'as far as possible the same forms have been preserved so as to reduce the number of castings.' 'Truth' is referred to again and again: 'Our drawings show that the framework of this design is of iron. The columns, instead of being cast imitations of stone forms are composed of four detached rods bound together by a spiral band.'

The argument was carried further by F. A. Skidmore of Coventry who was chosen as the prospective contractor for the church – and who carried out numerous church-furnishing commissions for the Ecclesiologist architects – in several lectures on iron architecture to the Ecclesiological Society, the Oxford Architectural Society and later to the Architectural Association.[89] The new material should not only be used 'as a cheap expedient, instead of giving to it that development in Christian art of which it is so capable'.[90] He admits that iron could appear 'thin in its general appearance' (cf. Ruskin above) but he praises the 'delicacy and sharpness of outlines'.[91]

No built or planned example of this Iron Church is known. On the whole, the attitude of the Ecclesiologists towards iron does not become clear and during the following years it underwent changes. First of all, there did not seem to be a consensus as to what a design in iron should look like, taking into account the conditions of the material. A commentator in one of the discussions in the Society 'expressed his doubts whether it [the Iron Church] was not more a stone church built in iron than a design built on purely metallic principles.'[92] And there did not seem to be agreement as regards the merits of the

WEST ELEVATION

155–156 W. Slater, model design for an 'Iron Church', 1856 (from
Instrumenta Ecclesiastica pl. 69 and 72).
Following the Oxford Museum, this design, according to the description,
fulfils the demands for truth to construction as well as for 'ecclesiastical
and architectural treatment'.

Crystal Palace in this respect; doubtless the phrase 'cast imitations of stone forms' refers to buildings like the Crystal Palace. Yet in the same comment on the Iron Church: 'undoubtedly they [the Crystal Palace etc.] show a legitimate use of the material. . . .'[93]

But secondly and more important: the desire to produce something reflecting the special properties of the material and not just something

201

economical, while a consideration, was not the highest aim of the
Society. Although the design could be executed very simply, 'where
poverty would forbid any unnecessary enrichment', it is 'obviously
allowing of any amount of characteristic ornamentation'. Furthermore, the design does not 'abandon architectural forms'. These forms
should be 'ecclesiastical in character and associations'. The well-
known judgment about the Crystal Palace is repeated: '[it falls]
within the province of engineering rather than architecture.' In his
book of 1858, *Remarks on Secular and Domestic Architecture,* Scott
reiterates many remarks of Skidmore's and mentions the Iron
Church.[94] But further on he says: 'Engineering works are very
irregular in point of beauty, some intrinsically fine, others basically
ugly.'[95] They depend on the amount of 'architecture', of 'architectural
touches' added: 'If iron mullions be used, they should assume the
form of pillars.'[96]

Subsequently, very few attempts were made to use iron in more than
a subsidiary way: in architectural discussions iron was refused
'architectural' value.[97] Generally it can be observed that iron buildings
became more ornate. One only needs to compare the two large green-
houses at Kew, the Palm House of 1844 and the Temperate House of
1860, both designed by the same architect.[98]

The attitudes of the Ecclesiologists, Ruskin, and Scott to iron were
influential on another feature of commercial architecture, shop fronts.
Already in the forties criticism was voiced which Scott took up in his
book: he rails against glazed shop windows with the masonry of the
upper storeys supported by thin iron posts: 'to see how a building
is supported is utterly ignored, and fronts of towering altitude are
erected with no apparent substructure but plate glass.'[99]

This problem was avoided, somewhat paradoxically, in that with
the help of hidden iron ties – which Ruskin had allowed explicitly –
very flat segmental arches took the place of the architrave of the
ground floor. One of the first and most characteristic examples of
that is J. H. Chamberlain's nos. 28–29 Union Street, Birmingham, 1856,
already mentioned [Plate 147].[100] On the whole the low segmental
arch became one of the most typical features in the compromising
second half of the century.

Epilogue: the end of High Victorianism eight

Rather than following up the later influence of High Victorian design until it petered out in the late seventies, we might try to look into what caused the end of High Victorianism. In a way, this also means rounding off the story, because, as has been mentioned, several of the most ardent followers of the movement were the main instigators of the new tendencies.

No mention has so far been made of one of the most fascinating architectural personalities of the whole nineteenth century, who began his career in the late fifties: Philip Webb.[1] Like Shaw and Sedding, he was one of the many architects who had served in Street's office. Webb was Street's chief assistant from 1856 to 1859. His first projects are only recorded in descriptions: they seemed to adhere closely to his master's, displaying massiveness together with unusual combinations of motifs.[2] In 1859 he started his first building, Red House at Bexley Heath, outside London, for William Morris.[3] Red House can still be called the most famous building of the later nineteenth century. Since about the start of this century, it has been held to be the beginning of simplicity in modern architecture, at least in domestic design.[4] In recent years, however, historians have pointed out that Webb took over the simplicity from the schools and vicarages of Street and Butterfield. But this is only one aspect of Red House. It is important to state that among the Ecclesiologists' work up to that time, no smaller house in brick could be found which was not built in conjunction with the church or a school. It seems therefore that the Red House can claim to be the first house – suburban house, we would say today – which was built in the purposely simple manner of the Ecclesiologist cottage-type. But there is yet another aspect to Red House: its interior was very richly decorated with paintings and painted furniture, executed by Morris and his group of artists from the younger Pre-Raphaelites. Morris' famous firm for the design and production of church and domestic fittings was more or less started in Red House in 1861. Ornate, story-telling furniture and wall decorations with motifs from nature in Red House – what are the claims of its position as the beginning of simple domestic architecture, the 'Domestic Revival'? Was it not similar to Burges' demand to build simply in order to set off the pictorial decoration?

Tendencies in domestic design have been omitted in this account, except for the cottage. With regard to country houses, architects like Salvin and Clutton continued the earlier tendency of providing

203

totally different designs for different clients. In spite of all his practical recommendations, R. Kerr, with his book *The English Gentleman's House,* first published in 1864, remained within this tradition. Those High Victorians who occasionally did build country houses, like Scott and Seddon, applied their principles of brick and colour just as they did to any other building. The houses of Burges, Nesfield and Godwin of the early and mid-sixties firmly kept to the heavy Gothic manner. Perhaps Pearson's Quar Wood in 1857 [Plate 78], preceded by Teulon's Enbrook in 1853 [Plate 25], with their cottage-type roofs, come nearest to introducing simpler features in country houses: roofs with projecting eaves, tile-hanging, half-timbering, and a reduction of elaborate stone features. Norman Shaw's first house of this sort was Glen Andred near Groombridge (Sussex) of 1867, and in his larger and more famous Leyswood nearby many cottage features were used. A large number of architects followed these designs when they began to be published in 1871.

There were complementary developments in interior design. Ford Madox Brown had designed simple 'cottage' furniture in the fifties and Morris and Webb continued this type in the sixties. But, for Morris at least, 'art' and cottage furniture had to be kept distinct as two different categories. It was the fusion between these categories which brought about a new development in interior design. In 1864 C. L. Eastlake,[5] who later wrote the famous *History of the Gothic Revival,* advocated simple, convenient and truthful furniture. This was directed against manufactured elegance and also against Gothic art furniture, which was too expensive and too elaborate. Eastlake published his views in a book entitled *Hints on Household Furniture* in 1868. It might be called the first book on interior design in a 'modern' sense, because Eastlake purposely separated interior domestic design from architecture when he maintains that in most cases nothing can be done about the outside of town houses, so one should concentrate on the interior.[6] In spite of all their rationalism, it is un-thinkable that Pugin or Street would have practised a reform in a very limited and, for them, subordinate branch of architecture. In fact, as one would expect, neither Street nor Burges nor most of the older Ecclesiologists had any share in these developments of the seventies and eighties. Eastlake's rationalism was concrete enough to stress hygiene, to combine 'art' and hygiene was E. W. Godwin's professed aim in his furniture. One can observe his escape from Gothic heaviness towards light undecorated framework in a drawing for the interior of Dromore, c. 1867–8 [Plate 157]. Godwin understood 'art furniture' in the seventies to mean something light and 'hygenic' rather than heavy and painted.[7]

Eastlake's new style was 'Old English',[8] which meant the furniture of the English seventeenth century, sturdy, wooden and simple, similar to the 'Early French' of Pearson and others. By the late sixties

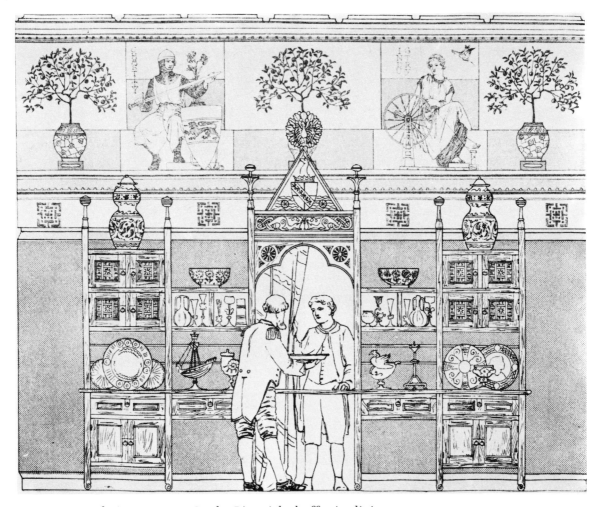

157 E. W. Godwin, Dromore Castle, Limerick, buffet in dining room,
c. 1867 (from the *Architect*, 20 Aug. 1870).
Godwin's furniture in these years is on the point of changing from heavy
carpenter-like Gothic to the lightness and simplicity of the Japanese
fashion and the Aesthetic Movement.

a new national tendency was developing. In 1864 a writer in the
Ecclesiologist had already maintained that the different kinds of
Gothic were a matter of the different sentiments of nations and
English Gothic was not 'grand' but 'homely and sweet', at a time when
Bodley had already turned to English models in his churches. 'Homely',
'comfortable', a certain desire for primitivism made architects search
for new modes of expression. Philip Webb had already found it: the
primitive English brick versions of classical architecture of the
seventeenth and early eighteenth centuries – flat pilasters, squat
columns, sash windows, with white-painted frames and glazing bars
contrasting with the colour of brick [Plate 158].

When all this was codified in the early seventies as the 'Queen

158 Philip Webb, London, 35 Glebe Place, Chelsea, 1869.
Eclecticism and counting on the external effects of materials, especially brick, were elements that the Queen Anne Revival took over from the High Victorian Movement. Gothic or generally arched motifs were abandoned in favour of simplified classical features. Yet there was no return to the simple classical manner of the early nineteenth century. The formal treatment is less orthodox: there is less constructional logic, no adherence to the flat wall surface. The effect is quaint, 'homely and sweet': in one word, vernacular.

Anne Style',[9] it meant the death-blow to further serious efforts in 'Gothic' except in churches. Clearly 'Queen Anne' continued Pugin's and the High Victorians' emphasis on the decorative value of colour especially in brick. But truth of construction was no longer taken so seriously. Not every detail had to be related to constructional logic. It could just be 'quaint'. Not unlike High Victorian Gothic, 'Queen Anne' was eclectic, it was thought to be classical with remnants of the Middle Ages. But it was not a 'high' style, and there was no perfection but that it seemed well suited to ordinary town houses: in short, it was a 'vernacular style'.

As we know through Henry-Russell Hitchcock's writings,[10] the story of High Victorian architecture continued in the United States. There is no need to summarize those developments here. There are many examples of High Victorianism in the States from about the mid-fifties until the late seventies, but they do not seem to amount to much more than a provincial version of the English development. From the mid-seventies it was rapidly replaced by the work and influence of H. H. Richardson and L. H. Sullivan. Richardson grew out of High Victorianism and 'Second Empire': he continued the concept of 'massiveness', but introduced a kind of regular surface-relief which gave his buildings a unity and a geometrical simplicity which no High Victorian work ever possessed.

Between the continent of Europe and England there seemed to be very few exchanges either way. A few continental examples of 'massiveness' in the forties and early fifties have been cited in Chapter 1. But the crucial difference from England was that there were fewer links between the Gothicists and the 'neo-sublime'. Gothic on the continent remained a matter of much more narrow-minded fighters for their symbolic cause. This was true for church architecture, as well as for some German Gothicists, like Ungewitter and Carl Schäfer, who in the fifties and sixties revived half-timbering and other vernacular methods of construction.[11] Only Cuypers, for a moment, seemed to attract the attention of the English. Later, in the seventies, probably influenced by Scott's projects, some German architects tried to combine classical and Gothic elements, such as Friedrich von Schmidt in his Town Hall in Vienna (1872). Viollet-le-Duc's outstanding contributions to architectural history were fully acknowledged, but he built very little. His major work, Saint-Denys-de-l'Estrée at Saint Denis (1864) seems influenced by a growing demand for 'massiveness' as well: spaciousness and height were not the aim of the Gothic constructional system here, but it was nevertheless carried out with great exactitude with all its pillars, shafts, and buttresses.[12]

In short, what the English observer would have missed on the continent in about 1860 were two things: the tradition of sensitivity to form, materials and colour, and the freedom to follow different beliefs and styles in architecture. Neither element reached the continent before the 1880s.

Notes

Abbreviations

AAS   *Associated Architectural Societies' Reports and Papers*

AR   *Architectural Review*

B   *Builder*

BE   *The Buildings of England,* edited by N. Pevsner, Penguin Books, from 1951

BN   *Building News*

CEAJ   *Civil Engineer and Architect's Journal*

Collins   P. Collins, *Changing Ideals in Modern Architecture,* Faber, 1965

Concerning Architecture
   Concerning Architecture, Essays on Architectural Writers and Writing presented to N. Pevsner, edited by J. Summerson, Allen Lane, the Penguin Press, 1968

DNB   *Dictionary of National Biography*

E   *Ecclesiologist*

EGR   Charles L. Eastlake, *A History of the Gothic Revival,* 1872 (new edition, J. M. Crook (ed.), Leicester, 1970)

EVA   H.-R. Hitchcock, *Early Victorian Architecture in Britain,* London and New Haven, 1954

GR   H. S. Goodhart-Rendel, *Index of Victorian Churches* (at the National Monuments Record and the RIBA)

ILN   *Illustrated London News*

JSAH   *Journal of the Society of Architectural Historians* (U.S.A.)

LE   *Library Edition* of the works of John Ruskin, edited by E. T. Cook and A. Wedderburn, 1903–12

RIBA   Royal Institute of British Architects

Str.   H.-R. Hitchcock, 'G. E. Street in the 1850s' in *JSAH,* XIX, 1960, no. 4, 145–71

Summerson, *Heavenly Mansions*
   J. Summerson, *Heavenly Mansions* (collected essays), Cresset Press, 1948

TP   A. W. N. Pugin, *The True Principles of Pointed or Christian Architecture,* 1841

VA   *Victorian Architecture,* edited by P. Ferriday, Cape, 1963

Chapter 1

1   J. Summerson, *Architecture in Britain 1530–1830* (4th ed.), 1964, 306.

2   H.-R. Hitchcock, *Early Victorian Architecture (EVA)* 1954, 612.

3   See Books for Further Reading.

4   B. Ferrey, *Recollections of A. W. N. Pugin . . . ,* 1861. Phoebe

B. Stanton 'Welby Pugin and the Gothic Revival', (unpubl.) Ph.D. thesis. Some comments on . . . Pugin', *RIBA Journal,* 3rd ser., Vol. LX, 1952, 47–54. 'Pugin, Principles of Design versus Revivalism', *JSAH,* XII, 1954, 20–5. 'Sources of Pugin's *Contrasts*', in *Concerning Architecture,* 120–30. *Pugin,* Thames & Hudson, 1971. A. Gordon-Clarke (Wedgwood), 'Pugin', in *VA.*

5 James F. White, *The Cambridge Movement, The Ecclesiologists and the Gothic Revival,* Cambridge, 1962 (cf. the review in the *Times Literary Supplement,* 22 February 1963). A. G. Lough, *The Influence of J. M. Neale,* 1962; cf. also C. F. Port, *Six Hundred New Churches, a Study of the Church Building Commission 1818–1856 and its Church Building Activities,* 1961. P. B. Stanton, *The Gothic Revival and American Church Architecture,* Baltimore, 1968, Ch. I.

6 The best known was the Oxford Society for Promoting the Study of Gothic Architecture, usually called the Oxford Architectural Society, founded 1839, see J. F. White, op. cit.

7 Cf. N. Pevsner, *Academies of Art,* Cambridge, 1940; Street: *E.,* XI, 1850, 40–2; cf. W. White, *B,* 1857, 361 (for the development of architectural professionalism in the fifties see Chapter 7).

8 Complete list of publications in J. F. White, op. cit.

9 See J. F. White, op. cit., 44–6; cf. also *E, V,* 1846, 33.

10 The first weekly architectural journal; cf. Arthur Cox, *These Stones, The Story of the Builder,* 1937.

11 Donald Pilcher, *The Regency Style,* 1947; cf. also D. Watkin, *Thomas Hope and the Neo-Classical Idea,* 1968.

12 See *EVA,* 211, 213, etc.; e.g. Gothic: the church at Deptford, St John, Lewisham Way (*B,* 1854, 533, *EGR,* No. 118, *BE London II,* 104); Brantham Court (1850–2, *BE Suffolk,* 101) is 'Elizabethan'; classical: Paddington Hotel (1851–3, *EVA,* 211–14, *BE London II,* 304). For discussions see, among others, the writings of J. Fergusson; Collins, 119; cf. *B,* 1848, 88; see below, note 16.

13 *EGR,* 233.

14 See L. Grote, N. Pevsner, H. G. Evers and others, *Historismus und bildende Kunst* (Discussion Fritz Thyssen Stiftung, nineteenth-century research project), Munich, 1965; C. L. V. Meeks, *The Railway Station,* London and New Haven, 1957; Jan Białostocki, 'Romantische Ikonographie', in *Stil und Ikonographie,* Dresden, 1965; Collins, Chapters IV–XIII.

15 The first opinion is shared by the majority of modern writers on Pugin's theories and buildings (cf. *EVA,* 84; S. Lang in *JSAH,* XXV, 1966, 267: ' . . . Pugin, under the guise of Gothic, achieved a highly original style'). The other interpretation is found in P. Stanton's article, 'Pugin, Principles of Design versus Revivalism' (see above, note 4).

16 Cf. Pilcher, op. cit., 67–76. For the discussions around 1850 see *EVA,* 604–6; for later discussions see Chapter 7.

17 See Walter John Hipple, *The Beautiful, The Sublime, and the Picturesque in 18th Century British Aesthetic Theory,* Carbondale, Ill., 1957; Samuel Monk, *The Sublime,* Ann Arbor, 1960; C. Hussey, *The Picturesque . . . ,* 1927 (1967); N. Pevsner, 'Price on

Picturesque Planning', 'The Picturesque in Architecture', reprinted in N. Pevsner, *Studies in Art, Architecture and Design,* 1968, Vol. I. Uvedale Price, *Essays on the Picturesque, as compared with the Sublime and Beautiful . . . ,* 1794; 'Essay on Architecture' is part of the 2nd Vol., 1798. J. C. Loudon (ed.), *Architectural Magazine,* 1834–8; idem, *An Encyclopedia of Cottage, Farm and Villa Architecture and furniture . . . ,* 1835. Sir Thomas Dick Lauder, *Sir Uvedale Price on the Picturesque,* Edinburgh, 1842. For a recent short discussion of the links between the theories and architecture in the eighteenth century see D. Wiebenson, ' "L'Architecture terrible" and the "jardin anglo-chinois" ', *JSAH,* May 1968, 136 etc.

18 *TP,* 63.

19 *E,* II, 1843, 147.

20 *EVA,* 185–7. For problems of proportion see further 'Proportion in Gothic Architecture', *E,* IX, 1848, 27–31.

21 See *EVA,* 88–90.

22 N. Pevsner, *M. D. Wyatt,* Cambridge, 1950, 41; see also P. Frankl, *The Gothic,* Princeton, N.J., 1960, 555.

23 In England the Ecclesiologists were reproached by rationalists, such as George Wightwick, who advocated 'convenience' and 'utility' in centralized plans (see J. F. White, op. cit., note 5, 130–1).

24 *TP,* 63.

25 *EVA,* 157.

26 *A Few Words to Church Builders,* 3.

27 *E,* V, 1846, 3. See also the introduction by J. Mason Neale and Benjamin Webb to the new edition of the medieval treatise *Durandus' Symbolism,* 1843 (i.e. Bishop of Mende, *Rationale Divinorum Officiorum*); cf. also G. A. Poole, *The Appropriate Character of Church Architecture,* 1842.

28 J. F. White, op. cit., 94.

29 *A Few Words to Church Builders,* 7.

30 See J. F. White, op. cit.; a more controversial feature was the chancel screen. See also Peter F. Anson, *Victorian Church Furnishings 1840–1940,* 1961.

31 *E,* II, 1843, 120. Cf. J. Summerson, 'J. Gandy', in *Heavenly Mansions.*

32 'On Sacristies' *E,* VI, 1846, 5–10; cf. also 'The Warming of Churches', *E,* III, 1844, 136 etc. According to Neale and Webb (introduction to *Durandus' Symbolism,* op. cit., note 27, p. xxvii) Pugin had planned in those years a 'work on the reality of domestic architecture', of which nothing is known otherwise, but his *Apology for the Revival of Christian Architecture in England,* 1843, contains many secular designs.

33 'On Parsonage Houses', *E,* II, 1843, 145–7.

34 See *EVA,* 231–2. Cf. A. Salvin's Scotney Castle (Lamberhurst, Kent), 1837, Pugin's own house at Ramsgate, 1841, the vicarage at Coalpit Heath (Glos.), 1844, by Butterfield and Wilburton House by Pugin, 1848 (*BE Cambs.,* 400). For the general development of

35 *E*, VII, 1847, 1–6; cf. M. Seaborne, *The English School, Its Architecture and Organization*, Routledge & Kegan Paul, 1971.

36 See note 35.

37 See W. H. Dykes, 'On the Arrangement of Monasteries', 1851, *AAS*, I, 293–306; see *TP*.

38 See note 35.

39 G. G. Scott, *Secular and Domestic Architecture*, 1858, 227.

40 ' . . . the science of so placing a church, as best to harmonize with the surrounding scenery, and to receive the greatest beauty from it . . . ' *E*, IV, 1845, 264.

41 Pilcher, op. cit., 89. A typical example is Baldersby St James by William Butterfield, see above pp. 70–3.

42 Cf. the Society's publication *Churches of Cambridgeshire and the Isle of Ely*, 1845, ill. by Butterfield; 'Architectural Localisms', *E*, X, 1849–50.

43 *E*, XI, 1850, 34–42; see also 'On the Distinctive feature of Middle Pointed Architecture of Cornwall', 1850, in *Exeter Diocesan Architectural Society Transactions*, IV, 1853, 86–102.

44 'Attempts to follow particular themes through the years from the mid thirties to the end of the century rarely convince' (H.-R. Hitchcock, 'High Victorian Architecture' in *Victorian Studies* I, 1957, 49).

45 *E*, II, 1843, 118–21.

46 *A Few Words to Church Builders*, 4.

47 *E*, VII, 1847, 41. See also W. Airy, 'Rubble or Rubbish, an Apology for Rubble Walls', *AAS*, I, 1851, 372–81.

48 See Alf Bøe, *From Gothic Revival to Functional Form, a Study in Victorian Theories of Design*, Oslo and Oxford, 1957; N. Pevsner, *Pioneers of Modern Design*, 1960; *M. D. Wyatt*, 1950.

49 Cf. Peter Nicholson, *New Practical Builder*, 1827, an imitation of J. B. Rondelet, *L'Art de Bâtir* (1st ed. 1802; see Collins, 203–4). For earlier developments of the moralistic problems see Eberhard Hempel, *Material und Strukturechtheit in der Architektur, Abhandlungen der Sächsischen Akademie der Wissenschaften zu Leipzig*, Philolog. Hist. Klasse, Vol. 48, Heft 3, Berlin, 1956.

50 See the first pages of *TP*; Collins, 211–14, Ch. 19; P. Frankl, *The Gothic*, Princeton, N.J., 1960; Wolfgang Hermann, *Laugier and 18th Century French Theory*, 1962; R. D. Middleton, 'Viollet-le-Duc and the Rational Gothic Tradition', unpubl. Ph.D. thesis, Cambridge, 1958 (see also idem in *Journal of the Warburg and Courtauld Institutes*, XXV, 1962, 278–320; XXVI, 1963, 90–124). For England see Frankl, op. cit.; for A. Bartholemew see G. G. Pace, 'Alfred Bartholomew, A pioneer of Functional Gothic', *AR*, 92, 1942, 92–102. For Whewell see N. Pevsner, 'W. Whewell and his notes on German churches', in *German Life & Letters*, Vol. XXII, Oct. 1968, 39 etc. For Willis see N. Pevsner, *R. Willis*, Smith College Studies in History 46, Northampton, Mass., 1970.

the parsonage see Anthony Bax, *The English Parsonage*, 1964; Alan Savidge, *The Parsonage in England, its History and Architecture*, 1964.

51 See Chapter 2, note 23.

52 *TP*, 45.

53 *TP*, 17, Plate II.

54 Cf. Marlow R. C. Church built in 1844, *BE Bucks.*, 198.

55 *E*, VI, 1846, 41–5.

56 'Manly' and 'austere' were the characteristics of Butterfield's All Saints, Margaret Street; ' . . . in spite of the smallness of scale he has approached the sublime in architecture' (*E*, XX, 1859, 186).

57 For Streatham see below, note 106; for Salvin (Peckforton, 1840s) see *EVA*, Ch. VIII; and for Alnwick (1854), *B*, 1856, 646, 673 and *BE Northumberland*, 68. Other styles; Louis XIV: Marbury Hall (Cheshire 1856); Classical-Renaissance: County Hotel, Carlisle, 1856.

58 'Simplicity of Composition', *E*, II, 1843, 118–22; Price, *Essays on the Picturesque*, 2nd Vol., 1798, 421; T. D. Lauder's edition (1842), 405. One of the passages from *Simplicity of Composition* may be given here in full: 'It must, nevertheless, be observed, that there is a wide and important difference between plainness and meagreness in church architecture. The former is simply the absence of ornamental detail, the latter is a scanty and stinted development of the essential parts of construction. A building may be plain, and yet perfectly graceful and pleasing; but if it be also meagre, it necessarily becomes ugly; . . . Costliness and ornament should be regarded only as a step in advance of plainness and simplicity. The same elements of beauty are contained in both, but only in one is it developed. The absurdity, therefore, of ornamental meagreness instead of simple massiveness is evident, since decoration was never intended as a substitute for, but only as an addition to, solid and substantial construction.'

59 See *EVA*, 73–5; *BE South Lancs.*, 350.

60 1842–4; illustrated in A. W. N. Pugin, *The Present State of Ecclesiastical Architecture in England*, 1843; *EVA*, 84–5; *BE Notts.*, 125–6.

61 Signed 'F.A.P.', probably Frederick Apthorpe Paley (1815–88), an amateur architectural historian (not to be confounded with the architect E. G. Paley).

62 Op. cit., 14.

63 See P. B. Stanton, 'Pugin, Principles of Design versus Revivalism', *JSAH*, XII, 1954, 20–5.

64 Cf. also Pugin's designs for Railway Stations in *An Apology . . . .*, 1843.

65 *A Few Words to Church Builders*, 1841, 16–18; *The British Critic*, No. 58, April 1841; Phil. Freeman, Lect. Eccles. Soc., 1841 (*Transactions of the Ecclesiological Society*, 1845, 105 etc.); *E*, III, 1843–4, 72 etc.; J. R. and R. A. Brandon, *Open Timber Roofs in the Middle Ages*, 1849; there is much less in later years; cf. G. A. Poole, *AAS*, II, 381–94. Wooden churches: see *E*, IV, 1845, 148; *E*, IX, 1849, 14; R. C. Carpenter's design for the *Instrumenta Ecclesiastica* (2nd Ser., 1851, pls. 19–26), a framework of heavy beams with windows cut out as lancets in thinner panels.

66 On this most prolific Victorian church architect see the *List of*

Works, compiled in the RIBA Library (Molesworth-Roberts) in 1957;
D. Cole, 'Some Early Works by G. G. Scott', in *Architectural
Association Journal,* LXVI, 1951, 98 etc.; D. Cole, 'G. G. Scott',
in *VA; EVA.*

67   E.g. Christ Church, Turnham Green, 1843 (*BE Middx,* 31).

68   Ramsgate, begun 1846; information kindly supplied by J. Edgar
     Ralph, Ramsgate. Alderney: *EVA,* 145; *ILN,* 5 October 1850.

69   E.g. St John the Evangelist, Leeds-Holbeck, 1847, destroyed, drawings
     in RIBA Collection; more about Scott in Chapters 5 and 7.

70   For Street see below, note 1 Chapter 3; see *EVA,* 145, 603. Hitchcock
     ascribes the tower of St Matthew's, City Road, to Street (1847,
     destroyed in the last war) and the 'plate tracery' of St John's
     Newfoundland (begun 1846; cf. further Basil F. L. Clarke, *Anglican
     Cathedrals outside the British Isles,* 1958, 55–7).

71   Additional sources for Par (besides *Str.* 146): plan in the church
     signed by Street, 22 February 1847; consecrated 1 November 1848;
     E, IX, 1849, 393–5; *Transact. of the Exeter Diocesan Architectural
     Society,* IV, 1853, 23; see also John Betjeman's recent pamphlet,
     An Appeal . . . , n.d.

72   Influenced by local medieval towers (Lostwithiel and Cubert)
     cf. below, Chapter 3 (information, Paul Joyce).

73   See *DNB* and obituary in the *Architect,* 2 January 1869.

74   On architectural drawing since Piranesi see H. Focillon, *Piranesi,*
     Paris, 1928; Ulya Vogt Göknil, *G. B. Piranesi, 'Carceri',* Zürich,
     1958; G. Eimer, *C. D. Friedrich und die Gotik,* Hamburg, 1963.

75   See J. Summerson, 'The Vision of J. M. Gandy', in *Heavenly Mansions.*

76   Cf. Ruskin, *LE* Index. For Pugin's drawings see *Photographs from
     Sketches by Pugin,* ed. E. W. Pugin, 2 vols, 1865.

77   Published again as *Remarks on the Principles of Gothic Architecture
     as applied to ordinary Parish Churches,* Oxford, 1846.

78   *Remarks on Church Architecture,* 1841, 41.

79   *Architectural Studies in France,* 178, 5.

80   *RIBA Transactions,* 1st Ser., Vol. for 1854–55, 97 ff.

81   Petit saw this building before the rebuilding by Ballu had started.

82   Illustrated in Petit, *Architectural Studies in France,* 79; Petit's
     books were very carefully reviewed; see esp. *Remarks, E,* I, 1842,
     87; *Architectural Character, E,* VI, 1846, 126–33; *Architectural
     Studies, E,* XVI, 1855, 100–10.

83   For the development of architectural polychromy see Collins, Ch. 2;
     for the earlier years, especially in France, see R. D. Middleton (op.
     cit., note 50). Cf. also H.-R. Hitchcock, *Architecture: Nineteenth
     and Twentieth Centuries,* 1958, 433 n.3. See also Michael G. Murray,
     'The Nineteenth Century External Polychromatic Revival, A Study
     of the Origins and Development of the Revival of External Colour in
     Victorian Architecture', unpubl. thesis, 1950. (I have to thank Mr
     Murray and Mr Middleton for their help.) For a recent discussion
     of the early archaeological controversies about polychromy in France
     and Germany see Karl Hammer, *Jakob Ignaz Hittorf, ein Pariser
     Baumeister,* Stuttgart, 1968, 101 etc; see also M. Steinhauser,
     Die Architektur der Pariser Oper, Munich, 1969, 63–5.

84 P. de Gayanos and Owen Jones, *Plans . . . of the Alhambra*, 1842;
F. O. Ward and Owen Jones, *Designs for Mosaic and Tesselated
Pavements*, 1842. For Owen Jones see D. T. van Zanten, 'J. W.
Mould, Echoes of Owen Jones and the High Victorian Styles in
New York 1853–65', *JSAH*, XXVIII, 1969, 41–57.

86 John Whichcord, 'Observations on the Polychromatic Decorations
of the Middle Ages', in *Weale's Quarterly Papers of Architecture,*
IV, 1845.

87 *E,* IV, 1845, 199–203.

88 Especially the Allerheiligen Hofkirche (by Klenze, 1826) and St
Bonifazius (by Ziebland, 1835); see Benjamin Webb, *Sketches of
Continental Ecclesiology*, 1848, 137–40.

89 'No one, except in the spirit of contradiction, would say that in
gilding stone, we wish to make people fancy it gold. We only
seek to bestow on it a beauty which it has not by nature; and
whether this is done by adding colour or calling forth form, can
make no difference to the principle of reality' (*E,* IV, 1845, 201).

90 See *EVA,* 81 etc.

91 A. Pugin, 'Some Remarks on Articles which have appeared in the
Rambler relative to Ecclesiastical Architecture and Decoration',
as reviewed in *E, X,* 1850, 393–7.

92 Cf. M. G. Murray (op. cit., note 83, 34): ' . . . the key to polychromy lay in the juxtaposition and colour contrast of natural
building materials . . . against colour obtained by superficial
application.' A compromise was coloured tiles, see *EVA,* 574.
The fact that stones used in architecture were of different colours
had, of course, been noticed before, but different effects were
advocated; in 1848 a writer still demanded: 'The tints of the
materials of a building should harmonize as much as possible
with the surrounding objects.' (*B,* 1848, 260). The term 'natural
polychromy' appeared already in 1837 in a description of the
interior of some Roman churches (*Architectural Magazine,* IV,
1837, 97–112). From 1845 onwards it was noticed more and more:
'A sort of natural polychromy is produced by the rich and varied
tints by which the stone is varied' (*E,* IV, 1845, 235, St Mark's,
Great Wyrley, Staffs., by T. Johnson, 1845); for other early
examples see *EVA,* 575, 578. Another term frequently used was
permanent polychromy' (J. Ruskin, *The Stones of Venice*, Vol. II,
1853, Ch. 3, para. 29).

93 *Transactions of the Ecclesiological Society,* 1845, 199–218.

94 Questions of ventilation formed an important part in architectural-
technical discussions of these years, cf. Collins 235, *EVA,* Ch. IX.

95 See *EVA,* 122 and ill.

96 Whereas a William Scott, M.A., in 'Some Notes on the Cathedral of
Las Palmas, with a few thoughts on Tropical Architecture', still
talked in a more general way about 'flatness' and 'speluncar interiors' (*E,* XII, 1851, 20), the Rev. J. F. Bourne, 'of Guinea', goes
much more into the actual practical requirements of the climate
('On Tropical Architecture', *E,* XII, 1851, 169). Cf. Plate 82 below.

97 *Continental Ecclesiology,* 252–3.

98 Op. cit., 246; cf. also the review of the book, not yet entirely favourable, in *E*, IX, 1849, 230.

99 *A Few Words to Church Builders*, 9.

100 In *Fourth Report of the Architectural Society of the Archdeaconry of Northampton*, 25–37.

101 *E*, VI, 1847, 98–101: ' . . . and from its exceedingly anomalous character it would hardly be safe to regard it as a model, yet we must confess that considering its material it is architecturally speaking a legitimate piece of construction and may in more ways than one afford valuable hints for the future' (cf. the *Ecclesiologist's* remarks about Butterfield's brick design for Adelaide Cathedral in 1847, Chapter 4).

102 *E*, VIII, 1848, 91–2; see *EVA*, 150 and ill.

103 'Medieval Brick Buildings in Germany', *B*, 1850, 112; Spain: J. B. Waring in *B*, 1851, 733; *B*, 1852, 37, 168, 180, 197.

104 See generally *The Victorian Vision of Italy*, Catalogue, Leicester Museum and Art Gallery, 1968; Thomas Hope, *Historical Essay on Architecture*, 1835; R. Willis, *Remarks on the Architecture of the Middle Ages, especially of Italy*, 1835; H. Gally Knight, *Ecclesiastical Architecture of Italy from the Time of Constantine to the 15th Century*, 1842–4; Street's comment in *Brick and Marble*, 1855, 101.

105 L. Runge, *Beiträge zur Kenntniss der Backstein-Architektur Italiens, nach Reiseskizzen . . .* , 2nd ser., Berlin, 1846–53. For German research on medieval Italy cf. Georg Friedrich Koch, 'Karl Friedrich Schinkel, und die Architektur des Mittelalters, die Studien auf der ersten Italienreise und ihre Auswirkungen', in *Zeitschrift für Kunstgeschichte*, Vol. 29, 1966, Heft 3, 177–222). The earlier continental developments of architectural polychromy as distinct from the archaeologists' arguments and Nazarene interior decoration have not been gone into so far. As far as external polychromatic detailing is concerned, probably the most interesting architect was Schinkel. He tended to use brick in his buildings of lesser standing, and occasionally used coloured bricks. Thus in his Berlin Bauakademie of 1832 he used, as he writes, coloured bands to emphasize the subdivisions of the buildings and to relieve the overall colour of the material (see K. F. Schinkel, *Sammlung architektonischer Entwürfe*, 1819 ff.).

106 Streatham: see *EVA*, 106–7, *BE London II*, 442; see T. James, op. cit., 36; J. Ruskin, *The Stones of Venice* I, Ch. 26 para. 4. Lincoln's Inn Library: see *EVA*, 313, *BE London I*, 278. For the general development of the brick-making industry see Alec Clifton-Taylor, *Patterns in English Building*, 1962, 222, 243. The development was speeded by the lifting of the brick tax in 1850 and by new and more mechanized methods of production.

107 *E*, XVI, 1855, 239; H. Bramsen, G. Bindesbøll, Copenhagen, 1959.

Chapter 2

N.B. In references for *The Seven Lamps* and *The Stones of Venice*, roman figures refer to the chapter, arabic figures to the paragraph.

1 For Ruskin see the *Library Edition* (*LE*), ed. E. T. Cook and A. Wedderburn, 39 vols., 1903–12; cf. introduction of vols. I–XIII for biography; cf. the general index, vol. XXXIX. For literature on Ruskin, see *LE* vol. XXXVII; cf. also *BN*, 1900, I, 149, 225. For more recent literature see John D. Rosenberg, *The Darkening Glass, A Portrait of Ruskin's Genius*, New York, 1961, London, 1963; Catalogue of the Exhibition *J. R.*, The Arts Council of Great Britain, 1964; *Ruskin Today,* chosen and annotated by Sir Kenneth Clark, 1964; *The Art Criticism of John Ruskin,* ed. R. L. Herbert, Garden City, N.Y., 1964; see, further, notes 2, 5, 10, 12, 16, 32, 51, 53, 54, 61.

2 Ruskin had dealt with the subject of cottage architecture in his articles on 'The Poetry of Architecture', 1836–7 (Loudon's *Architectural Magazine,* Vols. 4, 5 (*LE,* I); see Graham Hough, 'Kata Phusin', *AR,* 106, 1949, 279.

3 *Praeterita* II, VI, 1886–7 (*LE,* XXXV, 350).

4 *Modern Painters,* II, Epilogue 1883 (*LE,* IV, 346–7). Cf. the greater part of *Mod. Ptrs* Vol. I, part II, sect. I, Ch. VII, Par. 25, etc.

5 For Ruskin's drawings in general see J. H. Whitehouse, *Ruskin the Painter . . .* , 1938; see also *LE,* XXXVIII, 216f.

6 *LE,* III, 207, 208.

7 Drawings in pen and wash; for more details see Catalogue *LE,* XXXVII; Plates: Lucca, San Michele façade etc., *LE,* III, 206; Pisa, Santa Maria della Spina, 1840, IV, 136; Pisa, 1845, XXVII, 349.

8 *LE* XI.

9 For Pisa drawing, *LE,* XXVII, 349; *Praeterita: LE,* XXXV, 372–3; letter 1845, *LE,* III, 210. For photography and architecture see *B,* 1853, 61, *B,* 1856, 38, *E,* XVII, 1856, 219, *E,* XVII, 1856, 429–30, *AAS,* III, 340. Archit. Photogr. Soc. *B,* 1857, 249. See also A. Scharf, *Art and Photography,* 1968.

10 London, 1847, Ruskin's review appeared in the *Quarterly Review,* No. 81, June 1847, 1–57, *LE,* XII; cf. John Steegman, 'Lord Lindsay's History of Christian Art', *Journal of the Warburg and Courtauld Institutes,* X, 1947, 123–31; Francis G. Townsend, 'Ruskin and Landscape Feeling. A critical Analysis of his Thoughts during the Crucial Years of his Life 1843–56', *Illinois Studies of Language and Literature,* Vol. 35, No. 3, 1951.

11 2nd ed. 1855; cf. *LE,* pp. VIII, XXIII, LI, 278–9.

12 See Ruskin's own surveys of the contents of Chs. III and IV in IV, 43. For the links with older aesthetic and ethical theories see H. Ladd, *The Victorian Morality of Art, An Analysis of Ruskin's Ethic,* 1932 (recently reprinted).

13 II, 6–8, 14.

14 II, 18–20.

15 II, 9–10.

16 VI, 18. The argument however, is very diffuse. Ruskin deals with the role of architecture as an exponent of the time in which it was built, mainly thinking of the narrative sculpture of its decoration; 'delight in decay' (VI, 11 etc.) has only accidental value. But he goes on to state that 'picturesque or extraneous sublimity of

architecture has . . . just this nobler function . . . that it is an
exponent of age . . . the greatest glory of a building . . .' (VI, 16).
A building has to be five hundred years old 'to be considered
in its prime', but Ruskin then reasons that one should avoid
'mechanical degradation'. In the following paragraph (VI, 17),
after stating that the argument is very complex, he sums up that
hard materials go with purity of outline, whereas soft materials
gain in the state of decay. Then, again, 'the sweetness of gentle
line, which the rain and the sun had wrought' (VI, 18) are called
in to prove the anti-restoration argument. These opinions can also
be traced back into the mid-forties; in a letter from Venice in 1845
he wrote of the restoration of the Ca' d'Oro: 'I must do what I
can [i.e. draw], to save a little, the workmen were hammering
it down before my face . . .' (*LE,* III, 214, n.1). Later he was
even more sharply opposed to 'restoration' in his pamphlet *The
Crystal Palace,* 1854 (*LE,* XII; see N. Pevsner, *M. D. Wyatt,*
Cambridge, 1950, 22, 43). For the problem of restoration in these
decades see Martin S. Briggs, *Goths and Vandals . . . ,* 1952; Peter
Ferriday, 'The Church Restorers', *AR,* 136, 1964, 87–95; J. Summerson,
in *Historic Preservation Today, Essays . . .* (Williamsburg, 1963)
Univ. Press of Virginia, Charlottesville, 1966.

17 II, 18.

18 IV, 38–9; cf. Plate VIII, *The Stones of Venice,* I. In *Modern Painters,*
I, 1843, Ruskin still maintained that 'Colour is subjected to an
inviolable law of chiaroscuro' (*LE,* III, 299), but in *Modern
Painters,* II, 1846, he already wrote of 'brightness of unshadowed
colour' (*LE,* IV, 206, 324–51; see also his own survey on his
opinions about colour in *Modern Painters* V, *LE,* VIII, 414 ff.).
Cf. also Collins, 113–14; cf. below, note 21.

19 *The Stones of Venice,* Vol. I, XXVI, 6.

20 *The Seven Lamps,* III, 8.

21 *TP,* 29. Again the argument is more complicated; Ruskin has
to struggle with his own liking of broken surfaces: 'if breadth is
to be beautiful, its substance must in some sort be beautiful;
and we must not hastily condemn the exclusive resting of the
northern architects in divided lines, until at least we have
remembered the difference between a blank surface of Caen Stone,
and one mixed from Genoa and Carrara, of serpentine with snow.'
(III, 8.) A passage from the review of Lord Lindsay's book
might further elucidate these points: 'We have already alluded
to the great school of colour which arose in the immediate
neighbourhood of the Genoa serpentine. The accessibility of marble
throughout North Italy similarly modified the aim of all design,
by the admission of undecorated surfaces. A blank space of
freestone wall is always uninteresting, and sometimes offensive;
there is no suggestion of preciousness in its dull colour, and the
stains and rents of time upon it are dark, coarse, and gloomy. But
a marble surface receives in its age hues of continually increasing
glow and grandeur; its stains are never foul nor dim; its
undecomposing surface preserves a soft, fruit-like polish for

ever, slowly flushed by the maturing suns of centuries. Hence, while in the Northern Gothic the effort of the architect was always so to diffuse his ornament as to prevent the eye from permanently resting on the blank material, the Italian fearlessly left fallow large fields of uncarved surface, and concentrated the labour of the chisel on detached portions, in which the eye, being rather directed to them by their isolation than attracted by their salience, required perfect finish and pure design rather than force of shade or breadth of parts; and further, the intensity of Italian sunshine articulated by perfect gradations, and defined by sharp shadows at the edge, such inner anatomy and minuteness of outline as would have been utterly vain and valueless under the gloom of a northern sky; while again the fineness of material both admitted of, and allured to, the precision of execution which the climate was calculated to exhibit.' (*LE*, XII, 197–8.)

22 III, 6–10.
23 For Burke see *Enquiry . . . Ideas of the Sublime and the Beautiful*, 1757, Pt. II, Sect. 9 'Succession and uniformity'. For Boullée see Helen Rosenau, *Boullée's Treatise on Architecture* (*Architecture, Essai sur l'art*), 1953, 44, 84; Ruskin: 'machicolations', *The Seven Lamps*, III, 7.
24 III, 12–15.
25 *The Seven Lamps*, III, 21–23 and *The Stones of Venice*, II, Plate 12; cf. Whewell's review of *The Seven Lamps* in *Fraser's Magazine*, February 1850, 157.
26 IV, 35.
27 IV, 42.
28 Ruskin collected the material during winter 1849 and spring 1850; see *LE*, VIII, IX, Introductions. Second edition of the 1st Vol., 1858.
29 See Collins, chapters 18, 19.
30 *Stones of Venice* I, II, 15. E.g. the problems of the foundations of a building are reduced to a few lines (IV, 7).
31 IV, 5.
32 Ch. V; see Hélène Lemaître, *Les Pierres dans l'oeuvre de Ruskin*, Caen, 1965.
33 IV, 5.
34 XXVI, 1; IV, 6
35 IV, 4–6. Ruskin terms this part of the wall 'wall-veil', which means the same as 'wall body' (IV, 4); as this term was used very little at the time it is not used in the present context, either. Little special illustration is given; but cf. fig. 2 ch. IV and also Plates XIII and XXI.
36 *The Seven Lamps*, III, 5–8.
37 Ruskin resumed the discussion about masonry on several occasions. 'Masonry must be shown': he adopts the moralizing demands of the period and talks about rough masonry (*The Seven Lamps*, III, 11) but again he prefers smoothed surface. In *The Stones of Venice* he discusses the various kinds of laying the stones again, but he comes to the conclusion, similarly to the *Ecclesiologist* in 'On Masonry' (cf. above p. 13), that the best masonry is that in

which the division in the individual building stones is not
noticed (V, 7).

38   XV, 9–11.

39   V, 5.

40   *The Seven Lamps*, II, 23.

41   *The Stones of Venice*, II, VI, 110.

42   E. Lundberg (*Arkitekturens Formspråk*, Vol. X, Stockholm, 1960,
35) stresses the importance of Ruskin's 'materialistic' interpretation
of the columns as bearers of load as against the classical concepts
of symbolism and overall patterns; but it must be remembered
that in this point Ruskin stands firmly in the tradition of
Rationalism.

43   *The Stones of Venice*, I, XIX, 10, VIII, 30.

44   XIX, 11–14; the towers on the left in Plate VI, the Free Church
College at Edinburgh, built in 1846–50, with which the Campanile
is contrasted, are somewhat understated in their size. Cf. Pugin's
description of a medieval tower: ' . . . not formed of *detached
and misapplied* portions stuck over another to make up a height
[he speaks of Wren's towers] but solid buttresses and walls rising
from a massive base, and gradually diminishing and enriching as
they rise, till they were terminated in a heaven-pointing spire,
surrounded by clusters of pinnacles'. (*TP*, 49.) Here 'uprightness'
seems more concerned with outline than with mass.

45   XIII, 10.

46   XXIX, 4. Collins (285–6) briefly deals with the origins of modern
concepts of space and proves that the word 'space', or 'espace',
had rarely been used with modern architectural meaning before
the middle of the nineteenth century. In Ruskin's writings it still
has several meanings, the most frequent meaning is 'sphere'
or 'compartment': ' . . . other buildings are mere enclosures of
space, as ramparts and walls . . . and have no roofs at all' (*The
Stones of Venice*, II, VI, 130); very often it is synonymous with
'mass', 'masses of light and shade', 'spaces of light and
darkness' (*The Seven Lamps*, III, 13). One may, however, interpret
some lines in *The Stones* as a tendency to think of space as a
correlative to 'mass': 'horizontal bands of colour . . . , they
are valuable as an expression of horizontal space to the
imagination, space of which the conception is opposed and gives
more effect by its opposition, to the enclosing power of the
wall itself' (XXVI, 1). If 'enclosing power' is brought together with
'space' one may get something like the 'space-enclosing mass of
wall' of H. Lotze ('raumumfassende Mauermasse', in *Geschichte
der Aesthetik in Deutschland*, Munich, 1868, 'Die Baukunst', 531).

47   *The Stones of Venice* I, XIX, 2. Ruskin sometimes conventionally
lists the division of building types (*The Seven Lamps*, I, 2; *The
Stones of Venice*, I, III, 1), but he never goes into any detail. In
The Seven Lamps another remark may be interpreted in the same
way; when dealing with the importance of size he writes: 'The
limitation of size must be only in the use of the building, or in the
grounds at his disposal.' (III, 5.)

48 *The Seven Lamps,* IV, 25.

49 *The Stones of Venice,* I, XIX, 7, 8. See H. Ladd, op. cit., note 12 above.

50 *The Stones of Venice,* I, XIII, 6.

51 In the Chapter 'Obedience' in *The Seven Lamps.* 'Obedience' means one has to follow certain architectural styles. Ruskin recommends: '1. Pisan Romanesque; 2. The early Gothic of the Western Italian Republics advanced as far and as fast as our art would enable us to the Gothic of Giotto; 3. The Venetian Gothic in its purest development; 4. The English earliest decorated' (*The Seven Lamps,* VII, 7). No. 4 is least highly thought of; later he would have added the Gothic architecture of Verona, see *The Seven Lamps,* Preface 2nd ed., 1855, *LE,* VIII, 13. For Ruskin's studies at Verona see the Catalogue of the exhibition: *Ruskin a Verona,* Museo del Castel Vecchio at Verona, with comments by Terence Mullaby, 1966.

52 'Ruskin . . . was one of the earliest, and remains one of the most articulate, advocates of functionalism,' writes Rosenberg (op. cit., note 1 above, 60) and refers to ' . . . Gothic . . . the only rational architecture' (*The Stones of Venice,* II, VI, 38). This view can hardly be supported, as Ruskin's writings contain more anti-'functional' and anti-'rational' elements than those of most other architectural writings of the time. Collins holds a rather different view in that he denies any major rational elements in Ruskin's theories. This seems overstated, at least for the years before 1851; Collins' quotation, 'The science of inner construction has to be abandoned', does not come, as Collins (114) writes, from the first volume of *The Stones,* but from the second volume of 1853 (*The Stones of Venice,* II, IV, 31).

53 See *EVA,* 609–11; H.-R. Hitchcock, 'High Victorian Architecture', in *Victorian Studies,* Vol I, 1957; *Architecture: Nineteenth and Twentieth centuries,* 1958, 175–6; 'Ruskin and American Architecture . . .', in *Concerning Architecture.*

54 E.g. cf. N. Pevsner, *Pioneers of Modern Design,* 1960, Ch. 2; see also Alf Bøe, *From Gothic Revival to Functional Form,* Oslo, 1957.

55 *The Seven Lamps,* I, 1.

56 *The Stones of Venice,* I, II, 17 ('The Virtues of Architecture').

57 Collins, 210.

58 *The Stones of Venice,* II, IV, 47.

59 *The Seven Lamps,* I, 1.

60 *The Stones of Venice,* I, XIII, 6; see Townsend, op. cit., note 10.

61 For further exposition of Ruskin's views on architecture see *Lectures on Architecture and Painting,* 1854; For early detailed comments on Ruskin's architectural writings see further: the Rev. Edward Young, *Preraffaelitism* . . ., London, 1857; For the reviews in the *Builder* and in the *Ecclesiologist* see *EVA,* 582–3, 609 (*E,* X, 1849, 111, *E,* XII, 1851, 275, 341). For further contacts between Ruskin and the architectural world of his day see *E,* XXII, 1862, 252 ff.; *RIBA Transactions,* 1864–5, 139–56; *RIBA Transactions,* 1869–70. Street's comparatively unimportant church St Paul's, Herne Hill, (Ruskin belonged to that parish) was praised as a 'remarkable piece

of colouring' (see *LE*, XVI, 463). Of All Saints Church, Margaret Street, he spoke favourably in several places (*The Stones of Venice*, III, *LE*, XI, 229–30). In the later fifties he supported Scott's cause in the struggle of the Government Offices (see below Chapter 7); but in 1859 he wrote in a letter 'Neither Scott nor anybody else can build Gothic or Italian at present . . . all Modern architecture is spurious and must remain so until our architects become sculptors.' (*LE*, XXXVIII, 347.)

Chapter 3

1   *JSAH,* XIX, No. 4, Dec. 1960 (*Str.*). Literature on Street, in addition to Hitchcock (A. E. Street, *Memoir* . . . , 1888; *DNB*; *EVA*): R. Gradidge, 'The Vigorous Style', unpubl. thesis, 1958; Nicholas Taylor, *St Peter's Bournemouth,* Bournemouth, 1962; see also J. F. White, op. cit. (note 5, Chapter 1), K. Andrews, *The Nazarenes,* 1964, 78. List of Works exhibited in the Royal Academy, see the *Architect,* XXXVI, 1881, Dec. 24. For further literature on Street see below, note 50, Chapter 6. I am also indebted to Paul Joyce for information; see above, note 70, Chapter 1.

2   *EVA,* 604–5; *Str.,* 149. The article was printed in the *Ecclesiologist* in December 1850 (E, XI, 1850, 227–33).

3   Cf. R. C. Carpenter's St Mary Magdalene, Munster Square, London, begun in 1849, *E,* X, 1849–50, 64, 353; *BE London, II,* 361.

4   Paper for the Oxford Architectural Society, *E,* XIII, 1852, 247–62.

5   See note 43, Chapter 1.

6   On several pages he dealt with stained glass (257–9), where he paraphrased Ruskin, stressing the importance of the effects of colour as against subject matter. Street concluded with the glorification of the artist, where the religious aspect was now less emphasized.

7   *E,* XIV, 1853, 70–7; see also *B,* 1853, 140; *Str.,* 149–50. Practical considerations, had, however, already found their way into the literature on the history of domestic design: cf. T. Hudson Turner, *Some Account of the Domestic Architecture of the Middle Ages,* Oxford, 1851, 2nd Vol., 1853, by John Henry Parker (the best known of the Medieval archaeologists whose *Introduction into Gothic Architecture* ran to seventeen editions between 1849 and 1913).

8   *B,* 1849, 437 (Foundation stone September), ill.: *B,* 1849, 451; compl. *B,* 1850, 524; *EVA,* 578; *The Seven Lamps* had appeared in May 1849.

9   See Paul Thompson, 'The Writings of William White', in *Concerning Architecture.* I have to thank Paul Thompson for his help.

10   See Street, *Memoir* . . . , 1888, 11.

11   *Transactions of the Exeter Diocesan Architectural Society,* IV, 1851, 176–80.

12   *E,* XII, 1851, 305–13.

13   Cf. also 'Symbolism, its practical benefits and Uses' (1852), *Exeter*

Diocesan Architectural Society Transactions IV, 1853, 304. Other writings by White: 'On the Draining and Drying of Churches', *E*, XI, 1850, 153; 'On Proportion in Architectural Design', *E*, XIV, 1853, 313–28; *E*, XV, 1854, 293–97; on windows see above, p. 82; 'Architecture and its Practical Benefits to Man', Lect. Worcester Diocesan Architectural Society, 1856, 37–49, in *Reports and Papers of Archit. Societies Lincoln, Bedford, Worcester,* publ. at Lincoln.

14 Truefitt's little book *Architectural Sketches on the Continent*, 1847, contains hardly more than very sketchily drawn details of buildings, like spires, doors, and so on. Also it lacks colour, and it is only concerned with north-European examples; it can hardly be called the first in a series of important publications on the continent (Hitchcock in *EVA*, 577). Truefitt built very little (see below, note 108, chapter 4).

15 *Str.,* 146.

16 *E*, XI, 1850, 229; here especially Street's restorations of that time, most of them in Cornwall, should be examined; see *Str.,* 146; see List in *Memoir* (op. cit., note 1).

17 *Str.,* 150–1.

18 Beg. *E*, XII, 1851, 67; compl. 1852, *B*, 1852, 86.

19 *Str.,* 147; *E*, XII, 1851, 150, *E*, XIV, 1853, 136, *B*, 1853, 262; *BE Berks.,* 131. The building does not show later additions, as Hitchcock writes.

20 *E*, XIV, 1853, 136; *Str.,* 147, 151.

21 Compl. *B*, 1854, 582.

22 *E*, XV, 1854, 212, 430, *E*, XVII, 1856, 77, *B*, 1855, 365.

23 *E*, XV 1854, 429, *E*, XIX 1858, 315; *Str.* 154; see further below.

24 'First Pointed', rarely used in these years, at Wheatley (Oxon., *B*, 1856, 45, 88, *E*, XVII, 1856, 71). The smaller church at Watchfield (*E*, XVIII, 1858, 116, 126, *BE Berks.,* 259) continues the tradition of low pyramidal contours, with asymmetrically placed buttresses and an even heavier appearance of the whole. Hitchcock asks how much Street left in those years to his assistants (*Str.,* 168–9) and ascribes the little church at East Hanney (*E*, XIX, 1858, 116, 127; *BE Berks.,* 133) to Philip Webb. This church seems in fact to have little to do with Street's other work at that time (for the relationship of Webb to the Ecclesiologists see above p. 203); on the other hand it is known from later accounts that Street tended to design everything himself.

25 *Str.,* 148, *BE Berks.,* 255.

26 *Str.,* 153, *BE Berks.,* 253.

27 *Str.,* 151; 1852–4; alterations have taken place recently, cf. *Str.* ill; *BN*, 1875, 6 Aug., the *Architect,* 1 July 1876.

28 *EVA*, Ch. II; D. Pilcher, *The Regency Style,* 1947.

29 *E*, XII, 1851, 70; *Str.,* 147; *EVA*, 601–2; *BE Berks.,* 159.

30 Probably built with the church or a little later, 1851–3, see above, note 19; *BE Berks.,* 131.

31 *Str.,* 151.

32 Plans in the office of the Church Commissioners, London.

33 Plans in the office of the Church Commissioners, London; *Str.*,
170–1; the School dates from 1858 (*BN*, 1858, 181).

34 2nd Ser., Pl. 63, 64.

35 All Saints Grammar School *E*, XV, 1854, 398, *E*, XVII, 1856, 152,
Str., 151–2 (including comment by Dr Royston Lambert). An
illustrated prospectus of the school (n.d.) gives detailed information
about the complicated building history. Street's design of 1854 is
preserved at the school. I am grateful to the Registrar for help.

36 *Str.*, 154, begun probably 1855; *B*, 1856, 424.

37 For St Margaret's Convent at East Grinstead, which according to
Hitchcock dates from the mid-fifties, see below, Chapter 6, note 49.

38 See *Str.*, 150.

39 Street, *An Urgent Plea for the Revival of the True Principles of
Architecture in the Public Buildings of Oxford,* 12; Ruskin, *The
Stones of Venice,* I, XXX, 6.

40 *E*, XII, 1851, 59, 69, plate p. 235. In John Betjeman's *Cornwall*
(Shell Guide, 1964) the house is erroneously ascribed to Street.

41 *E*, XI, 1850, 417, *E*, XII, 1851, 59, 69. It is a hotel now; I have to
thank the manageress for her help.

42 An earlier building by White is the church at Baldhu (Cornwall)
begun in 1847 ('foundation stone July 1st,' *E*, IX, 1849, 262). It
seems rather advanced in not having buttresses, similar to Pugin's
contemporary churches (Ramsgate). Another early building of
White's is the small and coarse looking parish-school at St Probus
(*E*, X, 1849, 163, not by Street as *Str.*, 146 and *BE Cornw.*, 129).

43 For the Church Commissioners see K. Clark, *The Gothic Revival,*
2nd ed., 1962, Ch. 5, (see above, note 5 Ch. 1); for Christian see
J. Standen Atkins, in *RIBA Journal*, 3rd Ser., Vol. 18, 1911,
711 ff.; see file in RIBA library; also *Ewan Christian, Architect,*
printed privately, Cambridge, 1896 (information Roderick
Gradidge). St John, Kenilworth (Atkins, op. cit., 1851, *BE Warws.*,
389), St James, Leyland (*B*, 1855, 366, *BE North Lanc.*, 167); cf.
also St Stephen's, Tonbridge (*B*, 1851, 345, *E*, XIV, 1853, 454,
EGR, No. 101).

44 Godolphin: *E*, XII, 1851, 430; cf. the church at Illogan, 1849, still
with regular buttresses and conventional tracery. Halsetown:
E, XV, 1854, 191, 213, *BE Cornw.*, 68.

45 See H. Redfern, 'H.W.' in *Architect and Building News*, 1944,
178, 21–2, 44–5; Woodyer was an early pupil of Butterfield,
see Paul Thompson, *VA.*

46 *EVA*, Chs. IV, V; cf. also for his buildings in Sussex: *BE Sussex.*
Hurstpierpoint: 1851–3, *E*, XIV, 1853, 264; *BE Sussex,* 612.
Milton: 1854–6, later alterations For St Mary Magdalene, Munster
Square, see above, note 3.

47 For Teulon see below, note 52. Enbrook: see *EVA*, 23, *B*, 1854,
487 ill.; Ferrey (1810–1880) see *EVA*, 44, *DNB*; the small church at
Fairfield Belbroughton (Worc., 1854 GR). T. H. Wyatt (1807–
1880), cf. Nannerch (Flints., *B*, 1853, 656; see also *BE Wilts.*);
Joseph Clarke (1820–1888), e.g. Culham College, nr. Abingdon,
(*E*, XIV, 1853, 149, *EGR*, No. 102).

48 'Rogue Architects of the Victorian Era', *RIBA Journal*, 3rd Ser., Vol. 56, 1949, 251 etc.

49 *E*, XIII, 1852, 299; *B*, 1855, 486–7 with plates, *E*, XXII, 1861, 328 (compl.); *EGR*, 291, *BE London II*, 197.

50 Cf. Kilkhampton church, ill. in *BE Cornw.*, pl. 19a.

51 Beg. 1853, *E*, XV, 1854, 267, *B*, 1855, 500, *BE Cornw.*, 159; J. Betjeman, *Cornwall* (Shell Guide, 1964).

52 Obituary *B*, 1873, 384. See also *EVA*, Ch. VIII; for his early churches of the forties in Suffolk see *BE*. Some of his churches also belong in the group of low-and-heavy ones: St James, Edgbaston, Birmingham (Charlotte Road; compl. *B*, 1852, 263, *BE Warws.*, 165).

53 *E*, XX, 1859, 69, *B*, 1857, 351 with ill., *EGR*, No. 145; *BE Sussex* 522.

54 *E*, XVII, 1856, 72; *B*, 1859, 841 ill., *BN*, 1857, 140, with ill.; *BE North Soms.*, 325.

55 See *EVA*, 32, 560, about his early projects in the *Architectural Magazine* in the thirties.

56 1850, *EVA*, 159, *BE Yorks. NR*, 304.

57 Compl. *B*, 1859, 492, *BE Surrey*, 183.

58 *B*, 1854, 462 with ill.; *BE Suffolk*, 303.

59 *B*, 1856, 409, *BN*, 1857, 44 with ill. Cf. the sculptural effect of the tower of West Hartlepool church (*ILN*, 1854, 1, 301; *BE Durh.*, 160). His vicarage at Great Kimble (nr. Wendover, Bucks.) may also be mentioned here, a picturesque composition, yet with the decorative framing of its gables quite different from contemporary buildings of the Ecclesiologists (*B*, 1858, 83).

60 *BN*, 1860, 439.

61 *B*, 1866, 779; *BE London II*, 360.

62 *BE Surrey*, 158.

63 *E*, XIII, 1852, 58–9.

64 The subject of 'originality' in architecture has hardly been gone into historically. Collins (243–8) discusses some aspects of 'novelty' and 'ugliness'. But as far as the 1850s are concerned the tools of differentiation have yet to be sharpened. Collins opposes rational and visual (aesthetic) elements, which he equates with regular development and wilfulness respectively. But, as has been shown, in the fifties, aesthetic elements and demands in the visual sphere could be combined with regularity and opposed to trends of individual irregularity.

Chapter 4

1 Paul Thompson, *William Butterfield*, London, Routledge & Kegan Paul, 1971. I am greatly indebted to Paul Thompson for information on many buildings. A complete list of literature on Butterfield will be found in the catalogue of the RIBA Drawings Collection, to be published soon. See also *DNB*; *Encyclopedia of World Art*, London and New York, 1960, Vol. II (by Sir John Summerson); Paul Thompson, 'W.B.' in *VA*; J. P. H. House, 'The Architecture of W. Butterfield 1814–1900', *Transact. Anc. Mon. Society*, II, 1963.

2 *E*, X, Oct. 1849, 64; *E*, X, 1850, 432–3; *B*, 1850, 507, 531, *E*, XIV, 1853, 273, *B*, 1853, 57, 8; *ILN*, 1853, I, 268, *E*, XX, 1859, 184, *B*, 1859, 365, 377, 1473, *ILN*, 1859, I, 376; for further references see in P. Thompson, below note 4; *BE London II*, 325; E. Lundberg, *Arkitekturens Formspråk*, Stockholm, 1960, Vol. X, 86–90; J. F. White, op. cit. (note 5, Ch. 1), 195–7 etc.; Paul Thompson, 'Butterfield's Masterpiece Re-assessed . . .', *Country Life*, 14 January 1965.

3 *AR*, 98, 1945, 166–75; reprinted in *Heavenly Mansions*.

4 In *Architectural History*, vol. 8, 1965, 73–87.

5 *EVA*, 584–94.

6 See *DNB*.

7 As Paul Thompson told me, there are indications in letters that Butterfield had been in Italy himself. Butterfield also drew the few, rather inconspicuous illustrations in B. Webb, *Continental Ecclesiology*, 1848.

8 *EVA*, 115, 145.

9 *EVA*, 145, 185 etc.

10 Probably built in 1847 with the church; *BE Yorks. NR*, 338.

11 Beg. 1850, P. Thompson, *VA*, 71.

12 Probably built at the time of the church, *E*, X, 1849, 67–8; *BE Sussex*, 372.

13 1850, *BE London II*, 372; destroyed in 1964.

14 Cf. also Butterfield's design for cemetery and chapel, *Instrumenta Ecclesiastica*, 2nd Ser. (1850), Plates 1–5.

15 Cf. above pp. 47 ff.

16 *E*, VIII, 1848, 361–2 with plate; *E*, XII, 1851, 23; for the present state of the building see Basil F. L. Clarke, *Anglican Cathedrals outside the British Isles*, 1958, 56–8, and P. B. Stanton, *The Gothic Revival and American Church Architecture*, Baltimore, 1968, 140–53.

17 I am indebted to the Provost, the Very Reverend W. B. Currie, for help; *E*, XII, 1851, 24–9; *E*, XX, 1859, 377–8. The *Ecclesiologist* criticized the chimney as exaggerated (1850).

18 Cathedral of the Isles, Millport, Isle of Cumbrae; compl. *B*, 1851, 533, *E*, XX, 1859, 380–83; Paul Thompson in *VA*, 169. I am grateful to the Provost for help.

19 This was also a gift of Beresford-Hope; *E*, IX, 1849, 1, *EGR*, 225–8, *EVA*, 154; Guide-book, Canterbury 1952.

20 *E*, XV, 1854, 59.

21 At Holbeck; *EVA*, 595; destroyed c. 40 years ago. Drawings in the RIBA Drawings Collection.

22 c. 1849–52; *BE Yorks. WR*, 17, 272.

23 See above, note 8, Chapter 3; cf. Pugin's Bishop's House of Birmingham Cathedral (destroyed) c. 1840, plate in A. W. N. Pugin, *The Present State . . .*, 1843.

24 See above p. 21.

25 In the early fifties the *Ecclesiologist* did not like 'the large blank walls which are so often seen in Mr Butterfield's churches' (in this case St Ninian's, Perth, *E*, XII, 1851, 28). That the *Ecclesiologist* changed its opinion in the course of the fifties is shown by a

remark on a church by Street (St Paul's, Herne Hill: 'Mr Street is not afraid of blank walls . . .' (*E*, XX, 1859, 65).

26 *E*, VIII, 1848, 141 (cf. B. F. L. Clarke, op. cit., note 16, 111–12); Beresford-Hope, *The English Cathedral of the 19th century*, 1861, 104; a remarkable earlier example of brick was A. W. N. Pugin's St Chad's Cathedral, Birmingham, of 1839–41.

27 M. D. Wyatt, *Specimens of the Geometrical Mosaics of the Middle Ages*. In principle Butterfield's decorations go back to Pugin and Owen Jones in the early forties.

28 *EVA*, 591.

29 *B*, 1853, 56.

30 For the rich furnishings of All Saints, dating from 1853 to 1859 and later, Paul Thompson in *Architectural History*, VIII, 1965, must be consulted.

31 *E*, XX, 1859, 185.

32 Only the bands of coloured tiles in the interior of Yealmpton church have to be mentioned here (c. 1850, see James Furneaux, 'On Y. Church', 1852, *Exeter Diocesan Architectural Society Transactions*, IV, 1853, 245–9; *BE Sth. Devon*, 314.

33 *E*, XIV, 1853, 267; *EVA*, 596–8.

34 *E*, XI, 1850, 54; plan *E*, XI, 142; *BE London II*, 248.

35 2nd ser., Pl. 49–54; see also *E*, XIV, 1853, 116.

36 Some of Clarke's schools have been executed: Foxearth (Essex), Brabourne (Kent).

37 Near Snaith, beg. *B*, 1853, 470, compl. *B*, 1854. Paul Thompson in *VA*, 172–3. I am grateful to the Rev. J. P. Woodger of Balne for his help.

38 Cf. note 65, Chapter 1.

39 *B*, 1854, 609; *BE Yorks. NR*, 404–5.

40 Paul Thompson, *VA*, 173. The church was begun in 1856, see below, note 56; for school and vicarage see below.

41 Cf. the Rev. Thomas James, 'On Labourers' Cottages', 1849, *AAS*, I, 24–36; Fred Pollock, 'Labourers' Cottages', *B* 1851, 145; for G. Godwin and the reform of working-class housing see Anthony King, 'Another Blow for Life, G. Godwin . . . ' *AR* 136, 1964, 448–52; cf. also N. Pevsner, 'Model Houses for the Labouring Classes' (1953) in *Studies in Art, Architecture and Design*, 1968, Vol. II; Nicholas Cooper, in *Country Life*, 25 May and 8 June 1967.

42 Paul Thompson in *VA*, 172–3.

43 See Paul Thompson in his article on All Saints, *Architectural History*, *VIII*, 1965 and in *VA*, 173 f.

44 School and teacher's house at Alvechurch (Worcs., 1856, loc. inform.), the tiny school-room at Letcombe Bassett (Berks., *B*, 1859, 7) etc.

45 Alvechurch: 1856, inscription. Baldersby: probably built with the church, 1856–7, see below, note 56.

46 Beg. 1854, compl. 1855–6 (inf. P. Thompson); built for his brother-in-law; *Country Life*, 23 Oct. 1969.

47 See further: Schools at Langley (Kent, probably c. 1855, see note 49) and Aldbourne (Wilts., 1857–8, *BE Wilts.*, 73).

48 Brick, in the succession of Yorkshire churches; Braishfield,
Hants, '1854' (GR; BE Hants, 135).

49 Loc. inform. ; P. Thompson in VA, 171.

50 B, 1856, 461, B, 1857, 709, P. Thompson, VA, 171.

51 B, 1857, 452.

52 1858–65, BE Middx., 27.

53 'Erected 1858' in church, BE Northu., 149.

54 Beg. B, 1857, 613, BE North Soms., 200.

55 E, XVII, 1856, 137, E, XIX, 1858, 241 etc.; B, 1859, 401 etc., EGR,
261; designs in the collection of the Victoria & Albert Museum,
London.

56 BN, 1857, 1060, compl.; BE Yorks. NR, 70.

57 B, 1857, 565, BN, 1858, 1036; BE Wilts., 260.

58 Glenthorne Road, 'half finished' in E, XIX, 1858, 341, compl. E,
XX, 1859, 323, tower 1880s; BE London II, 175.

59 E, XXII, 1861, 317, B, 1862, 443; Summerson in Heavenly
Mansions, 170; BE London II, 205.

60 B, 1860, 500; the vicarage has been preserved, drawings at RIBA.
The school in Enmore Road also of the same date (BE Berks., 182).

61 E, XV, 1854, 284, B, 1855, 189, school E, XVI, 1855, 65.

62 E, XIII, 1852, 438, B, 1854, 429; BE Sussex, 266.

63 E, XV, 1854, 356, B, 1854, 414; drawings in the Church Commissioners Institute in London (I have to thank Mr Robinson,
Records Officer, for his help).

64 Compl. E, XV, 1854, 357.

65 'Chaplain's cottage', E, XV, 1854, 287.

66 For the workman's cottage by Olbrich, 1907, see J. M. Olbrich,
Catalogue, Darmstadt, 1967, and for Tessenow's houses at Hellerau,
see H. Tessenow, Hausbau und dergleichen, Berlin, 1920.

67 Cf. also White's design for a church in the Diocese of Cape Town,
which is half-timbered throughout (see the Catalogue The
Gothic of Gothick, B. Weinreb Ltd., London n.d.; I am indebted
to Messrs Weinreb for their help).

68 E, XV, 1854, 357.

69 E, XVII, 1856, 135, 159; B, 1857, 709, BN, 1857, 1286;
BE Hants, 275, 506.

70 E, XVIII, 1857, 50, 63; BE Bucks., 159.

71 E, XVIII, 1857, 67.

72 E, XVIII, 1857, 67.

73 E, XVII, 1856, 75, 159, formerly 'St Michael's and All Angels
institution for training domestic servants'; BE Berks., 254.

74 B, 1855, 378, 379 with pl., E, XVI, 1855, 190.

75 E, XVIII, 1857, 28 (Architectural Exhibition).

76 Compl. E, XIX, 1858, 199.

77 E, XVII, 1856, 319–30.

78 323.

79 For the development of the consideration of practical aspects of
house-building see Pilcher, The Regency Style, 1947, 152 etc.

80 White continued the discussion about regularity and irregularity
in 'Architectural Uniformity and its Claims' (BN, 1860, 132–3).

81 *E,* XIX, 1858, 414.

82 *BN,* 1859, April (tenders list).

83 *E,* XXI, 1860, 115; vicarage and school contemporary (local inform.).

84 *E,* XXI, 1860, 325, later altered.

85 *E,* XXI, 1860, 114.

86 St Michael and All Angels, beg. 1859; *E,* XX, 1859, 288, *B,* 1859, 669 etc.; *EGR,* 292,; *BE Hants,* 326. The design for the competition at Istanbul (Constantinople Competition, see above, p. 93) showed a very complicated arrangement, too, as well as an 'excessive use of colour' (*E,* XVIII, 1857, 106); the same can be said of the Bishop's residence, Gowton, near Clyst Honiton (Exeter, 1860 *EGR,* No. 195).

87 *E,* XV, 1854, 431, *E,* XVII, 1856, 72, 422; *B,* 1856, 314 with pl.; *EGR,* No. 121; *BE London II;* ' . . . no buttresses . . . , red brick, capacity and conditions of the material have been well considered.'

88 Church beg. *B,* 1849, 333.

89 *B,* 1856, 583.

90 *E,* XVII, 1856, 76 (not far from St John the Evangelist, a slightly earlier church by Teulon, see *BE Warws.,* 137).

91 *E,* XVII, 1856, 230, *B,* 1857, 661, *BE Lincs.,* 207.

92 Beg. March 1859, compl. *B,* 1860, 724; *BE Berks.,* 166.

93 Compl. *E,* XXI, 1860, 187, 193; *BE Essex* 319; see also *The High Victorian Cultural Achievement,* Victorian Society Conference Report, 1965, 28.

94 Beg. *E,* XXI, 1860, 324.

95 *B,* 1860, 331, ill., *BE Hants,* 210.

96 Holy Trinity. *B,* 1855, 65; *BE Salop,* 220.

97 *B,* 1856, 596 etc.

98 *B,* 1858, 699.

99 Withers built little; an early work: School at Poyntington (Dorset, *B,* 1848, 559 pl., *E,* XI, 1849, 265).

100 *B,* 1856, 661; beg. *B,* 1858, 486; *BN,* 1859, 830, 840 ill.

101 *E,* XX, 1859, 70–1.

102 *E,* XX, 1859, 287 with ill., see J. F. White, op. cit., note 5, Ch. 1, ill. VIII, 256; *BE Lincs.,* 298.

103 *B,* 1859, 360 with ill.

104 *E,* XV, 1854, 257–9; for Clutton's earlier brick-churches in the East End see *EVA,* 116.

105 Beg. 1853, *B,* 1855, 611, *E,* XVII, 1856, 37; extended later, *B,* 1858, 507 etc., *BE Berks.,* 305.

106 *B,* 1856, 348, *E,* XVIII, 1857, 195.

107 *E,* XVII, 1856, 308; *BE Salop,* 160. A few years later the churches at Sambrook (Newport, with vicarage and school, *BE Salop,* 240) and Scropton (*B,* 1856, 541, *BE Derbys.,* 213) are characterized by nearly-flush tracery.

108 In the case of Truefitt one has to resort to descriptions: ' . . . The walls are without buttresses or stringcourses, and a simple chamfer instead of all mouldings. The windows are mere piercings in a plane of stone – a kind of austere plate tracery . . . giving . . . a forcible

effect of light and shade.' (*E*, XVII, 1856, 71, unexecuted design for
St John, Hulme, Manchester). The design for the Constantinople
competition was described in similar terms (*E*, XVIII, 1857, 107–8).
In 1858 these characteristics may be seen in the illustration of his
Catholic Apostolic Church, Duncan Street, Islington (*B*, 1858,
798); see also his St George's in Tufnell Park (*BN*, 1867,
65 ill.)

109   *E*, 1859, 185 etc.: 'a work of 10 years before'; see also A. J.
      Beresford-Hope, *The English Cathedral of the 19th Century*, 1861, 234–5.
110   *EGR*, No. 199; the chapel dates from 1872; *BE Warws.*, 388.
111   *EGR*, No. 246; *BE Hants*, 706.
112   1868–74; *BE Sth. Devon*, 292.
113   *EGR*, No. 252, 1864.
114   *B*, 1867, 551; *BE Sth. Lancs.*, 337.
115   *EGR.*, No. 340; *BE London II*, 243.
116   Beg. *B*, 1868, 323; ill. Chapel *B*, 1885, Jan. 3.
117   *E*, XXVII, 1866, 251, *B*, 1867, 551 ill.; *BE London II*, 229
118   Another ambitious work of the sixties is Humewood (Wicklow,
      Ireland, *B*, 1868, 588 ill.; *EGR*, No. 287 *Country Life*, 16 May
      1968, 1212, 1282), a late example of the 'castellated style'.
      Churches adhering to 'English' motifs: Merifield (Anthony, *BE
      Cornw.*, 27) and St John, Masborough (Rotherham, *BE Yorks.
      WR*, 421), both 1865.

Chapter 5

1   Most sources are listed in *Str.*, 158–9. The most important
    descriptions are to be found in *E*, XVII, 1856, 80–105; *E*, XVII,
    1856, 161. Additional sources to Hitchcock: E. Hautecoeur,
    Histoire de Notre Dame de la Treille, Lille, 1900; Report in
    *Annuaire de l'Institut des Provinces, des Sociétés savantes et des
    Congrès Scientifiques*, XI, 1859. My thanks go to Mgr. Lepoutre,
    Archiviste Diocésain, Lille, for his help in finding the original
    designs of the first three prizes. None of these designs was
    executed; the building was started shortly after the competition
    from the designs of the local architect Leroy and is still unfinished.
2   See *Str.*, 158–9 for sources. Most important the detailed
    descriptions in *E*, XVIII, 1857, 98–114. For the competition itself
    see *BN*, 1857, 240.
3   *Str.*, 150.
4   See *Str.*, 149–50; see Foreword to the 1874 edn.
5   *E*, XVI, 1855, 75.
6   *Brick and Marble*, 267.
7   *Brick and Marble*, 186.
8   See *Str.*, n. 31; 'Naumburg', *E*, XV, 1854, 381; 'Lübeck', *E*, XVI,
    1855, 21; 'Erfurt and Marburg', *E*, XVI, 1855, 73; 'Münster and
    Soest', *E*, XVI, 1855, 361; 'German Gothic architecture', *E*,
    XVIII, 1857, 162. Various other parts from Street's diaries etc.
    were published later in a book by the Hispanic Society of America,
    1916 (ed. Gordon King).

9 'Altogether about the noblest pointed church in the North of Italy' (*Brick and Marble*, 76–9).

10 See esp. *Brick and Marble*, 264–5, 79.

11 85–6.

12 265–7.

13 269.

14 90.

15 *AAS,* III, 1855, 355.

16 *E*, XVIII, 1857, 8; he had recommended it before in his 'True Principles', *E*, XIII, 1852, 261.

17 For other instances of polychromy see *Str.*, 149.

18 Compl. *B*, 1854, 414; Colnbrook: see above, plate 19.

19 Cf. also the comment on a church by Ferrey, 76.

20 Cf. Street's opinion of Ste Clothilde at Paris (1846–59 by Gau and Ballu) in *Brick and Marble*, Ch. 1, or his comments on the new parts of Cologne Cathedral – 'thin and attenuated' (*E*, XVI, 1855, 365).

21 *Str.*, 160; *B*, 1857, 162–3 ill.

22 *ILN*, 1857, II, 412; *Str.*, 162.

23 Cf. Hitchcock's description: ' . . . orderly monumental design in terms of function'. I cannot agree with his interpretation of the top of the tower ' . . . spiky incidents that contrast with the essential dignity and straightforwardness of the design'. In several of his designs Street shows that he seeks the contrast between those two elements, which is for him also a contrast between various materials. These details should certainly not be likened to the generally 'spiky', regular details of earlier 'Neo-Gothic'; in fact, Street's details are considerably more spiky.

24 *Str.*, 162–3; the design is mentioned *E*, XVIII, 1857, 392.

25 Churches of Blymhill (Staffs., formerly Salop, *E*, XVII, 1856, 233, *B*, 1859, 636), Pitcombe (Soms., *E*, XIX, 1858, 127 etc.), Winterbourne Down (Winterbourne Ducis, Glos., *E*, XVIII, 1857, 392 etc.; I am grateful to the Rev. R. C. Bulley for his help). Street contrasts the rough surface with windows of hewn stone, with porphyr-shafts in the interior. Similar: Hollington (Staffs., *E*, XX, 1859, 287); Chapel of the Wantage Sisterhood (1858; *Str.*, 153).

26 *E*, XVIII, 1857, 393; *E*, XVI, 1855, 389 (col. decoration not mentioned).

27 *E*, XIX, 1858, 127; *BE Lincs.*, 235–6.

28 *E*, XVIII, 1857, 127, *B*, 1858, 14. Cf. Street's Holy Trinity School, not far away, built of hewn stone (*B*, 1860, 128).

29 Cf. the small school and schoolmaster's House at Colnbrook (Bucks., *E*, XX, 1859, 72), Schools at Blithfield and Leigh (*E*, XVIII, 1857, 66, *B*, 1857, 135, *CEAJ*, 1858, pl. 51) are more polychromatic.

30 See Nicholas Taylor, *St Peter's, Bournemouth*, 1962.

31 *Str.*, 166–7, *BE Bucks.*, 300; for Street's rebuilding of St Paul's, Herne Hill, see above, note 61, Chapter 2, note 25, Chapter 4.

32 *E*, XX, 1859, 65 etc., *BE Yorks. NR*, 400.

33 *E*, XX, 1859, 135, compl. *B*, 1860, 563.

34 *Str.*, 167, *E*, XX, 1859, 206 etc., *CEAJ*, XXII, 228, ext.; photo of the

design for the interior at the National Monuments Record.

35   *Str.,* 163–6; *E, XX,* 1859, 197, 205, 426 ill., *E, XXII,* 1861, 317, 414, *B,* 1859, tenders, May, etc., *B,* 1862, 187, largely completed. Ill. in: *B,* 1861, 411; *B,* 1862, 187, the *Architect,* 6 Jan. 1872. *BE London II,* 12, 429, John Betjeman, *An Appeal . . .* (publ. by the church), 1961. There is an old model in the church. The schools have a different appearance in the ill. in *B,* 1861, 411; the school on the corner as it is today dates perhaps from the mid-sixties (the one next to the tower is much later).

36   *E, XX,* 1859, 206, *B,* 1859, 795, *E, XX,* 1859, 389–393, controversy of the Oxford Architectural Society with Street, see also *BN,* 1859, 1033; beg. *B,* 1860, 317; *BN,* 1861, 713 ill. *Str.,* 167: St Philip and St James 'begun in 1860 . . ., initiated a new period', to which I cannot agree.

37   See D. Pilcher, *The Regency Style,* 1947, 80.

38   *E, XVI,* 1855, 142 etc., also printed as an appendix to *Secular and Domestic Architecture,* 1858.

39   See above, p. 170.

40   *EGR,* No. 169; *BN,* 1869, I, 158 ill.

41   Obituary *B,* 1897, II, 514, *AR,* I, 1896–7; a short résumé on the 1850s can be found in *BE Surrey,* 409. In his first churches he followed Pugin: Ellerker (1824 *GR, Yorks. ER*), and Holy Trinity, Bessborough Gardens, Westminster (*E, XII,* 1851, 221–2; destroyed in the war). Eastoft church (*BE Yorks. WR,* 189; 1855) is typically 'rural' with a wide, low roof; Devoran (1854, *BE Cornw.,* 50) very simple and massive.

42   *E, XXI,* 1860, 48–9.

43   *BN,* 1858, 1099.

44   Titsey: *E, XXI,* 1860, 48, *EGR,* No. 171, *BE Surrey,* 409. Daylesford: *E, XXI,* 1860, 48; *BN,* 1863, 365 ill.; *EGR,* No. 170. The little church at Broomfleet (Yorkshire, 1859, inf. kindly supplied by the vicar) has got nothing of this elaborate shaft-work; the vicarage, as well as the schools behind St Peter's, Vauxhall (1860, ill. *B,* 1860, 497), show White's cottage manner.

45   Near Stow on the Wold, *EGR,* 304 ill., built for the Rev. R. W. Hippisley.

46   See *DNB,* Obituary, *B,* 1907, 11, 447–8 etc. Bodley was, like Street and White, a pupil of Scott.

47   Compl. *E, XV,* 1854, 143.

48   'Des. in 1854', *CEAJ,* 1858, 317 pl.

49   *E, XV,* 1854, 140, *BE Herefs.,* 241.

50   *E, XVI,* 1855, 50, 62; *B,* 1856, 277.

51   Cf. also the small, low church at Bicknor (Kent, *E, XX,* 1859, 76, 141).

52   *E, XVIII,* 1857, 106.

53   *E, XX,* 1859, 67, *B,* 1860, 141, *BN,* 1864, 695 ill. etc., *EGR,* No. 176; *BE Sussex,* 434.

54   Obit.: *B,* 1872, 1002.

55   *E, XX,* 1859, 287, compl.

56   *E, XVII,* 1856, 108, *E, XXI,* 1860, 142 ill.

57 *E*, XXII, 1862, 158, plan, ill.; *BN*, 1867, ill.; *BN*, 10 April 1868 ill.,

58 1856 *GR*; cf. also the chancel at Martham (Norf., *E*, XVII, 1856, 265, *BE North Norf.*, 194).

59 Welsh Bicknor: *B*, 1859, 302, 318; *BE Herefs.*, 226. Greetland: *B*, 1859, 476; *CEAJ*, 1859, 148 ill.; *BE Yorks. WR*, 226.

60 *BN*, 1899, II, 582; e.g. St Mary, Aberdare (Glam.), *CEAJ*, 1864, 85 ill., St Paul, Haggerston (*B*, 1860, 201 ill.); see also note 100, Chapter 7. Other names which ought to be mentioned here: Richard Poplewell Pullan competed for Lille and Constantinople (there are books with photographs of both designs in the RIBA Library); the Belfast architects Lanyon and Lynn (Seamen's Church, Belfast, *B*, 1857, 407 ill.).

Chapter 6

1 *EGR*, 319.

2 See *E*, X, 1849, *E*, XI, 1850; for Viollet-le-Duc and England see also *Catalogue Viollet-le-Duc*, Paris, 1965 (publ. Caisse Nationale des Monuments Historiques) 233–6. See also 'England and France', *E*, XVI, 1855, 351.

3 *Essay on the Military Architecture of the Middle Ages*, transl. M. Macdermott, 1860.

4 See *RIBA Papers*, Vol. 1863–4, xxxvii.

5 *Lectures on Architecture*, 1877–81; for the translator Benjamin Bucknall, his earlier contacts with Viollet-le-Duc and his country house, Woodchester Park (Glos.) see D. Verey, 'Woodchester Park', in *Country Life*, 6 Feb. 1969.

6 *E*, XX, 1859, 178–9.

7 *E*, XVIII, 1857, 342.

8 *E*, XXII, 1861, 70, 213, 250, 312.

9 *BN*, 1859, 1127 ill.

10 *E*, XIX, 1858, *E*, XX, 1859.

11 *E*, XXII, 1861, 140.

12 *BN*, 1864, 459–62.

13 *VA*, 187–220; for other articles see below, note 24 and note 115. I am greatly indebted to Mr Handley-Read for several pieces of information. For reproductions of many of Burges' designs see R. P. Pullan, *The Architectural Designs of William Burges*, 1883.

14 For the Lille Competition see Chapter 5, note 1.

15 *Facsimile of the Sketchbook of Wilars de Honecourt* . . . Descript. by Lassus and Quicherat, translated . . . by R. Willis, 1859.

16 *B*, 1858, 758.

17 *RIBA Transactions*, 1860–61, 15 etc.

18 *BN*, 1864, 459 etc.

19 *E*, XXIII, 1862, 336.

20 *BN*, 1864, 460.

21 *E*, XVII, 1856, 89.

22 For the competition see above, Chapter 5, note 2; Burges' design is illustrated in *B*, 1857, 150–1 with a comment by Burges, drawings in the RIBA Collection, including the smaller versions of 1858.

23 Brisbane: *BN*, 1860, 991 ill., see also in A. J. Beresford-Hope, *The*

English Cathedral of the 19th Century, 1861. Waltham: *BE Essex,* 371.

24 *E,* XXIV, 1863, 213 ill.; *E,* XXIX, 1868, 312. See C. Handley-Read in *AR,* June 1967, 423 etc.

25 Fleet: *E,* XXI, 1860, 322; *BE Hants,* 234. Lowfield: *BE Surrey,* 304 and *BE Sussex,* 204.

26 See *Country Life,* 6, 13, 20 April 1961.

27 See D. Harbron, *The Conscious Stone,* Life of E. W. Godwin, London, Latimer House, 1949; for Godwin's own comments later see the *British Architect,* 29 Nov. 1878. For most of the sixties Godwin was in partnership with the Bristol architect H. Crisp. Godwin moved to London in 1865.

28 *BN,* 1861, 893. *BE Northants.,* 316.

29 *B,* 1864, 529.

30 *BN,* 1865, July 21: not 'at Oxford' as the caption runs, but Nos. 43–4 Billing Road, Northampton (inf. kindly supplied by P. Joyce).

31 *BN,* 1871, April 21, June 9, ill.

32 BN, 1867, Nov. 1 ill.; see also above, pp. 204–5.

33 358.

34 *BN,* 1875, 441.

35 *British Architect,* 4 July 1879.

36 See *B,* 1888, I, 229; *AR,* 1, 1896–7.

37 The architect's drawings are in the Victoria & Albert Museum, London; Cloverley is mostly signed and dated 1865; *EGR,* No. 220. Combe '1863', '1864', see *EGR,* No. 202, *BE Warws.,* 237, *Country Life,* 4 Dec. 1909.

38 For Shaw see Sir R. Blomfield, *R. N. Shaw,* 1940, and N. Pevsner in *VA.*

39 *BN,* 1859, 422.

40 Drawings in the RIBA Collection. Another view was published (without giving Shaw's name) in *BN,* 24 March 1871.

41 *EGR,* No. 273; some of the drawings are in the RIBA Collection. The earlier version of the tower is illustrated in P. Howell, *Victorian Churches,* 1968, 22.

42 *BN,* 1873, I, 42–3 ill.; for Anglican churches overseas see the Publications for the Society of the Propagation of Christian Knowledge (Society for the Propagation of the Gospel in Foreign Parts, London) and the Colonial (Commonwealth) and Continental Church Society, London.

43 *E,* XIX, 1858, 364.

44 *E,* XX, 1859, 333.

45 *BN,* 1864, 920 ill. ext., 4 August 1865, ill. int.; *EGR,* No. 244, *BE North Soms.,* 387.

46 *BN,* 16 Oct. 1868, ill. int.; *EGR,* No. 306, *BE South Devon,* 293; the tower was built by A. E. Street in 1884.

47 *BN,* 15 July 1870, ill.; *BE Sussex,* 487; *EGR,* No. 265.

48 *BN,* 1868, 571 ill.; cf. also the small church at Westcott (1867, *BE Bucks.,* 281).

49 Hitchcock, *Str.,* 152, attributes the design for St Margaret's Convent

233

at East Grinstead (*BE Sussex,* 493) to these years. Yet there is hardly any documentary evidence that these buildings were designed ten years before construction started (the convent was founded in 1855). There is no word in the *Ecclesiologist* about a design at that time, but in 1865 it says: 'Mr Street has designed very extensive buildings for the Nursing Sisters of St Margaret's, East Grinstead' (*E,* XXVI, 1865, 234). It is hardly conceivable that Street would have used a design outmoded by many years for such an important commission. Hitchcock himself points out characteristics which belong to the sixties rather than to the fifties: 'There is little or no Butterfieldian crankiness here . . . the absence of un-English forms . . .'. Indeed, the quietness and evenness of surface, the more easy-going variation of features and the lack of 'constructional polychromy' are hardly datable into the mid-fifties, but can be closely related for instance to the Law Courts, as they were designed in 1866–7 (cf. *BN,* 1867, 392). Cf. also Street's design for the National Gallery in 1866 (Victoria & Albert Museum).

50 Inf. P. Joyce, *BN,* 31 Oct. 1873, ill. For Street's later work see J. Kinnard in *VA*; C. Meeks, 'Street's Rome Churches', in *Art Quarterly,* XVI, 1953, 215 f.; B. F. L. Clarke & John Piper, 'Street's Yorkshire Churches and Contemporary Criticism', in *Concerning Architecture.*

51 *BN,* 28 Dec. 1866, ill.; *BN,* 14 April 1871, ill.; *EGR,* No. 253; Seddon on his buildings in *RIBA Papers,* 1870–1, 148 etc.

52 On Bentley see W. De L'Hopital, *Westminster Cathedral and its architect,* 1919. A slightly earlier competition drawing for a church from the RIBA Collection is illustrated in P. Howell, *Victorian Churches,* 1968. For St Francis, Notting Hill: *EGR,* No. 209.

53 1858; *B,* 1863, 551 ill.; *BE Cty. Durham, 124.*

54 *BN,* 1865, 855; *Church Builder,* 1867, 3 ill.; *EGR,* No. 234; *BE Yorks. NR,* 65.

55 1865–7, *EGR,* No. 258; the school and parsonage are by Pearson as well; they are half-timbered.

56 *E,* XXII, 1861, 281; *BE Yorks. NR,* 434.

57 1862, *GR.*

58 *E,* XXII, 1861, 124; *E,* XXIV, 1863, 127–8; *EGR,* No. 247, *BE Cambs.,* 174; 'Mr Bodley has restricted himself to pure English forms. The time for a reaction from exclusively French or Italian types has at length arrived' (*E,* 1863). Recent inf. (A. Symondson, see *B,* 1870, 891): the traceried windows and the tower are results of redesigning in c. 1868.

59 *E,* XXV, 1864, 49; *EGR,* No. 219; *BE Sussex,* 529.

60 *EGR,* No. 235; *BE South Lancs.,* cf. also the strongly 'English' church at Sutton Veny by Pearson of 1866 (*BE Wilts.,* 454).

61 *B,* 1856, 243, *E,* XVII, 1856, 304, *BN,* 1860, 118, 127 ill.

62 *B,* 1858, 535 ill.; *BE Surrey,* 367.

63 West Derby: *B,* 1853, 293, *B,* 1856, 628, *BE South Lancs.,* 258. Hamburg: See *EVA*; J. Faulwasser, *Die St Nikolaikirche in Hamburg,* Hamburg, 1926; ill. int. *B,* 1858, 439.

64 *BN,* 1859, 1034, *BE Surrey,* 355.

65 Beg. 1858, *GR.*

66 Compl. *BN,* 1859, 1127 ill.

67 *E,* IX, 1848, 65, *BE Berks.,* 96; see Scott, *Personal and Professional
   Recollections,* 1879, 156.

68 See above, pp. 170–1.

69 A. J. Beresford-Hope, *The English Cathedral of the 19th Century,*
   1861, Ch. VI.

70 Op. cit., 261; see also J. F. White, *The Cambridge Movement,*
   1962, 190–1.

71 *E,* XXII, 1861, 45, 56–7; *E,* XXV, 1864, 272, *B,* 1865, 627 ill., *EGR,*
   No. 245, *BE London II,* 272; a larger tower was projected but not built.

72 For Brooks see *Church Builder,* 1870, 6 ff. St Michael's: *E,* XXIV,
   1863, 187–8; *BN,* 1863, ill., *EGR,* No. 274, *BE London II,* 383.

73 *E,* XXV, 1864, 245; *BN,* 15 Dec. 1865, ill.; *EGR,* No. 271, *BE
   London II,* 384.

74 1870; *BN,* 9 Sept. 1870, ill.; *BE Essex,* 282.

75 1867; *B,* 1869, 987 ill., *BE London II,* 382.

76 1868; *BN,* 9 Sept. 1870, ill., *EGR,* No. 293, *BE London II,* 382.

77 Chislehurst: 1868, *EGR,* No. 316. Clapton: *BN,* 5 Aug. 1870, ill.

78 *B,* 1874, 909 ill., *BE Sussex,* 430.

79 *E,* XXV, 1864, 223 ff.; cf. also *BN,* 1870, 203 etc. There were very
   few instances of really centrally-planned designs in those decades;
   e.g. Truefitt for Constantinople, *E,* XVIII, 1857, 108; later the
   'dome' was one of G. G. Scott's favourite forms (see below, note 43,
   Chapter 7).

80 *E,* XXV, 1864, 85–8; *E,* XXVII, 1866, 32–3.

81 See Bryan Little, *Catholic Churches since 1623,* 1966.

82 For E. Pugin see *BE Sth. Lancs.,* 41.

83 See the unpublished London University thesis on J. Hansom by
   Denis Evinson, 1965; I have to thank D. Evinson for information
   he gave me before completion of the thesis.

84 *B,* 1852, 104 ill.

85 *BN,* 1859, 464: 'in progress, under the plainest possible
   descriptions from motives of economy'.

86 *BN,* 1859, 565 ill.; *Dublin Builder,* 1859, 310 ill.

87 *B,* 1856, 344, *EGR,* No. 146, *BE Yorks. NR,* 323.

88 1862–4, *EGR,* No. 221, *BN,* 9 May 1873, ill.

89 1867, *EGR,* No. 289 ill.: *B,* 1868, 511, the *Architect,* 2 Oct. 1869.

90 See *BE Sth. Lancs.,* 41.

91 Arundel: 1868–9, *BE Sussex,* 90–1. Manchester: 1869–71, *BE
   Sth. Lancs.,* 307.

92 1863–4; H.-R. Hitchcock; *Architecture: Nineteenth and Twentieth
   Centuries,* 1958, 179; *BE Warws.,* 334.

93 1865, *EGR,* No. 261; *BE Beds.,* 164.

94 *B,* 1856, 222, *B,* 1859, 160; for Pollen see Anne Pollen, *J. H. Pollen,*
   1912.

95 *E,* XIX, 1858, 232–40; cf. also in *BN,* 1858, 219–24. For Bentley
   see above, note 52.

96 He goes on: 'and it is undoubtedly true that it is easier to design

with academical accuracy an ambitious imitation of a cathedral, than it is to devise and work out a really fine idea in stained glass, or a true vigorous, and beautiful treatment of a story, or even of foliage, in the tympanum of a doorway' (238–9). (Cf. Street in 1857, p. 95.)

97 Founded in 1849, among others by Ruskin (see Index *LE*).

98 For the PRB see William E. Fredeman, *Pre-Raphaelitism, A Bibliocritical Study,* Cambridge, Mass., 1965, and Leslie Parris *The Pre-Raphaelites,* Tate Gallery Publications 1966; J. D. Hunt, *The Pre-Raphaelite Imagination,* 1968. As regards painting up to the mid-fifties the Ecclesiologists seemed still to adhere to influence of the Nazarenes of the forties; see T. S. R. Boase, 'The Decoration of the New Palace of Westminster, 1841–63', *Journal of the Warburg and Courtauld Institutes,* XVII, 1954, 319 ff.; for the influence of Overbeck on Street see K. Andrews, *The Nazarenes,* 1964, 78; see the descriptions of Munich art in B. Webb's *Continental Ecclesiology,* 1848; for Overbeck's altarpiece for St Thomas, Leeds, see *Katalog der Sammlung G. Schäfer,* Germanisches National Museum, Nuremberg, 1966; for later references in Street see *Brick and Marble . . . ,* 114–16, 224; *AAS,* III, 1855, 348 ff.; see *E,* XIII, 1852; *B,* 1858, 160. Beresford-Hope, *The Common Sense of Art,* 1858; *BN,* 1859, 280; *E,* XXI, 1860, 247–8. See also T. Hilton, *The Pre-Raphaelites,* 1970.

99 In fact, as Leslie Parris, op. cit., points out, the PRB had also been much less esoteric at the beginning.

100 G. G. Scott, *Remarks on Secular and Domestic Architecture,* 191.

101 *E,* XVII, 1856, 385.

102 *B,* 1857, 730.

103 A. J. Beresford-Hope, *The English Cathedral of the 19th Century,* 1861, 249.

104 E.g. Street in 'True Principles . . .'; *E,* XIII, 1852, 257 ff.

105 Discussion Street—Scott: *B,* 1858, 202, 226, 228, 245. Apparently Ruskin had not solved the problem, see John Pollard Seddon, *Progress in Art and Architecture with Precedents for Ornaments,* 1852; *E,* XIV, 1853, 166; *B,* 1852, 774: 'copy of Ruskin'.

106 For list of publications of the museum see Catalogue of RIBA Library; see *E,* XIV, 1853, 24, 84, *E,* XVIII, 1856, 238; see also J. H. Markland in *AAS,* III, 1854, 140–2; see J. Summerson, *The Architectural Association,* 1947.

107 An example from the provinces indicates that by 1857 Ruskin's opinions had had a widespread influence. In 1857 the Baptist Church (Fishergate) at Preston by Hibbert & Rainford was decorated with sculpture where 'freedom was permitted to the carvers to produce them' (*B,* 1857, 707). For sculpture see further *E,* XVII, 1856, 220–1; for the Oxford Museum see p. 165.

108 See *Handbook to the Prince Consort Memorial,* 1872.

109 *E,* XXIII, 1862, 336.

110 *BN,* 1864, 461.

111 Anon., *B,* 1863, 798.

112 *BN*, 1864, 460.

113 *B*, 1858, 502; *BN*, 1860, 190; *E*, XVIII, 1857, 205.

114 See P. Thompson, *The Work of William Morris,* 1967.

115 See C. Handley-Read, 'William Burges' Painted Furniture',
Burlington Magazine, CV, 1963, 509.

116 *E*, XXIII, 1862, 337.

117 Drawing by Burges in the Victoria & Albert Museum; ill. *B,* 1858,
375; cf. his decorations for Gayhurst, *E,* XXI, 1860, 195; *BE Bucks.,*
138.

118 *E*, XVIII, 1857, 343.

119 *BN*, 1864, 460–2.

Chapter 7

1 See B. Kaye, *The Development of the Architectural Profession in
Britain,* 1960; *Frank Jenkins, Architect and Patron,* 1962; idem,
'The Victorian Architectural Profession', in *VA*; J. Mordaunt
Crook, 'The pre-Victorian architect: professionalism and
patronage', in *Architectural History,* XII, 1969, 62 etc.;
J. Summerson, *The Architectural Association,* 1947.

2 *E,* XVII, 1856, 284, 362; see also A. J. Beresford-Hope, *The Common
Sense of Art,* 1858.

3 See *E,* XVII, 1856, 107; for W. White: *B,* 1856, 402, *B,* 1857, 90.

4 *B,* 1858, 849.

5 Letter to *The Times,* 19 Oct. 1859, also in *E,* XX, 1859, 366 (by
'E.A.F.' = E. A. Freeman, an archaeological writer mainly active in
the forties).

6 *Remarks on a National Style in Reference to the Foreign Office,* 1860
(anon.).

7 See *EGR,* Ch. X.

8 G. G. Scott, *Personal and Professional Recollections,* 1879.

9 *E,* XXII, 1861, 13–15; for T. Harris see: D. Harbron, 'T.H.', *AR,*
92, 1942, 63. See also T. Harris' proposed houses at Harrow, *B,* 1860,
673 ill.

10 *B,* 1866, 368.

11 *E,* XXVII, 1866, 234; for more discussion of the problem see
R. Kerr, *The English Gentleman's House,* 1864.

12 See C. P. Curran, 'B. Woodward, Ruskin and the O'Sheas', in *Studies*
(Dublin), June 1940.

13 See Constantia Maxwell, *History of Trinity College, Dublin,* 1946,
with source material. See *B,* 1853, 420, *B,* 1854, 67, 425 ill., 443,
453 (controversy McCurdy–Woodward about the authorship of the
building), *E,* XV, 1854, 356 etc.

14 See Peter Ferriday, 'The Oxford Museum', *AR,* 132, 1962,
408–16; see *B,* 1854, 309, 590 etc. beg. *B,* 1855, 292 etc., *B,* 1859,
401, 735; *E,* XIX, 1858, 243; ill.: *B,* 1855, 291, *BN,* 1859, 819, *B,*
1859, 253, *BN,* 1860, 715, *B,* 1860, 399.

15 See J. Ruskin, *The Oxford Museum,* 1859 (1893; see *LE,* XVI).

16 'Already built' in *ILN,* 1857, II, 248. *E,* XIX, 1858, 243.
A building of the type: schoolroom plus teacher's house is the
Police Court at Dundrum (Dublin, not originally planned for this

purpose, loc. inf.; *B*, 1855, 450).

17 *ILN*, 1857, II, 348, *B*, 1857, 563 ill., *Str.*, 160–1.

18 *BN*, 1858, 948; *EGR*, No. 139.

19 House Doyne (St Austin's Abbey), *BN*, 1858, 948; the house was destroyed in 1922 by fire, only the porter's lodge remains intact. Another house: 'Thorncliffe', at Monkstown (Antrim; *BN* 1858, 948, inf. D. Richardson); 15 Upper Phillimore Gardens, Kensington, was destroyed (*EGR*, No 135, 1856; see A. T. Edwards, *Good and Bad Manners in Architecture*, 1924, ill. 31).

20 Nassau Street, *BN*, 1858, 948, *BN*, 1860, 49 ill.); *Dublin Builder*, 1859–61; *E*, XXIII, 1862, 335.

21 *BN*, 23 March 1866.

22 For lit. on Scott see above, note 66, Ch. 1.

23 That was also the *Ecclesiologist's* opinion about the book, *E*, XIX, 1858, 16–23.

24 An ardent propagandist for the symbolical value of 'Gothic' and a friend of Scott's was E. Beckett Denison (1816–1905), later Lord Grimthorpe, in his book *Lectures on Gothic Architecture*, 1854 (see P. Ferriday, *Lord Grimthorpe*, 1957). Scott at times was less doctrinal and used round arches where he had to deal with remains of previous buildings, e.g. Wren's St Michael's Cornhill, 1856 f., and for the completion of Charles Parker's Christ Church, St Albans (mid-fifties, loc. inf.; Parker's work dates from 1847; the vicarage in 'round-arched'-Gothic is probably also Scott's).

25 *E*, XVI, 1855, 142 f.; also printed as an appendix to *Secular and Domestic*. See also the discussion in the Ecclesiological Society, *E*, XVI, 1855, 181. Scott had been to Italy in 1851, where he went to see Ruskin in Venice (see *LE*, X, XXXIII; Scott, *Personal and Professional Recollections*, 1879, 157–64).

26 Cf. *The Stones of Venice*, Vol. I, Ch. VIII; Butterfield, All Saints; Viollet-le-Duc, *Dictionnaire raisonné de l'architecture française*, Vol. I (1854) article 'arcades'.

27 *Secular and Domestic*, 208–9.

28 Ibid., 215.

29 Ibid., 227–8; cf. also 220.

30 Ibid., 216.

31 *BE Essex*, 201.

32 *B*, 1854, 362 ill.; *BE London II*, 76: 'said to be the outcome of consultation with Ruskin'; no references in *LE*. Scott seems to have used coloured shafts already 1851–2 in Eastnor church (*BE Herefs.*, 122; *Country Life*, 21 March 1968); from 1854 onwards many fonts, funeral epitaphs etc. are known with such decorations; his best known monuments of this kind are the Crimean Column at Westminster (1859, *BE London I*, 493); and, later, the Albert Memorial in Kensington Gardens, 1862 f. (see above p. 156).

33 1857–8, see list, op. cit., note 66, Ch. I.

34 *B*, 1856, 63 ill., see H. J. Brandt, *Das Hamburger Rathaus*, Hamburg, 1957; drawings in the Collection of the RIBA; cf. Pugin's 'Hôtel de Ville', based on Ypres in *Contrasts*, 1836.

35 Drawings in the collection of the RIBA; see *B*, 1857, index; *ILN*,

12 Sept. 1857. Only one early example of specially rich sculptured decoration may be cited here, which ranks as one of the first examples of Ruskinian influence in that field, the portal of an organ factory in St Pancras, 1853 (*B,* 1853, 747 ill.). As an early example of 'constructional polychromy' Scott's church, St John's, Leicester (1853–4, *B,* 1854, 501; *BE Leics.,* 143), may be cited.

36   *B,* 1852, 289, *B,* 1854, 115 ill.; *BE London I,* 493.

37   See also Scott, *Personal and Professional Recollections,* 1879, 179; *BN,* 1857, 1122 ill. Cf. the former Manor-house Pippbrook at Dorking (1856, *BE Surrey,* 168, drawings at RIBA); and at Exeter College, Oxford, the Street fronts (c. 1854) with the Library (1856–8; *CEAJ,* 1858, pl. 26); the Sandbach Institute, Sandbach, Cheshire, 1858, *B,* 1859, 118.

38   *BE Notts.,* 86; M. Girouard, 'Kelham Hall', *Country Life,* 18 May 1967, 25.

39   *B,* 1860, 560 ill.; *BE Warws.,* 440; *B,* 1860, 560: 'local stone and bath stone for the dressings'.

40   Scott quotes a passage from Pugin's *True Principles* (61–3) that the elevation has to follow the plan; but Scott adds, 'the architect must neither make his plan independently of the elevation, nor his elevation of his plan' (*Secular and Domestic,* 120–3). However, Scott had second thoughts on the symmetry of his first Government design, the 1859 (*B,* 1859, 535 ill.) version shows more irregularity (see again *Personal and Professional Recollections,* 1879, Ch. IV).

41   *B,* 1862, 621 ill.

42   *CEAJ,* 1866, plates 37, 38.

43   G. B. Scott, *Lectures on the Rise and Development of Medieval Architecture,* 1879, Vol. II, 228; *Secular and Domestic,* 289.

44   *B,* 1864, 117 ill.

45   *B,* 1870, 707 ill.; *BN,* 1879, 19 Dec. ill. int.

46   See the *Architect* 1872, I, 316 etc.

47   *B,* 1868, 738, *BN,* 1869, 136, 274; see Jack Simmons, *St. Pancras Station,* 1968; N. Taylor, *Monuments of Commerce,* 1968.

48   *B,* 1857, 478 ill.

49   1870, Town Hall: *BN,* 135; *BE Yorks.,* WR, 124.

50   *BN,* 1859, 1063 ill.

51   See *DNB*; Xenia Norman, 'Life and Work of Waterhouse in and around Manchester', unpubl. thesis, Manchester, 1955; C. Stewart, *The Stones of Manchester,* 1956, *BE Sth. Lancs.,* 36. Stuart Allen Smith, 'A. Waterhouse', thesis, London University, 1970.

52   *B,* 1856, 26; coloured drawing in Victoria & Albert Museum.

53   *B,* 1858, 857, *ILN,* 1859, I, 149 ill., *BE Sth. Lancs.,* 107.

54   See X. Norman, op. cit., note 51.

55   *B,* 1859, 296, 326 ill., *B,* 1865, 136 ill., *EGR,* No. 177; A. Waterhouse on Assize Courts in *RIBA Papers,* 1864–5, 165 ff.

56   See N. Taylor, *Monuments of Commerce,* 1968. Drawings in RIBA Collection.

57   1867, *EGR,* No. 297.

58   1868, *EGR,* No. 318, *BE Cambs.,* 67.

59   1868, *EGR,* No. 334, *B,* 1868, 318 ill. pl., *BE Sth. Lancs.,* 280.

60 Eaton Hall, 1870, *EGR,* No. 339 (additions to an older building). Liverpool: 1868–71; *BE Sth. Lancs.,* 162.

61 *B,* 1868, 392 ill.

62 For the prehistory and history of the competition see M. H. Port, 'The New Law Courts Competition, 1866–7', in *Architectural History,* II, 1968, 75 etc. Most architects issued large publications of their designs. For Street see also his *Memoir* (ed. A. E. Street, 1888); *E,* XXVIII, 1867, 113 ff. Most designs are illustrated in Port. See also J. Summerson, *Victorian Architecture,* 1970.

63 *AR,* 105, 1949, 61–74; N. Taylor, *Monuments of Commerce,* 1968; see also *E,* XXIII, 1862, 333–6.

64 *BN,* 1858, 723 ill.; *EGR,* No. 125.

65 *B,* 1856, 661, *BN,* 1857, 1065 ill.

66 *E,* XVII, 1856, 33; see T. Harris, *Examples of Architecture of the Victorian Age,* Vol. I, 1862.

67 *B,* 1858, 719 ill.; for Bristol see R. Winstone, *Bristol in the 1850s,* Bristol, 1968; *EVA.*

68 *B,* 1861, 125 ill.

69 *BN,* 1860, 894–5 ill. Cf. also Somers Clarke's Merchant Seamen's Asylum, Snaresbrook, now Wanstead Hospital (*BN,* 31 Oct. 1862; *BE Essex,* 379).

70 H.-R. Hitchcock, *Architecture: Nineteenth and Twentieth Centuries,* 1958, ill. 113; *BE North Soms.,* 441.

71 See N. Taylor, op. cit., note 63; *BE London I.*

72 *EGR,* No. 255, 1862–5.

73 *E,* XXVII, 1866, 310, *BN,* 1866, 701, 780 ill.

74 *BN,* 1867, Jan. 11, ill.

75 See *From the Classicists to the Expressionists,* ed. E. Holt, 1966, 306.

76 Cf. 'Second Empire "avant la lettre" ' in *Gazette des Beaux Arts,* 1953, II, 115 ff.

77 *B,* 1855, 97, 103 ill.

78 *B,* 1856, 87 ill.; *BE Surrey,* 260.

79 *B,* 1855, 389 ill.; the Knowles will be the subject of a monograph by Priscilla Metcalf, to be published shortly; thanks are due to her for information and comment.

80 *B,* 1860, 755, *B,* 1861, 374 ill., *BE London II,* 453. See also C. Monkhouse, 'Station Hotels in Nineteenth Century England', thesis, London University, 1970.

81 *BN,* 1865, 726 ill. *BE London II,* 241.

82 For discussions in the forties see Collins, 135–8.

83 See *EVA,* 560; for Wyatt see N. Pevsner, *M.D.W.,* Cambridge, 1950; cf. Bunning's Coal Exchange, *EVA.* See also *Journal of Design and Manufactures,* III, 1850, 128, and IV, 1851, 12, 74.

84 *B,* 1851, 796.

85 *E,* XVIII, 1857, 29.

86 Second series, plates 67–72. Initially Carpenter had prepared a design or was supposed to prepare one, but he died in 1855; see *E,* XVI, 1855, 175, *E,* XVII, 1856, 62, 133–4.

87 See *EVA,* 527.

88 *Instrumenta Ecclesiastica,* 2nd ser., 1851, pl. 19–26.
89 *E, XV,* 1854, 124, *E, XVII,* 1856, 221–2, 333–8.
90 Quoted from Skidmore's letter accompanying the design.
91 *E, XVII,* 1856, 338.
92 *E, XVII,* 1856, 221.
93 For earlier comments from the *Ecclesiologist* on the Crystal Palace see *EVA,* 545. For William White's comments (*E, XVI,* 1855, 162–3) see P. Thompson, 'The Writings of William White', in *Concerning Architecture,* 234.
94 Scott, *Secular and Domestic,* 112.
95 Op. cit., 224.
96 Op. cit., 221.
97 See A. J. Beresford-Hope, *The English Cathedral in the 19th Century,* 1861, Ch. 2; W. White, 'On iron, its legitimate uses and proper treatment', in *RIBA Papers,* 1865–6, 15–30.
98 See *BE Surrey,* 280, 282.
99 *Secular and Domestic,* 117.
100 See above p. 190. Hitchcock writes that the fact that the 'forward line' of development lies with Street and not with those who erected the Crystal Palace, is a 'major historical paradox'. The paradox becomes even greater if one takes the 'iron activities' of the Ecclesiologists under consideration – until one knows the long-term outcome. Another attempt at modern materials was A. Blomfield's St Barnabas, Oxford, partly of concrete, adhering to plain walls and round arched forms (see *Church Builder,* 1870).

Chapter 8

1 See J. Brandon-Jones, in *VA*; ibid., 'Letters of Philip Webb and his Contemporaries', in *Architectural History,* Vol. 8, 1965, 52 f.
2 See *E, XIX,* 1858, 172.
3 Drawings in the Victoria & Albert Museum.
4 See N. Pevsner, *Pioneers of Modern Design,* 1960 ed., Ch. II; P. Thompson, *The Work of William Morris,* 1967; see esp. *BE West Kent,* 155–8.
5 C. L. Eastlake, 'The Fashion of Furniture', in *Cornhill Magazine,* IX, 1864, 337 ff.; see N. Pevsner, 'Art Furniture', (1952) in *Studies in Art Architecture and Design,* Vol. II, 1968; E. Aslin, *Nineteenth Century English Furniture,* 1962.
6 Eastlake, op. cit., 36 (1869 ed.).
7 See E. Aslin, *The Aesthetic Movement,* 1969.
8 See last chapter in *EGR.*
9 The history of 'Queen Anne' has to be traced in the discussions and illustrations of contemporary architectural periodicals, see *B, BN,* the *Architect* from c. 1873 onwards.
10 *Richardson as a Victorian Architect,* Smith College, Northampton, Mass., 1966; 'Ruskin and American Architecture, or Regeneration Long Delayed', in *Concerning Architecture.*
11 For German Neo-Gothic after 1850 see G. Kokkelink, *Die Neugotik Conrad Wilhelm Hases* in *Hannoversche Geschichtsblätter,* N.F., Band 22, Heft 1/3.

Note to
p. 207

12 For France see L. Hautecoeur, *Histoire de l'architecture classique
en France*, Vols. VI, VII, Paris, 1957. Hautecoeur (op. cit., Vol. VI,
340) concludes a brief comparison between English and French
gothicists (for the English side based, as it seems, on Basil F. L.
Clarke, *Church Builders of the 19th Century*, 1938, and *EVA*):
'ils [i.e. Viollet-le-Duc and the French] allaient plus loin que
Pugin', because Pugin insisted on Gothic for its own sake and
Viollet-le-Duc on Gothic for its principles. It seems that it was
just because of his abstract principles that Viollet-le-Duc did not
go 'as far' as the Ecclesiologists in the fifties and sixties. Cf.
also N. Pevsner, *Ruskin and Viollet-le-Duc,* 1969.

Further reading

Essential sources

A. W. N. Pugin, *The True Principles of Pointed or Christian Architecture*, 1841 (reprinted 1969)

J. Ruskin, *The Seven Lamps of Architecture*, 1849

J. Ruskin, *The Stones of Venice*, Vol. I, 1851, Vols II and III, 1853

G. E. Street, *Brick and Marble in the Middle Ages*, 1855

G. G. Scott, *Remarks on Secular and Domestic Architecture*, 1858

C. L. Eastlake, *A History of the Gothic Revival*, 1872 (new edition, J. M. Crook (ed.), Leicester, 1970)

Older works of interest

A. J. Beresford-Hope, *The English Cathedral of the Nineteenth Century*, 1861

R. Kerr, 'English Architecture Thirty Years Hence', *RIBA Transactions*, 1st series, Vol. 34 (1883–4), 218–30

J. Fergusson, *History of Architecture*, 1869 (Vol. 3, The Modern Styles) (Kerr and Fergusson are non-partisan to the movement)

T. F. Bumpus, *London Churches, Ancient and Modern*, 1881 and 1908

H. Muthesius, *Die neuere kirchliche Baukunst in England*, Berlin, 1901 (good for illustrations, especially later Victorian churches)

Criticism and careful evaluation of Victorian architecture based on later nineteenth- and early twentieth-century English architectural opinions

K. Clark, *The Gothic Revival*, London, John Murray and Penguin Books, 1928, 1950

D. Harbron, *Amphion, or The Nineteenth Century*, London, Dent, 1930

B. F. L. Clarke, *Church Builders of the Nineteenth Century*, A Study of the Gothic Revival in England, London, SPCK, 1938 (reprinted 1969)

D. Gwynn, *Lord Shrewsbury, Pugin and the Catholic Revival*, Westminster, Maryland, 1946

R. Turnor, *Nineteenth Century Architecture in Britain*, London, Batsford, 1950

H. S. Goodhart-Rendel, *English Architecture since the Regency*, London, Constable, 1953

W. Lethaby, *Philip Webb and his Work*, Oxford, 1935 (Lethaby stresses the continuity of rational and vernacular tendencies from Butterfield into the twentieth century)

Further reading   *More recently*

H. Casson, *An Introduction to Victorian Architecture*, London,
Art & Technics, 1948

J. Betjeman, *First and Last Loves*, London, John Murray, 1952

R. Furneaux Jordan, *Victorian Architecture*, Penguin Books, 1966

J. Summerson, *Victorian Architecture, Four Studies in Evaluation*,
Columbia University Press, 1970

R. Macleod, *Style and Society, Architectural Ideology in Britain 1835–1914*,
1971

Surveys of nineteenth-century architecture

H.-R. Hitchcock, *Architecture: Nineteenth and Twentieth Centuries*,
Penguin Books (Pelican History of Art), 1958

E. Lundberg, *Arkitekturens Formspråk*, Vols. IX, X, Stockholm, 1960

R. Zeitler and others, *Die Kunst des 19. Jahrhunderts, Berlin,* 1966
(*Propyläen Kunstgeschichte*)

E. G. Holt (ed.), *From Classicism to Impressionism* (Documentary History
of Art, Vol. III), Garden City, N.Y., 1966

H. Lietzmann, *Bibliographie zur Kunstgeschichte des 19. Jahrhunderts,*
Munich, 1968

D. Ware, *Short Dictionary of British Architects*, London, Allen & Unwin,
1967

T. S. R. Boase, *English Art 1800–1870*, Oxford (Oxford History of English
Art), 1959

Architecture of the last two hundred years seen from different angles

N. Pevsner, *Pioneers of Modern Design from William Morris to Walter
Gropius,* first published 1936, Penguin Books, 1960
(Victorian architecture and design as the negative background to the
Modern Movement)

P. Collins, *Changing Ideals in Modern Architecture*, London, Faber, 1965
(apart from a great amount of objective discussion of nineteenth-century
architectural problems, the emphasis is on the eighteenth- and nineteenth-
century rational tradition, not so much in England as in France, and
the Modern Movement is dealt with in the light of these traditions)

H. Sedlmayr, *Art in Crisis*, London, Hollis, 1967 (originally published as
Verlust der Mitte, Salzburg, 1948)
(The later nineteenth century and the Modern Movement are seen as the
outcome of Romanticism and contrasted to the religious integrity and
humanity of the old world up to the eighteenth century)

Essays on various aspects of Victorian architecture

J. Summerson, *Heavenly Mansions*, Cresset Press, 1948, New York, 1963

244   P. Ferriday (ed.), *Victorian Architecture*, London, Cape, 1963

N. Pevsner, *Studies in Art, Architecture and Design*, London, Thames & Hudson, 1968

J. Summerson (ed.), *Concerning Architecture, Essays on Architectural Writers and Writings presented to N. Pevsner,* London, Allen Lane the Penguin Press, 1968

The recent volumes of the *Architectural Review* and *Country Life* from the late thirties onwards contain a multitude of articles on nineteenth-century architecture.

Studies on Special Topics

Gothic Revival

S. Lang, 'The Principles of the Gothic Revival in England', in *JSAH XXV*, 1966 No. 4, 240–67 (a very useful short survey)

P. Frankl, *The Gothic, Sources and Interpretations through eight centuries,* Princeton, 1960 (an exhaustive survey)

The Gothic of Gothick, B. Weinreb Ltd., London, c. 1966 (useful bibliography)

Pre-Victorian

C. Hussey, *The Picturesque, Studies in a Point of View,* London, Cass, 1963

D. Watkin, *Thomas Hope and the neo-classical Idea*, London, John Murray, 1968

D. Pilcher, *The Regency Style*, London, Batsford, 1948

H. Ladd, *Victorian Morality of Art* (Ruskin), New York, 1932

Early Victorian

G. M Young (ed.), *Early Victorian England,* Oxford, 1934

H.-R. Hitchcock, *Early Victorian Architecture in Britain,* Architectural Press and New Haven, 1955 (a very detailed survey, more strictly concerned with the description of buildings)

J. F. White, *The Cambridge Movement,* Cambridge, 1962 (the history of the Ecclesiological Society)

P. B. Stanton, *The Gothic Revival and American Church Architecture,* Baltimore, 1968 (deals with the English Ecclesiologists as well)

N. Pevsner, *Matthew Digby Wyatt,* Cambridge, 1950 (problems of architecture and decorative design around 1850)

P. B. Stanton, *Pugin,* London, Thames & Hudson, 1971

High Victorian

H.-R. Hitchcock, 'High Victorian Architecture', in *Victorian Studies*, I, 1957 (a short survey)

L. G. Buckley, 'High Victorian Gothic, A dissertation on High Victorian

Further reading   Gothic Ecclesiastical architecture and a bibliography of the works in that sphere of A. Blomfield, G. F. Bodley . . . .' 1966 (MS., RIBA)

The High Victorian Cultural Achievement, Victorian Society Conference Report, London, 1965 (essays on various aspects of the period)

N. Pevsner, *Ruskin and Viollet-le-Duc,* London, Thames & Hudson, 1969 (some points of comparison)

H.-R. Hitchcock, *Richardson as a Victorian Architect,* Smith College, Northampton, Mass, 1966

P. Thompson, *William Butterfield,* London, Routledge & Kegan Paul, 1971

G. L. Hersey, *High Victorian Gothic, a study in associationism,* Baltimore, 1972

See further

P. Howell, *Victorian Churches,* Country Life—RIBA Drawing Series, 1968

N. Taylor, *Monuments of Commerce,* Country Life—RIBA Drawing Series, 1968

M. Girouard, *The Victorian Country House,* Oxford, 1971

A. Bøe, *From Gothic Revival to Functional Form, Study in Victorian Theories of Design,* Oslo and Oxford, 1957

E. Aslin, *Nineteenth Century English Furniture,* London, Faber, 1962

P. Thompson, *The Work of William Morris,* London, Heinemann, 1967

F. Jenkins, *Architect and Patron,* Oxford, 1961

J. Summerson, *The Architectural Association,* London, Pleiades Books for the Architectural Association, 1947

Topographical

N. Pevsner (ed.), *The Buildings of England,* Penguin Books, from 1951

B. F. L. Clarke, *Parish Churches of London,* London, Batsford, 1966

C. Stewart, *The Stones of Manchester,* London, Arnold, 1956

B. F. L. Clarke, *Anglican Cathedrals outside the British Isles,* London, SPCK, 1958

City Buildings Series, London, Studio Vista

Index

Numbers in italics refer to pages on which illustrations are to be found